W9-BFB-326

'INTH GRAD   PUS

Culture and Customs of Pakistan

Culture and Customs
of Pakistan

∽o∽

IFTIKHAR H. MALIK

Culture and Customs of Asia
Hanchao Lu, Series Editor

GREENWOOD PRESS
Westport, Connecticut • London

Library of Congress Cataloging-in-Publication Data

Malik, Iftikhar Haider, 1949-
    Culture and customs of Pakistan / by Iftikhar H. Malik.
        p. cm. — (Culture and customs of Asia, ISSN 1097–0738)
    Includes bibliographical references and index.
    ISBN 0–313–33126–X
    1. Ethnology—Pakistan. 2. Pakistan—Social life and customs. I. Title. II. Series.
GN635.P27M35 2006
    306.095491—dc22   2005029554

British Library Cataloguing in Publication Data is available.

Library of Congress Catalog Card Number:
ISBN: 0–313–33126-X
ISSN: 1097–0738

First published in 2006

Greenwood Press, 88 Post Road West, Westport, CT 06881
An imprint of Greenwood Publishing Group, Inc.
www.greenwood.com

Printed in the United States of America

The paper used in this book complies with the
Permanent Paper Standard issued by the National
Information Standards Organization (Z39.48–1984).

10   9   8   7   6   5   4   3   2   1

To the memory of my great grandmother,
whose prayers have always stayed with me.

Contents

Series Foreword

Geographically, Asia encompasses the vast area from Suez, the Bosporus, and the Ural Mountains eastward to the Bering Sea and from this line southward to the Indonesian archipelago, an expanse that covers about 30 percent of our earth. Conventionally, and especially insofar as culture and customs are concerned, Asia refers primarily to the region east of Iran and south of Russia. This area can be divided in turn into subregions commonly known as South, Southeast, and East Asia, which are the main focus of this series.

The United States has vast interests in this region. In the twentieth century the United States fought three major wars in Asia (namely the Pacific Wars of 1941–45, the Korean War of 1950–53, and the Vietnam War of 1965–75), and each had profound impact on life and politics in America. Today, America's major trading partners are in Asia, and in the foreseeable future the weight of Asia in American life will inevitably increase, for in Asia lie our great allies as well as our toughest competitors in virtually all arenas of global interest. Domestically, the role of Asian immigrants is more visible than at any other time in our history. In spite of these connections with Asia, however, our knowledge about this crucial region is far from adequate. For various reasons, Asia remains for most of us a relatively unfamiliar, if not stereotypical or even mysterious, "Oriental" land.

There are compelling reasons for Americans to obtain some level of concrete knowledge about Asia. It is one of the world's richest reservoirs of culture and an ever-evolving museum of human heritage. Rhoads Murphey, a prominent Asianist, once pointed out that in the part of Asia east of Afghanistan and south of Russia alone lies half the world, "half of its people and far more than half of its historical experience, for these are the oldest living civilized traditions." Prior to the modern era, with limited interaction and mutual influence between the East and the West, Asian civilizations developed largely independent from the West. In modern times, however, Asia and the West have come not only into close contact but also into frequent conflict: The result has been one of the most solemn and stirring dramas in world history. Today, integration and compromise are the trend in coping with cultural differences. The West—with some notable exceptions—has started to see Asian traditions not as something to fear but as something to be understood, appreciated, and even cherished. After all, Asian traditions are an indispensable part of the human legacy, a matter of global "common wealth" that few of us can afford to ignore.

As a result of Asia's enormous economic development since World War II, we can no longer neglect the study of this vibrant region. Japan's "economic miracle" of postwar development is no longer unique, but in various degrees has been matched by the booming economy of many other Asian countries and regions. The rise of the four "mini dragons" (South Korea, Taiwan, Hong Kong, and Singapore) suggests that there may be a common Asian pattern of development. At the same time, each economy in Asia has followed its own particular trajectory. Clearly, China is the next giant on the scene. Sweeping changes in China in the last two decades have already dramatically altered the world's economic map. Furthermore, growth has also been dramatic in much of Southeast Asia. Today, war-devastated Vietnam shows great enthusiasm for joining the "club" of nations engaged in the world economy. And in South Asia, India, the world's largest democracy, is rediscovering its role as a champion of market capitalism. The economic development of Asia presents a challenge to Americans but also provides them with unprecedented opportunities. It is largely against this background that more and more people in the United States, in particular among the younger generations, have started to pursue careers dealing with Asia.

This series is designed to meet the need for knowledge of Asia among students and the general public. Each book is written in an accessible and lively style by an expert (or experts) in the field of Asian studies. Each book focuses on culture and customs of a country or region. However, readers should be aware that culture is fluid, not always respecting national boundaries. While every nation seeks its own path to success and struggles to maintain its own identity, in the cultural domain mutual influence and integration among Asian nations are ubiquitous.

Each volume starts with an introduction to the land and the people of the nation or region and includes a brief history and an overview of the economy. This is followed by chapters dealing with a variety of topics that piece together a cultural panorama, such as thought, religion, ethics, literature and art, architecture and housing, cuisine, traditional dress, gender, courtship and marriage, festivals and leisure activities, music and dance, and social customs and lifestyle. In this series, we have chosen not to elaborate on elite life, ideology, or detailed questions of political structure and struggle, but instead to explore the world of common people, their sorrow and joy, their pattern of thinking, and their way of life. It is the culture and customs of the majority of the people (rather than just the rich and powerful elite) that we seek to understand. Without such understanding, it will be difficult for all of us to live peacefully and fruitfully with each other in this increasingly interdependent world.

As the world shrinks, modern technologies have made all nations on each continent "virtual" neighbors. The expression "global village" not only reveals the nature and the scope of the world in which we live but also, more importantly, highlights the serious need for mutual understanding of all people on our planet. If this series serves to help the reader obtain a better understanding of the "half of the world" that is Asia, the authors and I will be well rewarded.

Hanchao Lu
Georgia Institute of Technology

Preface

Writing about the cultural plurality and artistic evolution of Pakistan, understandably, proved a joyous journey in self-discovery. Having been born and raised in the young South Asian country, followed by extensive travels and formative encounters including decades of teaching and research on that part of the world, offered first-hand insight into its history, society, environment, and diverse cultures. The close interaction continued even after resuming a teaching career in 1989 in the United Kingdom; it allowed a comparative perspective on Pakistan and its historical and cultural trajectory beside a rigorous interface with the Diaspora across the North Atlantic region. All the way from its extreme northern borders with China to its southern reaches on the Arabian Sea, Pakistan has certainly been endowed with exceptionally high and majestic mountains, glacial valleys, mighty rivers, expansive deserts, and coastline. Most of all, Pakistan is a land of industrious people with vital traditions and customs emanating from the ancient Indus Valley and other powerful mainstreams including Islam. Eager to become a politically stable and economically secure society, Pakistanis, in their hearts, certainly remain quite traditional, hospitable, and frugal. Despite their country's position as a geopolitical hotspot and confronted with the recurring problems in governance, Pakistanis overwhelmingly share the vision of their founding fathers such as M. A. Jinnah (1876-1948) and Muhammad Iqbal (1873-1938) for a tolerant and forward-looking nationhood. One experiences the richness and plurality of Pakistani culture and arts across the labyrinths of rural hamlets, mountainous valleys, glacial plateaus, tribal settlements, nomad camps, and urban density. Underpinned by strong religious ethos, the historic, ethnic, and economic ingredients of these cultural and artistic pursuits reflect overwhelmingly agrarian and family-bound values.

Acknowledgments

Assistance and inspiration to write this volume were received from many individuals whose time and energy cannot be acknowledged just in a few customary words. In addition, they are too numerous to be acknowledged. During this sojourn that involved travel, extensive interviews, and photography, the hospitality and kindness of so many Pakistani friends and institutions remains unmistakably unsurpassed. My colleagues at Bath Spa University were, as always, supportive of my effort whereas my family stood in good stead all through the tedious months and usually late nights of my research and pounding on the computer. Sidra, a family expert on South Asian music and films, pointed me in the right direction in her area whereas Ayyub read the section on architecture. Nighat never failed to remind me of the Jinnahist dream of transforming Pakistan into an ideal synthesis of old and new, and of tradition and modernity, while Farooq and Kiran persisted with the questions expected of younger people. Appreciation is certainly due to Professor Hanchao Lu, the Series Editor of *Culture and Customs of Asia*, for commissioning me to write this book, whereas Greenwood editor, Wendi Schnaufer, kept me on the right track within the stipulated deadline. Her professional preening, added with the input from Emily Johnson and her colleagues, is deeply acknowledged. While appreciative of the published works and other related material consulted in this volume, I, as the author, accept the entire responsibility for any lapses in facts or figures.

Acronyms

AIML	All-India Muslim League
APWA	All-Pakistan Women's Association
GT Road	Grand Trunk Road
HRCP	Human Rights Commission of Pakistan
INC	Indian National Congress
JI	Jama'at-i-Islami
KKH	Karakoram Highway
MMA	Muttahida Majlis-i-Ammal (United Action Forum)
NCA	National College of Arts (formerly Mayo School of Arts in Lahore)
NWFP	North-West Frontier Province
PML	Pakistan Muslim League
PPP	Pakistan People's Party
PWA	Progressive Writers Association
WAF	Women's Action Forum

Chronology

712	Ibn Qasim conquers Sindh
997–1030	Mahmud of Ghazna's invasions of the subcontinent
1206	Establishment of the Slave Dynasty under Qutb-ud-Din Aibak in Delhi
1206–1525	Various Muslim Sultan Dynasties (Delhi Sultanate)
1288, 1293	Marco Polo visits southern India
1325–1351	Ibn Battutah visits India
1336	Founding of Kingdom of Vijaynagar
1345	Founding of Bahmini kingdom in Deccan
1469–1539	Baba Guru Nanak, the founder of Sikhism in Punjab
1526	Babur, the Mughal King, defeats Delhi sultan at Panipat
1600	East India Company established in London
1707	Aurengzeb, the last Great Mughal Emperor, dies
1757	East India Company defeat the nawab (Muslim prince) of Bengal
1799	Sultan Tipu is killed in Mysore
1857	Rebellion against the East India Company
1858	British Crown takes over India
1885	Indian National Congress established in Bombay
1906	All-India Muslim League founded in Dhaka
1913	M. A. Jinnah joins the Muslim League
1930	Muhammad Iqbal addresses the Muslim League at Allahabad
1940	Lahore Resolution of the Muslim League
1947	Independence of India and Pakistan
1948	Jinnah dies. Indo-Pakistani war over Kashmir
1958	General Ayub Khan's coup
1965	Second Indo-Pakistani war
1969	General Yahya Khan's coup

1

Introduction

Pakistan, a predominantly Muslim country and the heartland of the Indus Valley, was established in 1947 after the dissolution of the British Raj (colonial rule). In terms of its location, history, and culture, it is a meeting ground for various pluralistic traditions. It shares ecology, religious practices, languages, historical events, and ethnosocial commonalities with all its neighbors, and thus while located within South Asia, it is a bridgehead to the Western and Central Asian regions.

THE LAND

With an area of 803,940 square kilometers, of which 25,220 square kilometers are covered with water, Pakistan is slightly smaller than twice the size of California and has an estimated population of 159 million.[1] Surrounded by China to the north, the Arabian Sea to the south, and India to the east, Pakistan adjoins Afghanistan and Iran to its west. To its north lies the disputed Kashmir region—a former princely state—presently divided between India, Pakistan, and China. Pakistan and India share almost 3,000 kilometers of borders; with Afghanistan the boundary line runs through a mountainous region and accounts for 2,430 kilometers. China and Iran share 523 and 909 kilometers of common borders, respectively, with Pakistan, which has a coastline of 1,046 kilometers.

Its climate is mostly dry with extreme heat in the plains and deserts, while the mountains in the north share a cold and glacial climate. After Mount Everest, Pakistan has the world's eight tallest peaks in the world, straddling the Karakorams, Himalayas, and Hindu Kush mountains, which extend southward all the way into western regions of the country. K-2, the second highest and the most difficult mountaintop in the world, is located in northern Pakistan. It is also a land of big rivers—part of the world-famous Indus River system—feeding a growing population, divided into urban, rural, nomadic, and tribal sections.[2] Most of the rivers feeding Pakistan originate in the Himalayan regions of Tibet and Kashmir until they join the Indus in the Punjab, which empties itself into the Arabian Sea while passing through the plains and deserts of Sindh province. Pakistan is endowed with majestic and immensely tall mountains, low-lying hills, alluvial green plains, and sandy and graveled deserts, although climate-wise it is a tropical zone. Pakistan is a predominantly agrarian country, although only 28 percent of its land is arable, out of which 180,000 square kilometers are irrigated through complex systems of barrages and canals.

Pakistan's plains across the two provinces of Punjab and Sindh are vulnerable to periodic floods during the rainy season—monsoons—whereas the northern and western mountainous regions are prone to earthquakes. While lying on the proverbial Silk Road, Pakistan is connected with Central and West Asia through a number of passes including the well-known Khyber Pass, which has been the traditional route for immigrants and invaders since time immemorial.[3] Northern Pakistan has some of the world's largest glaciers, such

Rakaposhi Peak. Courtesy of the author.

Kalasha Valley. Courtesy of the author.

as Siachin, Saltoro, and Baltoro, which play a crucial role in determining the ecology of the country. Pakistan's main artery through these mountains—the Karakoram Highway (KKH)—is built on some of these glaciers, connecting Pakistan with China, and this road has to be repaired quite regularly because of slides and avalanches. The highway, built by the Chinese and Pakistani engineers, runs parallel to the Indus until near the town of Gilgit and then moves through Hunza and Shimshal before reaching the Indo-Chinese borders at the Khunjrab Pass, at the attitude of 18,000 feet. The KKH offers clear and immensely enchanting views of some of the most majestic natural scenery in the world at an unprecedented high altitude. It snakes through the mountain chains such as Nangaparbat, Rakhaposhi, Harmosh, and Shimshal Cones, all displaying their unique beauty and snow-covered peaks without any dust particle or industrial pollution blocking the view. The last section of the KKH remains usually snow-bound and is open only from May to October. In the neighboring and northwesterly regions of Chitral, the road crosses over the Loari Pass at the altitude of 12,000 feet before descending into the scenic and historic valleys of Chitral. Chitral is known for its non-Muslim communities, called Kalasha, and is bordered by its highest peak—Tirich Mir, which, unlike its Karakoram counterparts, remains hidden under the clouds.[4] The valleys between Gilgit and Chitral have been the oldest polo grounds, also located at such a high altitude.

Mankiyala Buddhist Stupa is the oldest and largest in the world. Courtesy of the author.

Pakistan has four seasons, although the summer is usually the longest with temperatures often reaching 120 degrees Fahrenheit (45 degrees Celsius) and higher. Summer months continue from late April to early September, whereas winter occurs from November to late January until spring provides a transition between a departing winter and a steadily warming summer. Summer days, except for mountainous regions in the north and to the west, are very long and hot until the rainy season sets in from late June to late August. Despite humidity, rains offer a welcome change from scorching heat and coincide with the arrival of ripe mangoes and juicy melons. The country is certainly known for a wide variety of vegetables and fruits, also dependent upon seasons and varying volume of rains. Most of the rain accumulates during the rainy season and then in January, when two main seasonal harvests need it the most. Wheat, grams (or, chickpeas), peanuts, and mustard—called the *Khareef* crops—are sown in the late autumn to be harvested in early April, while corn, sugar cane, millet, and a wide variety of beans—known as *Rabih* crops—are grown during the summer months. Summer heat and water result in a wide variety of vegetables and flowers, especially several varieties of roses, jasmine, dahlias, bougainvillea, radishes, cucumber, gourds, okra, tomatoes, and tropical vegetables, whereas winter months have pansies, daisies, sunflowers, marigolds, peppers, spinach, lettuce, apricots, pomegranates, guava, and loquats.

Winters in Pakistan are usually exceptionally sunny, but nights in the plains and deserts can get immensely cold with fog engulfing the atmosphere until the late morning when sun burns it out. Pakistan's spring is rather brief but flowery and fragrant, although the rainy season also arrives in the spring with the lush greenery across the plains until the autumn turns the terrain brown. The winter months are cold, dusty, and dry; people often complain of cold arctic winds coming from Siberia and the Himalayas. The northern passes in Chitral, Gilgit, Hunza, Baltistan, Kaghan, Swat, Dir, and Kurram become snowbound, whereas passes toward the west remain dry yet very cold during the night. Rain is not only needed for crops but also as a respite from the dust and nasal infections.

Despite a unique system of irrigation canals, the entire water supply and power generation is dependent upon the supply from dams and barrages on the Indus and River Jhelum. Under the arrangements of the Indus Basin Treaty with India in 1959, the three tributaries to the Indus flowing through Indian territories are only meant for supplying water to India, whereas the Indus and Jhelum rivers are solely for Pakistan's irrigation and power generation purposes. The waters of the Chenab, Ravi, and Sutlej were allocated to India for use, whereas the other two rivers were allotted to Pakistan and, additionally, a system of canals and dams was recommended by the World Bank so as to maximize the water utility for various purposes. Although there are thousands of tube wells across the country, during the long summer months the water table drops considerably. Pakistan is not as vulnerable to floods as is Bangladesh or northeastern India where the Gangetic system has been periodically causing havoc. Pakistan's coast and its inland regions are usually able to cope with some abnormalities in water levels. Otherwise, the country needs more water for its growing needs. Pakistan, during the 1960s and 1970s, built huge dams to manage water resources properly and also to generate electricity. The Tarbela on the Indus and Mangla on the Jhelum have been landmark achievements, but the plans for any new dams become contentious, especially among the low-lying provinces, which fear reduction in their water supplies. Except for the capital city of Islamabad, all the other urban centers, such as Karachi, Lahore, Faisalabad, Hyderabad, Gujranwala, Quetta, Rawalpindi, Multan, and Peshawar are already over-populous. The country reflects an interesting mix of old and new, rural and urban, tribal and nomadic. It is certainly a land of diverse ecology, pluralistic community, rich folk traditions, and historical vicissitudes.

PEOPLE

Pakistanis have descended from the ancient Indo-European communities who either lived in the Indus regions since time immemorial or ventured in as invaders and immigrants. Certainly, the ancient Indians were of Dravidian stock, but with the advent of Aryans, Persians, Greeks, Arabs, Mongols, Turks, Afghans, and other such central Asian tribes over the centuries in the past millennia, the Indus Valley became a nexus for various ethno-regional groups. While Pakistanis resemble other North Indian population groups in their appearances, cultures and customs, they are also akin to their West Asian counterparts in many ways. Since the spread of Islam from the seventh century, followed by centuries of Muslim rule, West Asia emerged as the dominant factor in Pakistani demography. Interestingly, many Pakistanis—especially the Muslim groups—seek their genealogies from Persia, Central Asia, and the Middle East, while there are some Muslims in Karachi and coastal areas of Balochistan whose ancestors came from Africa.

Whereas religion, history, and ecology generally unify Pakistanis as a homogenous national group, their linguistic and regional roots determine their respective ethnicities. Thus, the country's population is divided into five or six major ethnic groups who are not confined to their own specific territories. For instance, the Punjabi ethnic group—the largest of its type in Pakistan—is spread all over the country. They make up about 60 percent of the country's population. Seeking their origins from the valleys of the five rivers, they also trace their roots from the ancient Indian and West Asian tribes.

The Sindhis—the second largest ethnic group accounting for 20 percent of the country's population—live mostly in rural Sindh and are perceived to be the descendants of Dravidians along with some Persian and Arab background. They live in lower Pakistan, which, since 1947, has been the host to another predominantly urban ethnic group, known as Muhajireen (immigrants), who account for around five to six percent of the nation's population. These are the Urdu-speaking immigrants and the descendants of refugees from India who trace their origins from different provinces of India.

Town of Chaman on Afghanistan border. Courtesy of the author.

In Upper Pakistan, Pushtu-speaking Pushtuns share their ethnicity with Afghan Pushtuns settled across the Pak-Afghan border and are divided into rural, tribal, and urban communities. Pashtuns make up around 12 percent of Pakistani society. High up in the mountains in northern Pakistan, there are several smaller population groups who descend from ancient Central Asian, Tibetan, and Persian tribes. Southwestern Pakistan largely comprises Baloch tribes who claim to share kinship with the Kurds—not with the Arabs—and also seek common ancestry with the smaller Baloch communities in Iran and Afghanistan. While many Pakistanis in the lower half trace their origins from Baloch ancestors, there are around three million Baloch within the province of Balochistan itself. There are more Baloch people settled in Karachi than anywhere else in the country. In upper and western Balochistan, an equal number of Pushtun tribes account for the other half of the provincial population.

It is quite interesting to see ethnic Pakistani intellectuals debating and claiming their respective genealogies from the Semitic, Turkic, Kurdish, Persian, and Dravidian roots. The migrations from outside the country, especially during 1947, and an added mobility within the country have broken down the traditional territorial boundaries of these ethnic groups as they live side by side in most of the urban centers of Pakistan. Other than these predominantly Muslim ethnic groups, the Hindus, Sikhs, and Christians of Pakistan originate from the ancient Indians.

Pakistan, with its population of 159 million, is a significantly youthful society. Pakistan's annual population growth rate is still around two percent. The region has been a frequent recipient of some of the mass-based migrations from abroad, especially since 1947, when the country itself came into being. Life expectancy in Pakistan has improved in the last half century from a low of 32 years during the 1940s to 63 years in 2004 because of comparatively better health and nutritional facilities. However, the country is still confronted with big income gaps and poverty remains a major issue.[5]

Territorially, Balochistan—equal to the size of France—is the largest province, although only with a small population of about 6 million, but in terms of population, Punjab remains the largest of all because of its major share (almost 60%) in the country's populace, followed by Sindh (22%) and the North-West Frontier Province (NWFP) accounting for the remainder (13%). Although all the provinces of Pakistan are pluralistic, they also include some age-old ethno-lingual identities such as Balochi, Punjabi, Sindhi, and Pushtun. But these ethnic identities are not so clear-cut, as there are further regional and lingual variations within each province. In 1947, when Pakistan (then known as West Pakistan) received about 12 million Muslim refugees from India, the country's urban centers such as Karachi, Hyderabad, Lahore, Multan, Faisalabad, and others became more pluralistic.[6] It is generally the language and region that determine the ethnic origins of Pakistanis. The

Table 1.1.
Pakistani Population by Language Group

Language	Population (%)
Punjabi	48
Saraiki (a variant of Punjabi)	10
Sindhi	12
Pushtu	8
Urdu	8
Balochi	3
Baruhi	1
Barushaski, Shina, and Others	9

Note: The country has been holding its census every ten years and the next one is due in 2007. Sometimes, the figures are contested as they involve resource allocations, political representation, and jobs, so communities may even inflate their respective figures but the trends usually remain stable.

Urdu-speaking immigrants from the interiors of India and their descendants like to be called Muhajireen.[7] Table 1.1 offers an overview of Pakistani ethnic pluralism based on the usage of a mother tongue:

Urdu remains the national language of Pakistan, but a growing number of the elite use English for business, official work, and scientific instruction. At another level, Pakistan, although overwhelmingly a Muslim nation, is still a multi-religious society where eight to nine percent of Pakistanis come from Hindu, Christian, Sikh, and Zoroastrian backgrounds. Among the Muslims, Sunnis account for 77 percent and 20percent follow Shia sect—although both of these major sects include several doctrinal denominations. Pakistani Hindus and Christians are almost equal, totaling six to seven million each, whereas Sikhs, Parsis, Bahais, and Buddhists are rather smaller communities.[8]

LITERACY AND EDUCATION

The literacy rate is around 50 percent and is lowest among the rural and tribal women. Pakistan has a multitiered educational system. It has two dozen public universities and several private universities, and there are thousands of colleges and schools located across the country with varying degree of standards and facilities. Most of the academic institutions are administered by the provincial and local governments while private foundations and entrepreneurs have also introduced Westernized school systems, catering to the middle and upwardly mobile classes in the country. During the colonial era, the European missionaries opened some of the earliest private, English-speaking schools. Since independence, various governments have been slowly expanding the facilities for an ever-increasing demand. Schools are the largest employer of women in the country, whereas the armed forces and education recruit the maximum number of their male counterparts. Other than highbrow private institutions and state-sector schools and colleges, most of the mosques retain their own attached seminaries—*madrassas*—imparting religious knowledge to the poor children.

GOVERNMENT

Pakistan is a federation with four provinces and some federally administered tribal and border regions. Constitutionally named the Islamic Republic of Pakistan, the federation's capital is Islamabad—a new metropolis. A president heads the country, a parliamentary system is headed by an elected prime minister, and the cabinet runs the government. The parliament is divided into an upper house—the Senate—and the National Assembly, or the lower house. The Senate has an equal representation from all the four provinces and the capital territory, whereas the National Assembly is elected through universal suffrage from all the four provinces and tribal regions, and 33 percent of its seats are reserved for women.[9] Given all the vital amendments made since the military take-over by General Pervez Musharraf in 1999, Pakistan's constitution allocates vital powers to the president and stipulates a strong central government, although the Supreme Court decides on contentious constitutional matters.[10]

ECONOMY

Still a predominantly agricultural country, Pakistan's other vital economic sectors, such as services and manufacturing, have been steadily growing, although a huge population offers formidable challenges in areas such as education, housing, and employment. Its turbulent relations with India over the last several decades and instability in neighboring Afghanistan have not allowed the country to fully direct its energies and resources to unrestrained economic development. In addition, the absence of land reforms and a limited resource base have further hindered its economic growth. However, its toiling masses, a major number of trained professionals, and a vibrant Diaspora, remain positive attributes of a long-awaited take-off.

However, good governance, regional peace, and a prioritized social sector are the keys to a prosperous Pakistan. Pakistan's economy suffered from sanctions imposed on the country during the 1990s, especially after its nuclear tests in 1998, although the country had been a front-line state for the United States during the Cold War and played a key role in pushing the Soviets out of Afghanistan in 1989. The tragedy of September 11, 2001 and the subsequent fall-out also hurt Pakistan in the areas of trade and investment.

The country, already spending a stupendous amount on defense and debt servicing, was, however, gradually recovering by 2005.[11] Poverty, illiteracy, and urban violence proved major stumbling blocks in addition to a massive nondevelopment sector that stipulated vast allocations to defense, debt servicing, and bureaucracy.[12] By early 2003, Pakistan's GDP (Gross Domestic Product, indicating purchasing power parity) stood around $300 billion with an annual growth rate between five and six percent. Although the per-capita income remained quite low, the purchasing parity was about $2,200, with the remittances from expatriates making a significant contribution to Pakistan's growing foreign exchange reserves.

With a labor force totaling 45 million, 42 percent of it was still engaged in agriculture and 40 percent involved in services and 16 percent in industry. Heavily dependent on oil imports, Pakistan has 700 billion cubic meters of natural gas, although there has been concern of its eventually running out unless new sources were to be discovered in Balochistan and Sindh.[13] Pakistan's external debt in 2005 was $37 billion with about $13 billion in foreign exchange reserves, and the country was not in the threat of any immediate default. Pakistan has about 9,000 kilometers of railways and 10,000 kilometers of gas pipeline. Karachi is the country's main port, although efforts have been begun to develop Gwadar as an alternative. Pakistan's main exports are textiles, cotton, leather products, sports goods, surgical tools, rugs, spices, rice, fruits, and numerous handicrafts. The country imports pharmaceutical and other sophisticated industrial products and arms for its forces. Millions of Pakistani expatriates in the Gulf countries and North Atlantic regions send in the well-needed foreign exchange earnings. With an ever-expanding youthful society, there is a constant demand for more jobs and better services.

HISTORY

The Indus Valley Civilization

Areas making up present-day Pakistan have been the core regions of the ancient Indus Valley civilization, known for its towns, agriculture, trade, and social system, all under the leadership of priest-kings. The arrival of the Aryans from the north between 1500 and 2000 BC marginalized the indigenous cultural traditions, and soon Hinduism evolved as the dominant religion of this region.[14] The Hindu classics were written in Sanskrit long before the advent of the Christian era. In the next few centuries, India—the land of Indus—saw the emergence of Buddhism, Jainism, and Zoroastrianism, until Hinduism underwent another revival at the beginning of the Christian era.[15] It was in Taxila, the ancient capital of what is now Pakistan, that Hindu, Buddhist, Persian, Greek, and Christian political and cultural institutions flourished.[16] The evolution of Islam in South Asia during the seventh and eighth centuries largely is because of its simple message and egalitarianism, as represented by the Sufis (Muslim mystics) and traveling publicists. Islam had entered an immensely pluralistic subcontinent through the coastal areas and from West Asia. Streams of mystics, immigrants, and fortune seekers moved across the Indus and Gangetic basins.

The establishment of dynastic Muslim political rule during the medieval period under the Delhi Sultans and the development of a blended Indo-Islamic culture strengthened Muslim presence both in the western and eastern regions (largely making up present-day Pakistan and Bangladesh), although the political power was in otherwise Muslim-minority areas such as Delhi and the adjoining regions of northern India. The Mughal dynasty (1526–1857)—a Timurid/Turkish house—was contemporary with two other similar Timurid dynasties of the Persian Safwids and Ottoman Turks and ushered in a golden age in Indian cultures, crafts, literature, sciences, music, cuisine, architecture, and arts. It was also under the Great Mughals (1526–1707) that the Indian interaction with Europe began. During the 150-year long decline all the way from the death of Emperor Aurengzeb (1707) until the Indian Rebellion of 1857, the British East India Company was able to gradually consolidate its de facto position as the premier political force in South Asia.[17]

Not only a weakened Muslim central rule in Delhi became dependent upon the discretionary policies of the Company—even other regional Hindu, Muslim, and Sikh princes became solely dependent upon it. The rebellion sealed the fate of the Mughal rule as the British Crown directly assumed the responsibility over Indian affairs, and the later half of the nineteenth century turned out to be the high-point of the British Empire—also called the Raj. The British undertook major projects in industry, communications, agriculture, and education, and even in politics to reconstruct India in their own image, especially as Queen Victoria became the Empress of India. After the establishment of the Indian National Congress (INC) in 1885 as an intermediary channel between the Raj and the loyal Indian notables, Muslim elite also began their organizational activities.

It was in December 1906 that the Muslim delegates from all over British India met in Dhaka to form the All-India Muslim League (AIML), offering a united platform to obtain political, economic, and cultural safeguards for the world's largest Muslim community. Divided into several ethno-regional groups, South Asian Muslims, despite being in majority in the western and eastern zones, were still a scattered and generally underprivileged minority across the subcontinent. Except for the princely state of Kashmir, ruled by a Hindu Maharaja, most of the 565 princely states had Muslim minorities, whose local religious organizations usually kept them in touch with their traditional culture and past. In the British provinces such as Punjab, the United Provinces, Bengal, Bombay, and the Frontier, the Muslim professionals tried to achieve some competitive gains for their coreligionists. In 1913, M. A. Jinnah (1876–1948), the London-trained barrister, joined the Muslim League and tried for a rapprochement between the INC and the AIML through an agreed set of mutual safeguards. His efforts to seek out a common cause against British colonialism reached fruition at a joint session of both the political parties at Lucknow in 1916. Contemporary India was already astir with political agitation because of two main interrelated developments during the war years.

The British had imposed severe restrictions and censorship on political rallies and comments through some new stringent rules, whereas the future of a debilitated Muslim caliphate in Turkey appeared absolutely dismal. The struggle for the protection of the caliphate received support from certain Hindu groups as well, now led by Mohandas Karamchand (Mahatma) Gandhi (1869–1948), an Indian trained as a barrister in London. Gandhi had undergone a change while practicing law and espousing equal rights for Indians in South Africa and, in his simple native Indian dress, he now defied the Raj through peaceful boycotts, anchored on his philosophy of non-violence (*ahimsa*).

During the 1920s, Indian politics began to assume divisions on religious lines. Although both the INC and the AIML remained mainstream parties, they were largely sidelined by newer ethno-regional and sectarian constellations. Since 1909, the British government had been gradually introducing some political and constitutional reforms in India through periodic acts, so as to transfer some selective administrative powers to the Indians—elected through a narrowly defined franchise—which made party politics more competitive and even conflictive on occasions. It was, in fact, the outbreak of the Second World War and India's massive participation in the war efforts that led to more distinct political espousals by its parties. Led by Gandhi and Pundit Jawaharlal Nehru (1890–1964), the INC was deeply affronted by the British unilateral decision to commit India's human and natural resources to the war without even consulting Indians. The INC demanded complete independence for the subcontinent and pursued the Gandhian strategy of noncooperation, while the AIML, led by Jinnah, intensified its organizational efforts to transform itself into a formidable forum for Indian Muslims. Whereas Lord Linlithgow's government in Delhi filled jails with the defiant Congress workers, including its top leadership, Jinnah advocated the case for durable Muslim safeguards in view of an eventual British withdrawal from South Asia.

By the 1920s, the Indian elite knew that the British rule would certainly come to an end in the near future, yet a cohesive nationalist program incorporating the participation of various regional and religious communities was not available. The Indian Muslims were soon divided into three groups: one group subscribed to a composite Indian nationalism; another group articulated Muslim separatism, and the last one only focused on regional identities. All of them, invariably, used Islam, history, and politicoeconomic factors to justify their respective stances, although Islamists mostly fell within the first category, as they remained suspicious of territorial identities over and above communitarian or pan-Islamic loyalties. The preeminent Muslim poet-philosopher, Sir Muhammad Iqbal (1873–1938), had vacillated between an all-Indian nationalism and pan-Islamism, yet finally advised for a larger Muslim statehood, thus offering an intellectual justification for Muslim separatism. This position became the mainstay of the AIML's demand for a separate statehood in its annual convention in Lahore on March 23, 1940. Its historic resolution, embodying the demand for a Muslim statehood based on Muslim majority regions, resulted in a state named Pakistan—the Land of Pure (believers)—a term originally coined by a Muslim student at Cambridge University in 1933. Chaudhary Rehmat Ali, through his books and lectures, had urged a reorganization of the Indian provinces as sovereign Muslim states, working toward a larger inception of pluralistic composition. A pan-Islamist, Ali, like many other Muslim intellectuals, feared further marginalization of Indian Muslims in a united and sovereign India, where the Hindu majority might define as well as dominate the cultural and political ethos. His scheme, like the League's Lahore resolution, was quiet on the extent of separatism, status of minorities in the new arrangement, and other related issues such as the transfer of populations.

The British government led by Winston Churchill was reluctant to offer complete independence to India while the war went on and was not prepared even to make a commitment on any timetable for transfer of power. In 1945, with the end of the hostilities and a weakened Britain led by Labour Prime Minister Clement Attlee, India finally appeared to be heading toward independence. The British wanted to leave a united India behind, as they considered it to be their premier achievement, yet they demanded that the Indian leaders find a mutually acceptable formula on the transfer of power. Whereas the elections of 1945–1946 reaffirmed the salience of the INC as an India-wide party speaking for a unitary nationalism, the AIML also proved its credentials as the "sole" representative of Indian Muslims.

Amidst growing chaos and bloodshed, the Attlee government sent Lord Mountbatten as the last viceroy of India, who soon decided in favor of partition. He even brought forward the date of transfer of power to August 1947, which, without proper mechanisms in place, only worsened the communal situation, besides escalating the population movement across the supposed boundaries of the two emerging states. Jinnah, Nehru, and other Indian leaders including the princes accepted the partition plan within the backdrop of communal riots and dislocation of minorities. A special commission to demarcate the boundaries of two new states by partitioning the provinces of the Punjab, Bengal, and Assam was appointed by Britain. The world watched the largest migration of people across these new borders. Both India and Pakistan, despite being the beneficiaries of decolonization and sovereign nationhood, witnessed ethnic cleansing of monumental proportions, which left permanent scars on both sides.

While Mountbatten was asked to continue as the governor-general of independent India, Jinnah—now known as the Quaid-i-Azam or the Great Leader—assumed the headship of the largest Muslim state to emerge on the world map.[18] On August 14, 1947, Pakistan came into being with its capital at Karachi. A total of 1,100 miles separated its two provinces, located in the extreme west and east of what used to be the Muslim majority regions in British India, besides the incorporation of some princely states. Some 14 million people, each with harrowing stories, were already on the move when the two nations inaugurated a new phase in their history. Around one million of them never made it to their new home. Women, children, and even some elderly refugees were slaughtered mercilessly by organized armed gangs. Religious and nationalist divides were used to wreak vengeance on these hapless refugees in 1947. The unending caravans of impoverished, disorganized, and vulnerable refugees consisting of pedestrians, bullock carts, and cycles took to the dusty roads in millions to seek new homes and hearths in the scorching months of that South Asian summer of 1947. Even six decades after independence the bitter memories continue to dictate policies of mutually hostile neighbors while historians continue debating the inevitability of Partition or even any other possible alternatives to this decolonizing process. Those tragic events of 1947 have made the South Asian historiography one of the most widely contested, hotly debated, and immensely diverse scholarly pursuits in recent history.[19]

Founding the State

The evolution of the largest Muslim state and the fifth largest country in the world on August 14, 1947 was an event of historical significance both for South Asia and for the Muslim world at large. The creation of Pakistan, owing to a protracted struggle fought largely through constitutional means by barristers such as M. A. Jinnah and his fellow members of the Muslim League, was itself a formidable challenge. The separation of the two disparate wings with a hostile and bigger neighbor in between was quite anomalous given all the newness of this nation. India's encroachment on princely states such as Kashmir and Junagarh, and its refusal to share due assets with the predominantly young state, and, worst of all, stoppage of water supply to the

Indus canal system in Punjab, all signaled a stillbirth for a tormented nation that sought its mooring amongst chaos and hopes.[20]

Jinnah desired a democratic, decentralized, and tolerant Pakistan. He laid out his vision through his speeches and special addresses across "the new nation yet an old country." Jinnah, like Gandhi and Nehru of India, believed in a parliamentary form of government, which, to him, would not only guarantee an equal participation for all but also an acceptable balance between the country's eastern and western wings. Jinnah's ideal of a *Muslim* Pakistan, despite an overwhelming Muslim majority, was meant to offer equal rights and opportunities to its non-Muslim citizens. He fully realized that through peaceful and constitutional institutionalization the country would obtain a stable nationhood, as he firmly believed in its human and natural potentials. Jinnah, despite being deeply saddened by the refugee influx and problems with India over Kashmir, still desired a friendlier relationship with the larger neighbor, which decisively sat between his country's two wings and had also inherited most of the British educational, industrial, administrative, economic, and military institutions.

Pakistan, a country of 75 million inhabitants in 1947, had only two universities, very few industrial concerns, and no countrywide infrastructure to guarantee its cohesion and independence. Only the province of Punjab, now sundered because of the boundary division of 1947, had some agrarian and limited industrial potentials; otherwise East Pakistan, the NWFP, and Sindh were largely rural and agrarian regions mostly bordering on deficit. Balochistan was not yet a province and had been ruled through an amalgam of anachronistic colonial and tribal intermediaries. Karachi had been the only main port, while Chittagong, the new port in East Pakistan, was hundreds of miles away and also cut off from the major international sea-lanes. East Pakistan, smaller in size than West Pakistan, was a delta land vulnerable to floods and cyclones. During the early 1940s, this region had suffered one of the worst famines in human history, which had cost three and a half million lives. Rice, tea, and jute were the main crops in that region. With Calcutta gone to India, East Pakistan's jute mills were also left in India until Pakistan had to undertake some emergency measures. Jinnah enthused his people in his calm manner, but his death on September 11, 1948—just 13 months after independence—left it like an orphaned family with numerous problems still unresolved.

East Pakistan had a slightly bigger population than West Pakistan, yet in area West Pakistan was many times bigger. While most East Pakistanis spoke Bangla/Bengali, West Pakistanis spoke four major mother tongues. Punjabi, Sindhi, Pushtu and Balochi were not merely regional languages, they were the bedrocks of provincial identities, and thus promulgation of Urdu as a national language, however genuine for creating a strong nationalist ethos, invoked resentment from Bengalis, Sindhis, Pushtuns, and Balochis. The resentment against Urdu was stronger in East Pakistan, where Bengali was the language of the largest number of Pakistanis. Among the West Pakistanis, Punjabis accounted for a dominant share in the senior military and civilian jobs in 1947 and further on, which engendered a growing sense of alienation in East Pakistan. These pressure groups routinely opted for a centralized system with smaller provinces, harboring a grave sense of alienation. Eventually by 1953, bureaucracy and the military emerged as the strongest ruling axis with politicians playing only a peripheral role. Instead of resolving the issues of regional representation and economic redistribution through mutually agreed processes, the administrative prerogatives widened the gulf between the Eastern and Western wings. Bengali politicians and middle-class professionals felt dismayed with the bureaucratization of the young state on top of the marginalization of their own province, despite it being the most populous of all.

Quest for Nationhood, 1947–2005

The history of Pakistan for the last six decades has been a series of achievements and mishaps, all often appearing in a cyclic manner. Despite its emergence from a political and constitutional struggle, the country has been mostly ruled by strong men beholden to its army while politicians were either incapacitated in establishing enduring democratic institutions or simply proved incompetent. From 1953 to 2004, more than a dozen prime ministers were dismissed by the army command, with the country periodically falling under longer military rule or martial law. Whereas from 1953 to 1958, the military generals indirectly asserted their power on domestic and external policies, between 1958 and 1971 and from 1977 to 1989, and again from 1999 onward, they have directly ruled the nation. Pakistan's erstwhile division into two separate wings, hostilities with India, and the resultant emphasis on a centralized defense, contrasted with the weaker political traditions and a diverse populace not fully integrated within an energized and participatory political culture, hampered efforts toward democratization.

The bureaucratic-military axis formidably disallowed evolution of an all-encompassing empowerment and sabotaged efforts for an accountable setup. Over the decades, politicians and even bureaucrats in some cases have turned weaker, with the army brass running almost every major section of the nation's life. The absence of democratic institutions, with the frequent resort to strong-arm tactics and extra-constitutional measures not only dismayed major sections of the society, they also hastened the separation of East Pakistan in 1971 after a public uproar augmented by an Indian intervention.[21] A country born with so many problems and almost no industrial and scientific base became the first Muslim nation to acquire nuclear capability despite all the testing pressures. That its Diaspora has persistently helped the economy, often in unfavorable circumstances, and the country's hospitality to millions of refugees from Afghanistan and Iran since the 1980s are certainly no mean achievements if one looks at its continuous problems of governance and location in an extremely turbulent region.

Muslims, scattered all over the subcontinent in the pre-1947 era, demanded a *Muslim* state for their majority regions, along with seeking safeguards for their minority communities elsewhere. Agreeing on a common Islamic platform to run this young state turned out to be a major challenge. The regional, ethnic, sectarian, and class-based differences, without any practical model of a given Islamic state available despite all the idealism to that effect, made consensus almost impossible.[22] Most of the Pakistanis desired a welfare state guaranteeing an honorable and secure life free from exploitation, and they would not shirk from acquiring knowledge and inspiration from any direction. However, when the politicians, bureaucrats, and generals dithered on constitution making or, because of their own specific interests, used Islam to whitewash their ad hoc policies, the mundane differences within the nation turned more acute. The narrowly defined Islamic ethos, as applied both by the regimes and the diverse class of clerics *(ulama)*, only exacerbated social divisions and disillusionment. Instead of sustained efforts toward nation building, Islam was used as a convenient legitimizer by authoritarian regimes merely to skirt the issue of representation and accountability, and the country was sundered in 1971. Again, during the 1980s, its civil society suffered gravely from a selective use of Islamic penal codes under another military dictator, General Zia-ul-Haq. Earlier, General Yahya Khan's brutal suppression of East Pakistanis in 1971, despite a fervent avowal of Islam, could not stop the evolution of Bangladesh, and General Zia-ul-Haq's discretionary use of Islam from 1977 to 1988 only aggravated sectarian schisms besides imposing repressive measures, which almost debilitated Pakistan's reforming classes.[23]

After the Indo-Pakistani War of 1971, East Pakistan transformed itself into the sovereign state of Bangladesh and began its new chapter in history under the leadership of recently freed Sheikh Mujibur Rahman. In West Pakistan, the generals reluctantly gave way to Zulfikar Ali Bhutto, the leader of Pakistan People's Party (PPP), to put the house in order. Bhutto did enthuse his people, sought help from the Muslim countries, negotiated with India on the return of POWs and on Kashmir, and also led the efforts for a new constitution for Pakistan. The Constitution of 1973 retained a parliamentary form of government where the president enjoyed only ceremonial powers and the prime minister represented the majority vote. The upper house—the Senate—like its American counterpart, offered equal representation to all four constituent parts in Pakistan, while the lower house received representation on the basis of population.

However, Bhutto soon fell to his own authoritarian tendencies and while trying to neutralize any threat from the army or religious opponents, tried to outdo them. He chose General Zia-ul-Haq as the new army chief. Although Zia-ul-Haq was the junior of all his colleagues. Bhutto thought Zia-ul-Haq's religious and conservative disposition might deter him from staging a military coup. Bhutto was soon proven wrong. Political opposition to Bhutto had begun a public agitation in early 1977 to dislodge him after the allegations of rigging in national elections. Opponents also accused him of murdering a political opponent, Nawab Ahmad Khan Qasuri. The street agitation soon turned violent, finally allowing General Zia-ul-Haq to stage a coup on July 4, 1977 resulting in Bhutto's dismissal and his subsequent execution in April 1979.[24] General Zia-ul-Haq led Pakistan through the third martial rule in the country's history and suspended the erstwhile constitution. His military courts dished out quick and often harsh decisions on various civic issues, and soon the Islamist generals began to implement a strict religious penal code, skirting the issues of governance and democracy.[25]

General Zia-ul-Haq was helped by the Soviet invasion of Afghanistan in December 1979, where a fledgling communist government had been struggling against a growing threat in the name of *Jihad* (holy war). With the Cold War, the United States and other Western allies soon began to provide covert assistance to the Afghan warriors *(Mujahideen)* with Pakistan operating as the conduit for aid as well as a sanctuary for them. The Soviet invasion of this land-locked Muslim region caused an outflow of five million Afghan refugees with more than three million pouring into Pakistan. Zia-ul-Haq soon assumed a leading profile in the resistance against the Soviet Union and thus consolidated his domestic position by crushing political opposition.[26] By this time, Bhutto's eldest daughter, Benazir Bhutto, had taken the mantle of the leadership and her return to the country in 1986 from London strengthened a marooned PPP. However, by then, Zia-ul-Haq had been able to make drastic amendments in the constitution to suit his own personal imperatives besides indemnifying all his laws and ordinances. His drastic amendments took away the powers from the prime minister as well as from the parliament, while concentrating them in the office of the president—in this case General Zia-ul-Haq himself.

Zia-ul-Haq's rule ended with his mysterious death on August 17, 1988 in an air crash in southeastern Pakistan along with the death of the U.S. ambassador and several senior generals. This incident allowed democracy to return to Pakistan with Benazir Bhutto becoming the first elected woman leader of a Muslim nation. However in 1990, after just 18 months, her government was dissolved by Zia-ul-Haq's civilian successor, Ghulam Ishaque Khan, who had retained the crucial powers to dissolve parliament and the prime minister.[27] The new elections in 1990 resulted in the victory of a resuscitated Muslim

League, led by a Punjabi businessman, Mian Nawaz Sharif, who himself soon fell afoul of the president. As in the case of Benazir Bhutto, Sharif was accused of incompetence and corruption.[28] However, with the intervention of the Supreme Court, Sharif was restored to his office; yet his conflict with Ishaque Khan (as well as with Benazir Bhutto) continued until the Army generals dismissed both of them in early 1993.

After another round of elections in late 1993, the PPP won the majority of seats and Benazir Bhutto started her second term as the prime minister. Her problems with President Farooq Leghari—himself from the PPP—weakened Bhutto, and her government was dismissed in 1996 by Leghari on the grounds of incompetence and corruption. Another round of elections offered yet another opportunity for Nawaz Sharif to assume prime ministership in 1996, and he began to roll back unilateral amendments introduced by Zia-ul-Haq a decade earlier. Despite amassing all the powers and a solid parliamentary majority, Sharif still remained apprehensive of ambitious generals. In May 1998, following India's suit, Sharif ordered the testing of Pakistan's hitherto secretly developed nuclear arsenal, which, in fact, had been begun by Zulfikar Ali Bhutto in the mid-1970s after the Indian nuclear test of 1974.[29]

In February 1999, Sharif welcomed the Indian prime minister A. B. Vajpayee, to Lahore for a summit aiming to end a five- decade-old hostility. This visit, however, was not appreciated by the military and religious leaders in the country. Sharif felt quite insecure and tried to replace the army chief, General Pervez Musharraf, with his own favorite in October 1999, while the general was on his way back from Sri Lanka. The other generals supported Musharraf and overthrew Sharif and implicated him in the case of a conspiracy to hijack Musharraf's plane with intent to kill him. The Supreme Court found Sharif guilty, but the generals allowed him and his family to seek exile in Saudi Arabia. Benazir Bhutto was already in exile since her second dismissal, and thus General Musharraf ruled the country, promising new reforms, clean government, and an accountability drive to check corruption in the country. In fact, both Benazir Bhutto and Nawaz Sharif had squandered the entire decade of the 1990s by fighting each other in a culture of corrupt cronyism. Thus, for many Pakistanis, Musharraf's coup on October 12, 1999 was welcome.

The overthrow of Sharif and his trial at the behest of generals was not appreciated in the West. Pakistan soon became a pariah state in the global community. It was suspended from the Commonwealth, and Islamabad's relations with India were also put on the hold. However, the events of September 11, 2001 changed the entire geopolitical scenario. Pakistan, the erstwhile supporter of the Taliban regime since its inception in 1994, not only withdrew its crucial support from the regime but also joined the U.S.-led coalition against terror.[30] General Musharraf, by now a self-assumed president, soon emerged as a close ally in London and Washington. Relations with India, after a nosedive in 2002, began to improve with U.S. persuasion. Like the preceding generals, Musharraf cashed in on his external support and introduced vital changes in the country's already marooned constitution by concentrating powers in his own twin offices of the president and the army chief.[31] Like Generals Ayub Khan and Zia-ul-Haq, he opted for local elections first. After a dubious referendum in April 2003, he was appointed as the president for five years. After further unilateral changes in the constitution through a Legal Framework Order (LFO), General Musharraf held the national and provincial elections in such a way that the mainstream national parties such as the PPP and the Muslim League received only a split vote while the religiopolitical parties were able to stage an unprecedented comeback. Manipulated through the intelligence agencies, the country's political system, despite a weak and disempowered parliament, remained vulnerable to official machinations. However, the economy under Musharraf certainly improved and its global isolation largely disappeared. But, Pakistan in 2005, even after almost six decades, still lacked a proper and durable political system and seemed adrift, thanks to so-called strong men who have always prioritized their personal and specific interests over the national interests.

NOTES

1. According to the Washington-based Population Reference Bureau. Quoted in *Dawn* (Karachi), 20 August 2004.

2. For an interesting work on the region's biodiversity, see *The Indus River: Biodiversity, Resources, Humankind,* ed. Azra Meadows and Peter Meadows (Karachi: Oxford University Press, 1999).

3. While Khunjrab Pass and other less traversed passes open into western China, the Tochi, Gomal, Khojak, and Bolan Passes lead into West Asia. The borders with India outside Kashmir are across plains, deserts, and through the Indus delta.

4. It is said that the famous English writer, Rudyard Kipling, sought among these people the locale of his story, *The Man Who would be King* and popularized the myth of these non-Muslim Chitralis seeking their origins from the Greek armies of Alexander the Great, who had, in fact, passed through this region in the fourth century B.C. Imperial campaigners like George Robertson and modern-day writers such as Eric Newby and John Keay have written extensively on these regions and their recent past. For a fascinating travelogue through this region, see Geoffrey Moorhouse, *To the Frontier* (London: Hodder and Stoughton, 1984).

5. Pakistan's performance in terms of education, health, and basic needs is not very impressive compared with that of some other countries in the region. Its ranking had fallen down to 147 in 2004. For a country-specific report on Pakistan, see *Pakistan: National Development Report 2003, Poverty, Growth and Governance,* http://www.un.org.pk.nhdr/.

6. The refugees from the Indian part of Punjab spoke Punjabi and were allotted lands vacated by outgoing Hindu and Sikh refugees, and in the same manner, Urdu-speaking refugees were allocated to cities and adjoining areas. The gradual urbanization and Green Revolution led to north-south migration within the country during the 1970s, and cities like Karachi became the most pluralistic megapolises, where competition over jobs, housing, and transport often took the shape of ethnic strife. Demographically, Pakistan has undergone radical changes over the last few decades. For instance, there are more Baloch in Karachi now than in Balochistan province, which accounts for 43 percent of the country's territory. Karachi is also the biggest Pushtun city and not Peshawar or Mardan on the Frontier. The Punjabi refugees assimilated themselves into the local culture and institutions successfully, whereas the tensions between the refugees and the local Sindhis in Sindh occasionally turned volatile. For details, see Iftikhar H. Malik, *State and Civil Society in Pakistan: Politics of Authority, Ideology and Ethnicity* (Oxford: St. Antony's-Palgrave Series, 1997).

7. For a very useful and holistic study, see Tariq Rahman, *Language and Politics in Pakistan* (Karachi: Oxford University Press, 1996).

8. There is not enough information available to Pakistani students on the non-Muslim ratio in their population, as the emphasis remains on Muslim national identity. For further information on religious pluralism, see Iftikhar H. Malik, *Religious Minorities in Pakistan* (London: Minority Rights Group, 2002).

9. The system is duplicated at the provincial level, where unicameral legislatures, elected through universal suffrage, run the administration. Governors, appointed by Islamabad, head the provinces, whereas the chief minister and the cabinet represent the majority party in the provincial legislature. All four provinces have their own capitals and raise funds through local taxes and contributions from the federation (central government) and have their respective higher courts. Azad Kashmir—the Pakistan-administered part of the disputed territory—has its own president, prime minister, legislature, and higher and lower courts. The Northern Areas, comprising Gilgit and Baltistan, are administered by the federation and do not have any representation in the federal legislature because, as part of an erstwhile princely state their legal position remains undefined. However, tribal regions on the Frontier and within Balochistan enjoy legislative representation but are internally governed by customary tribal laws and through political agents.

10. There are several political parties in Pakistan with the Muslim League, Pakistan People's Party, Jama'at-i-Islami, Jamiat-i-Ulama-i-Islam, and Jamiat-i-Ulama-i-Pakistan being nationwide, while regional and ethnic parties also abound. However, frequent military take-overs have not allowed a smooth running of party politics. The tribal and feudal landlords lack party commitment and mostly end up supporting whoever holds the power. The army, certainly, remains the most powerful pressure group and actor in Pakistani national life, and its chiefs have frequently captured power through coups. Thus, the problems of governance remain endemic to Pakistan, which itself was achieved through a political and constitutional struggle led by Muslim leaders in British India.

Between 1947 and 2005, Pakistan had 16 prime ministers and not a single one of them could complete the full term. Most of the dismissals were at the behest of the army generals who would rule the country indefinitely and bring in their own favorite type of political system. The country had several constitutions over the last 60 years, but they were either suspended by the generals or amended to suit their own personal interests. The problems of governance have deeply harrowed the country since the death of its founding father, Mohammad Ali Jinnah, in 1948. See Ian Talbot, *Pakistan: A Modern History* (London: Hurst, 2005); Lawrence Ziring, *Pakistan in the Twentieth Century: A Political History* (Karachi: Oxford University Press, 1997); Paula Newberg, *Judging the State: Courts and Constitutional Politics in Pakistan* (Cambridge: Cambridge University Press, 1995); and Iftikhar H. Malik, "Pakistan in 2001: The Afghanistan Crisis and the Rediscovery of the Frontline State," *Asian Survey* 42, no. 1 (2002): 204–12.

11. Claiming a major chunk of national resources, the defense sector employs nearly two million troops in all the three active forces. The country imports most of the hard equipment for its army, navy, and air force, and, given a pronounced emphasis on security vis-à-vis India, it ends up paying salaries, pensions, and other expenditures at the cost of billions of rupees. The defense sector is largely a tax-free area and the expenditure on nuclearization has been quite massive and equally unaudited. Many defense-related housing, commercial, and other such schemes account for an economic sector that is not open to competition or taxation. For statistics on military personnel and hardware, see the annual surveys such as those published by reputable think tanks such as the International Centre for Strategic Studies, London.

12. Officially, as admitted by General Musharraf in 2003 and further corroborated by various sources, 35 percent of the population was living in poverty.

13. For useful information on Pakistan's economy, see the annual *National Economic Survey*, published by the government. The subject-specific annual reports on South Asia by the Human Development Centre in Islamabad have a wide array of useful comparison with other neighbors. For comprehensive information on the subject, see S. Akbar Zaidi, *Issues in Pakistan's Economy* (Karachi: Oxford University Press, 1999).

14. Mark Kenoyer, *Ancient Cities of the Indus Valley Civilization* (Karachi: Oxford University Press, 1998).

15. For a compact and illustrated history since ancient times, see John Keay, *A History of India* (New York: HarperCollins, 2000). Also, see Hermann Kulke and Dietmar Rothermund, *A History of India* (New York: Routledge, 2004).

16. R.E.M. Wheeler, *Five Thousand Years of Pakistan* (London: Royal India and Pakistan Society, 1950).

17. For more details, see Aziz Ahmad, *Studies in Islamic Culture in the Indian Environment* (Delhi: Oxford University Press, 1999) (reprint); S.M. Ikram, *Modern Muslim India and the Birth of Pakistan* (Lahore: Research Society, 1995) (reprint); Farzana Shaikh, *Community and Consensus in Islam: Muslim Representation in Colonial India, 1860–1947* (Cambridge: Cambridge University Press, 1989); and, David Lelyveld, *Aligarh's First Generation: Muslim Solidarity in British India* (Delhi: Oxford University Press, 1996) (reprint).

18. For more on the Quaid-i-Azam (the Great Leader) M.A. Jinnah, see Stanley Wolpert, *Jinnah of Pakistan* (Berkeley: University of California Press), 1984.

19. There is an impressive historiography on modern South Asia including the freedom struggle. For more on Pakistan, see Ayesha Jalal, *The Sole Spokesman: Jinnah, the Muslim League and the Demand for Pakistan* (Cambridge: Cambridge University Press, 1985) (reprinted in 1993); Francis Robinson, *Separatism among Indian Muslims: the Politics of the United Provinces' Muslims* (Cambridge: Cambridge University Press, 1974) (reprinted in 1993); and, Mushirul Hasan, *Legacy of a Divided Nation: India's Muslims Since Independence* (London: Hurst, 1997).

20. These issues, especially the dispute with India over Kashmir, have continued to undermine Indo-Pakistani relations. For more on the Kashmir dispute, see Alastair Lamb, *Birth of a Tragedy: Kashmir 1947* (Hertingfordbury: Roxford Books, 1994), and Alastair Lamb, *Kashmir: A Disputed Legacy, 1846–1990* (Hertingfordbury: Roxford Books, 1991).

21. For more details, see Hasan Zaheer, *The Separation of East Pakistan* (Karachi: Oxford University Press, 1994); and, Richard Sisson and Leo E. Rose, *War and Secession: Pakistan, India and the Creation of Bangladesh* (Berkeley: University of California Press, 1990).

22. For more on this, S. Akbar Zaidi, ed., *Regional Imbalances and the National Question in Pakistan* (Lahore: Vanguard, 1992).

23. For further information on ideological issues and the role of Islam in Pakistani politics, see Iftikhar H. Malik, *Islam, Nationalism and the West: Issues of Identity in Pakistan* (Oxford: St. Antony's-Macmillan/Palgrave Series, 1999); and Seyyed Vali Reza Nasr, *Mawdudi and the Making of Islamic Revolution* (New York: Oxford University Press, 1996.)

24. For biographical details on Z. A. Bhutto, see Stanley Wolpert, *Zulfi Bhutto of Pakistan: His Life and Times* (Karachi: Oxford University Press, 1993).

25. Other than exacerbating the problems of governance, General Zia-ul-Haq's Islamization further marginalized minorities and women. See Khawar Mumtaz and Farida Shaheed, *Women of Pakistan: Two Steps Forward. One Step Back?* (London: Zed Books, 1987).

26. For an interesting exposé of the operation that cost billions of dollars and involved the United States, Pakistan, Egypt, Saudi Arabia, and several other actors, see George Crile, *My Enemy's Enemy: The Story of the Largest Covert Operation in History. The Arming of the Mujahideen by the CIA* (London: Atlantic Books, 2003).

27. Benazir Bhutto wrote an autobiography, *Daughter of the East* (London: Hamish Hamilton, 1988).

28. For a journalistic overview, see Christina Lamb, *Waiting for Allah: Pakistan's Struggle for Democracy* (London: Penguin, 1991).

29. For early background, see George Perkovich, *India's Nuclear Bomb: The Impact on Global Proliferation* (Delhi: Oxford University Press, 2003) (reprint); and Ziba Moshaver, *Nuclear Proliferation in the Indian Subcontinent* (London: Macmillan, 1991). For more recent commentaries, see http://www.sacw.com; http://www.saan.com; http://www.satribune.com; and http://www.paktribune.com.

30. See Bob Woodward, *Bush at War* (New York: Simon & Schuster, 2002). For a well-informed analysis of the Taliban, see Ahmed Rashid, *Taliban: Islam, Oil and the New Great Game in Central Asia* (London: I B. Tauris, 2000).

31. For an interesting overview by a Western journalist, see Owen B. Jones, *Pakistan: Eye of the Storm* (New Haven, CT: Yale University Press, 2002). Also, Stephen P. Cohen, *The Idea of Pakistan* (Washington, DC: Brookings Institution, 2004). For the sites maintained by the government and related departments of Pakistan, visit: http://www.pakistan.gov.pk.

SUGGESTED READINGS

Cohen, Stephen P. *The Idea of Pakistan.* Washington, DC: Brookings Institution, 2004.

Keay, John. *When Men and Mountains Meet.* Karachi: Oxford University Press, 1993.

Lamb, Alastair. *Birth of a Tragedy: Kashmir 1947.* Hertingfordbury: Roxford, 1994.

Malik, Iftikhar H. *State and Civil Society in Pakistan: Politics of Authority, Ideology and Ethnicity.* Oxford: St. Antony's Series, 1997.

Meadows, Azra, and Peter Meadows. *The Indus River: Biodiversity, Resources, Humankind.* Karachi: Oxford University Press, 1999.

Murphy, Dervla. *Where the Indus Is Young.* London: Century, 1977.

———. *Full Tilt.* London: Flamingo, 1995.

Talbot, Ian. *Pakistan: A Modern History.* London: Hurst, 2005.

Wheeler, R.E.M. *Five Thousand Years of Pakistan.* London: Royal Society, 1950.

Zaheer, Hasan. *The Separation of East Pakistan.* Karachi: Oxford University Press, 1994.

Ziring, Lawrence. *Pakistan: At the Crossroad of History.* Oxford: Oneworld, 2003.

2

Thought and Religion

The humanitarian traditions of *sufism* spread Islam in the Subcontinent, and Hindus, Sikhs, Christians and Muslims were equal before God. The inspiration derived from Sufi character was an advantage to our faith, and the tolerant and refined image of Islam was the ideal that was accepted.

—Maulana Abdus Sattar Edhi,
the preeminent Pakistani charity worker, 2000[1]

Pakistan, literally meaning, "the Land of the Pure," is overwhelmingly Muslim. Around 11 percent of Pakistanis are non-Muslim, and even among Muslims there are various sects.[2] However, religion plays a very important and often dominant role in the private as well as public life. Religion, being the bedrock of a collective life, feeds into a pluralistic national ethos and, with a strong accent on traditional values, significantly translates itself into a powerful national characteristic. Religious diversity, intra-Muslim pluralism, and ethnic identities, collectively underwrite the thought processes, cultural norms, and pervasive outlook of the Pakistanis.

Certainly, in a country of that size, there are individuals with ultra-modern lifestyles, yet the society predominantly remains traditional, family-oriented, and consciously religious. Religion provides overarching bonds, while history, a shared ecology, and uniform textbooks underwrite national attitudes. The lifestyles inherited from the ancient Indus Valley feature shared traditions within a visible and decisive Islamic context. They allow cultural variations, although it is not difficult to seek out pluralistic and historic antecedents of various norms and practices. Migrations, political upheavals, wars with India, instability in the neighboring Afghanistan, and a cherished desire to build bridges with the Muslim world—without resisting modern amenities—characterize the attitudes of Pakistanis, whose pan-Islamism coexists with a stronger national identity. Under these two predominant identity markers, diverse religious and regional expressions persist as subterranean realities.

Thus, while it is easy to demarcate the individual characteristics of a national culture, it is equally possible to discern its numerous and often diverse manifestations. Not only the regional proclivities, even the global geopolitical developments further strengthen both the religious and national embodiments. For instance, the events of September 11, 2001 and the invasions of West Asian regions by the United States and Britain have added emphasis to Islamic values, weakening the penchant for a Westernized modernity. Often, it appears as if Muslimness predominates over national, regional, or other such identity markers. From the name of the country—the Islamic Republic of Pakistan—to the far-away rural and tribal settlements, Islam is a visible and powerful reality that one encounters in private discussions and collective customs. The country's capital—one of the newest and most well-planned cities in the world—is itself called Islamabad, or the city of Islam. The important national documents, speeches by leaders, television and radio broadcasts, and even the textbooks begin by invoking Allah, the Prophet, and the Muslim beliefs. From the country's inception to its external policies and educational system, Islam is a major determinant and also an important collective experience even for smaller Muslim sects. On occasions, more than national or ethnic identity, it is the Muslimness that turns out to be the most-shared characteristic. As in Iran or Saudi Arabia and Bangladesh, being Muslim, at times, seems to subsume every other collective identity, new or old.[3]

Among the 159 million Pakistanis, 140 million are Muslims, 6 million are Hindus, and almost the same number are Christians.[4] Most of the Hindus left present-day Pakistani regions at the time of impendence in 1947, but some communities remain in rural Sindh and the interiors of Balochistan. They are mostly rural or small-town commercial communities that, due to the Indo-Pakistani hostilities and Hindu-Muslim riots in India, maintain a low-key profile. Life in a feudal situation such as in Sindh, despite its traditional reputation as a safe zone, hinders equal citizenship for these non-Muslim Pakistanis. Most of the Christians live in the Punjab province, with a sizeable presence in Karachi and Quetta, and they pursue menial jobs. Christianity was reintroduced in South Asia during the colonial period with the arrival of missionaries and generally involved indigenous people from the poorer and underprivileged sections. Thus, despite having established very good schools, Christians have been the victims of social biases and after September 11, 2001 there have been some attacks on their churches.[5]

Hindu temple inside the Rohtas fort. Courtesy of the author.

The human rights groups have been highlighting their predicament, but the fact remains that from the textbooks to media, these communities are less known to most Pakistanis. In the same vein, after the declaration in 1974 by the Pakistani parliament that Ahmadis were non-Muslims because of their views on the finality of prophethood, one can add at least two million more people as another minority. Mostly based in Punjab, with an affluent diaspora in Western Europe, these people share ethnicity and kinship with other Pakistanis but, many Muslims would avoid matrimonial relations with them. In the same vein, Ahmadis also shun religious and marriage ties with the other Muslim sects.[6] There are a few thousand Sikhs, who are found in the Punjab and the Frontier, including some in the tribal belt, who have not been threatened by any majoritarian backlash. A few hundred Parsis in Karachi and Lahore are the descendants of the traditional Zoroastrian families of India and have been usually well placed on the socioeconomic ladder. Indeed, some Parsis, such as Dorab Patel, A. Kaikous, Ardsher Cowasjee, Behram Avari, and Bapsi Sidhwa are national role models.[7]

ONE ISLAM, MANY MUSLIMS

Islam is one of the world's fastest-growing religions, and, compared with other Middle Eastern religions such as Judaism, Zoroastrianism, and Christianity, it is comparatively young. Even compared with Hinduism, Jainism, and Buddhism, it is certainly a younger tradition. Literally, "Islam" means submission, peace, and safety. Muslims believe that Prophet Muhammad (570 A.D.–632 A.D.) was not its founder but rather the facilitator of the same message that the early Judeo-Christian prophets had brought. To them, Islam originated with Adam and Eve and is, in fact, the religion of every newborn child until society inculcates another ideology into him or her.

The Prophet remains the core figure as well as the reference for all their beliefs and practices. The Prophet Muhammad's life is recounted from his early years to prophethood at the age of 40, migration to Medinah, battles, and the formation of the pioneering Muslim community. The intermingling of religion with the mundane made the early prophetic era into an ideal classical age for generations of Muslims to come.[8] Muhammad's humble, poor, and unschooled childhood resonates with most of the poor. His kindness, honesty, and tolerance become the ideals, whereas his occupation as a merchant, love marriage to a senior woman (Khadija), devotion to his companions, and then his disenchantment with the contemporary religious practices have always found sympathy with the ordinary, oppressed, and toiling people.[9] His modesty and kindness to non-Muslims, women, and animals, and the emphasis on purity, probity, and devotion through personal examples offer a human precedent to all Muslims.

The divine revelations transmitted through the Prophet and then fully illustrated by personal examples *(sunnah),* accompanied by oral guidance *(hadith)* offer a written corpus for Muslims. The Prophet taught the importance of beliefs in the unity of God (Allah), prophethoods of the earlier prophets and the validity of their messages, the existence of the angels, and the inevitability of the Day of Judgment. The Quran is Allah's exhortation, providing the guidelines for a fulfilling life in the interest of a greater life

Shah Jahan mosque, Thatta. Courtesy of the author.

hereafter. Prophet Muhammad epitomized the divine will on worship and human rights, thus making the Quran and Muhammad deeply interrelated. Muhammad's example as the perfect human being *(Insaan-i-Kaamil)* became the touchstone for his companions and descendants, who are much revered by the followers.[10] The Muslim duties to Allah—*huqooqul Allah*—include daily prayers, fasting, the pilgrimage to Makkah (formerly Mecca), and charity, and they are as important as the obligation to fellow human beings—*huqooqul Ibaad*—encompassing dependents, relatives, neighbors, and the world at large.

Soon after the Prophet's death, Muslims established empires that included several pluralistic regional and cultural traditions across the three continents of Africa, Asia, and Europe and promoted learning, research, and arts. Their intellectual achievements and scientific pursuits from the early Prophetic period to the decline of Muslim political rule and the emergence of European colonialism in the late eighteenth century are frequently highlighted through literature, sermons, and such other collective activities. Muslims all over the world, including Pakistanis, believe that the Muslim decline resulted from the ineptness of the elite and because of partisan external interventions.

The West is admired for its scientific and economic achievements, but its political and often divisive role in the Muslim world is problematic. The political situation in such places as Palestine, Chechnya, Bosnia, Kashmir, Afghanistan, Iraq, Moroland, Abkhazia, and cases of foreign invasions have become sad reminders to Muslims of the incompetence and corruption among their elite, where politicized Islam is perceived as the redeemer and healer. In the last several years, various forms of political Islam have used the ideology of holy war *(Jihad)* to wrest control of postcolonial states, and the war on terror has certainly intensified both the anger and anguish. Although there is a greater curiosity around the world to understand Islam, Muslims grieve over their own continued disempowerment. Apologia, aggression, and moderation characterize common Muslim responses, although more and more Muslims are trying to revisit their heritage within the changed times. Countries such as Pakistan see Islam as a binding force, yet people within remain divided if not polarized across the sectarian, ethnic, and national fault lines. The Muslim traditionalists and revivalists would like to relive the past by following the early scriptures to the letter; the modernists and reformers would seek solutions in conjunction with modernity. The scripturalists see in Islam more than a mere religion and a rather holistic order; the modernists would insist on synthesizing Islamic values with mundane solutions borrowed from elsewhere. While to scripturalists and purists, including the religiopolitical parties in Pakistan, Islam is the solution, to the secularists, it does not deter from acculturation.

SCRIPTURALISTS AND SUFIS

Scholars may go on debating the unity as well as the diversity within the Islamic experience. Unity may symbolize the universality of faith and basic rituals while diversity may reflect denominational, ethnic, and class-based variations. One may endlessly reflect on "High," "Low," and "Folk" Islam given the interpretations and practices, but two larger categories among Muslims are dealt with here. Islam, according to many clerics—*ulama*—has to be perceived within the strict and literalist code of its classical sources. In other words, the Quran, Hadith, and Sunnah, forming the Islamic corpus, are sufficient and competent for all the times to come without needing any new interpretations or contextualization. The various parties and groups among Muslims include such literalists. They would, usually, rule out the role of intermediaries—saints—and consider any bridgehead between the Creator and humanity merely as innovation.

Parallel to them are Muslims who believe that truth can be reached through intermediaries and Islam can coexist with all kinds of other ideological groups. Such a view was upheld by Sufis or mystics, who consider the Prophet Muhammad and his family and companions as the mainstream of Islamic mysticism. The Arabic word, *suf,* which literally means *wool,* is the origin of Sufism harkening to the austere life that the Prophet himself led. He usually carried a blanket over his shoulder, and some of his companions lived in his mosque wearing simple woolen clothes. Lambs, especially the newly born, symbolize innocence as in several other religious traditions, and its wool is used both for headgear and for protection against cold. Muslim mysticism considers love for Allah to be the true love and the ultimate goal for a lover, while Muhammad is the guide as well as a beloved to lead to the sublime light *(Noor)*. Accordingly, other than physical needs, it is the spirituality that has to be harnessed by a less mundane world and greater respect for other human beings irrespective of their creed, color, or class. Thus, Sufism is both a socializer and equalizer while allowing a common search for higher love under the guidance of a mentor *(Murhsid)*. Soon after the Prophet's death, Muslim expansion led to the development of scriptural as well as Sufi doctrines, occasionally both complementing each other.[11]

Other than the eminent clerics in Muslim history codifying Islamic history and law, there have been several Sufi orders *(silsilahs),* who presented a very simple and egalitarian face of Islam. These Sufis spread Islam in Africa and Central, Southern, and South-Eastern Asia, where egalitarian Muslim practices usually attracted the oppressed and underprivileged masses. While scripturalists might try to impose a more puritanical version of Islam, Sufis tolerated and even adopted many non-Muslim customs and costumes, making it into a more blended tradition.[12] To many contemporary observers, literalists represent High Islam of a fundamentalist nature, whereas Sufis embody Folk Islam, which may be on decline due to urbanization, education, and greater emphasis on purist interpretations.

However, most of the Pakistani Muslims follow Sufis and visit shrines and listen to Sufi music called *qawalli*. On the other hand, a growing middle class of Muslim purists consider dance and music to be latter-day influences from non-Islamic sources, which have to be shunned. All across Pakistan, as elsewhere, there are especially built tombs of the past Sufi masters whose descendants stay in touch with their followers and hold periodic functions where food, music, and sermons are featured for several days. In some cases, these persons, locally known as *pirs* (spiritual leaders), hold special prayers for the sick and distressed and may offer charms for the eradication of any discomfort. The shrines offer free food, which are, in fact, offerings from the disciples. Some of these *pirs* are very influential in local politics and have large property holdings, bought with the income from the shrine. Thus, to many educated people, such practices not only encourage irrational customs, they also stem from an exploitation of the underprivileged sections of the society. However, even in the diaspora—excluding Saudi Arabia—visiting Pakistani *pirs* are widely entertained by their disciples, who shower them with money and presents.[13]

THE INDO-ISLAMIC CULTURE

Islam arrived in the South Asian subcontinent because of two factors: Sufis and conquerors. Within the first century of Islam, Muslim publicists, traders, and Sufis had embarked on travels to distant lands in Asia, Africa, and Europe. Their interaction with the indigenous communities led to the early conversions, especially from among those who had been either oppressed because of their color, caste, or class, or were simply eager to adopt a new, austere, and dynamic creed. Muslim Sufis as well as regular publicists, in their own ways, reflected Islam as an egalitarian, focused, and self-assured way of life without demanding any total denial of the past cultural heritage and languages. Muslim Arabs formally invaded the Indus Delta in A.D. 712 and conquered areas all the way into southern Punjab, making present-day Pakistan an integral part of the Muslim caliphate in Damascus. Led by a youthful general, Muhammad ibn Qasim, Muslim armies defeated the local Hindu ruler, Raja Dahir, but strictly avoided forcibly converting the subjects to Islam.[14]

In fact, Ibn Qasim and his soldiers befriended the local populace, and it was mainly because of their tolerance as well as an efficient administration during chaotic times that Islam began to attract new converts. The Sufis and the future Muslim ruling dynasties, accompanied by artists, publicists, and adventurers mostly entered India through the western mountain passes and spread across the breadth and length of the subcontinent. In addition, Muslim sailors and businessmen reinvigorated their contacts with the coastal areas of Balochistan and western India, although such multiple contacts with the Middle East and Africa had predated the beginning of the Islamic era. However, Islamic conquest and the commercial and cultural relationship with India resulted in the region's integration into a larger cultural and political zone, now under Muslim control. The most significant component of this new interface, among several other important developments, was the evolution of a rich, multifarious, and highly sophisticated Indo-Islamic culture that combined the best of several traditions. Whereas Iranian, Turkish, and Arab Muslims adopted Indian skills and sciences, their synthesis with the Greek and African traditions and technologies ushered in a unique form of globalism combining these disparate regions into a new cultural entity.

Within India, Muslim rule extended for more than a thousand years, all the way from the conquest of Sindh by Ibn Qasim until the beginning of British rule in the late eighteenth century, although Muslims generally remained a sizeable minority across a vast and equally polyglot subcontinent. Although most Muslim *ulama* would have wanted to convert everybody to Islam, the Muslim rulers of all dynasties, except for one or two individuals, avoided undertaking this mission.[15] As in Ottoman Turkey and earlier in Muslim Spain and West Africa, Islam was synthesized with several cultural traditions instead of obliterating them. In particular, the Sufis played a vanguard role in intermingling with local cultures and peoples. From the arrival of Islam in India until recent times, this cultural interaction became the mainstay of a highly sophisticated and diffused Indo-Islamic culture, where Persian emerged as the literary and official language of the entire region. This cultural diffusion included areas such as language, literature, arts, cuisine, architecture, music, urban planning, and an overall celebration of India. The conquerors, within a few years of arrival in India, would adopt it as their home by becoming a part of this enriching Indo-Islamic culture, which expressed itself through the Persian language. After the early Arabs, most of the Muslim rulers of India were of Turkic stock, but, once in India, they adopted Persian both as a literary and court language. Of course, Arabic remained the language of the Muslim classics and the medium of prayers, but it was Persian that overtook all other languages. By this time, Sanskrit had become too elitist and was confined to a few Hindu ecclesiastic circles and Indian Persian emerged as the lingua franca.

For centuries, literature in Indian Persian excelled over its Iranian counterparts, given the vast Indian resources at the disposal of the literati and the official patronage. Some of the greatest writers, such as Baidil, Badayuni, Bairam Khan, Abul Fazl, Faizi, Khan-i-Khannan, Naziri Nishapuri, and Mirza Ghalib, were Indians, whereas emperors such as Jahangir or princesses such as Gulbadan Begum and Zaibun Nissa—the Mughal royals during the sixteenth and seventeenth centuries—wrote their biographical and literary works in their native Persian. These Muslim ruling elites even tried to revive Sanskrit, as under the early Mughals such as Akbar the Great (d. 1603). Great poets such as Kali Das composed in this classical language, and Tan Sen sang classical epics. Akbar's great-grandson, Prince Dara Shikoh, was a great scholar of Sanskrit and Persian and made several efforts to combine Sufi and Hindu mystical traditions. The Mughal era in India, especially during its heyday from 1526 to 1707, is viewed by all as the golden age of this Indo-Persian culture where emphasis was on cooperation and synthesis. Even in the Indian south, generally known as Deccan, the various regional and religious traditions were celebrated by the ruler of Bijapur, Ahmadnagar, and Vijaynagar.[16]

As late as the 1780s and 1790s, Muslim rulers of Mysore—Sultan Hyder Ali and Sultan Tipu—were actively resisting the British onslaught. Tipu Sultan, a valiant ruler, is celebrated both in India and Pakistan as an eminent freedom fighter, who died fighting the forces of the British East India Company at Saranagapatam in 1799. During the Sikh rule over Punjab in the early nineteenth century, Persian remained the official language, and most of the ministers and administrators in Lahore Darbar were, in fact, Muslim.

The Indo-Islamic culture flourished within a tolerant and blended milieu where Sufi poetry and similar mystical literature by Hindu Bhagats and Sikh Gurus flourished concurrently. It was only in the nineteenth century when Persian gave way to English, while Urdu and Hindi emerged as two main literary expressions among the Muslims and Hindus, that they became the identity markers for two major communities in British India.[17] Mirza Ghalib (d. 1869), the great Indian poet often known as "the Shakespeare of India," wrote both in Urdu and Persian, yet preferred his Persian poetry. By his time, Indian lingual unity had begun to be challenged not only by English but also by traditional "vernacular" languages. Muhammad Iqbal (1873–1938) was the last eminent writer to use English, Persian, and Urdu in his philosophical and poetical works.

Other than Persian or subsequently Urdu as the bedrock of this Indo-Muslim culture, costumes, jewelry, music, urban lifestyles, and even statecraft showed the prevalence of this multiculturalism. Incoming Muslims from elsewhere brought with them the West and Central Asian architecture, which, combined with the classical Indian traditions, presented a unique blend, symbolized by the world-famous masterpieces such as the Taj Mahal at Agra, Shalimar Gardens in Lahore and Srinagar, Thatta Mosque, Jamia Mosque in

Delhi, palaces in Fatehpur Sikri, and countless gardens, castles, tombs, canals, and roadways all across India. The beautiful arches with elaborate motifs, delicate stone masonry, slender marble columns, rich calligraphy, well-designed gardens, elaborate fountains, and ornate palaces all characterized this impressive Indo-Muslim culture. In the same manner, meat and vegetable dishes, rice, and puddings all were part of Muslim culture and so were scents, jewelry patterns, and, most of all, the traditions of romance, including poetry, plays, and musical instruments.

This entire experience was not totally without its tensions and challenges, especially during the decline of the Muslim empire in the late eighteenth century. While non-Muslims persisted with their economic and cultural activities all across India, the feeling of being a scattered minority now engendered a deeper sense of loss among Muslims, and the political fall motivated some Muslim religious elites to assume various ideological and political postulations so as to fight the malaise. Thus, it was in British India, especially during the late nineteenth century, that one sees the emergence of clusters of such ideological groups, which eventually became further politicized and, after Pakistan's independence, turned into regular religiopolitical organizations.

SUNNIS AND SHIAS

Pakistani Muslims are divided into two main sects: Sunnis (80%) and Shias (20%). The other smaller groups such as Zikris are mostly in the Karachi and Makran districts, although their concentration is mainly in southwestern Balochistan where their spiritual center, Koh-i-Murad, is located. However, their recent migrations to Karachi have tilted the balance in favor of urban Sindh. Both Sunnis and Shias are further subdivided into several doctrinal sects, although all of them agree on the basic beliefs and practices; it is only on the interpretations of their religion and the early Muslim history that they differ. Practicing Muslims pray five times a day and gather in mosques for congregational prayers on Friday. They fast during the month of fasting *(Ramadan),* offer alms *(zakat),* try to go on pilgrimage to holy places in Saudi Arabia, and believe in the prophethood of Muhammad and the unity of God (Allah). They also believe in other prophets, take Quran as the last revealed book, and have conviction in the Day of Judgment. Like Christians and Jews, they also believe in angels as messengers of the holy word. The Muslim prayers are always in Arabic, offering meditation on human actions and the ultimate reward or punishment. While praying, Muslims face toward Makkah in Saudi Arabia, where the earliest mosque (Holy Ka'aba), along with some other Abrahamic relics, is situated. They undergo an ablution before praying and eat properly slaughtered *(hallal)* meat while strictly avoiding pork.

Pilgrims in Sehwan Sharif. Courtesy of the author.

Other than specific religious practices, Islamic influences are clearly visible in the other mundane activities and also in arts and literature. A Muslim child, at birth, is expected to listen to the Quranic verses as an initiation, and males are circumcised Both the boys and girls are expected to read the Quran in Arabic in its entirety, which means learning to read 75,000 words with almost perfect pronunciation. Prayers, fasting, and an element of piety and restraint are also expected from adolescents. Most families would not look favorably at the free mixing of boys and girls, and premarital sex is totally forbidden. Reading the Quran, visiting Sufi shrines, and giving alms while being mindful of the world hereafter are collectively reflected in the various daily activities. Celebration of the end of Ramadhan through the Eid festival and the commemoration of Abraham's sacrifice of his son are major happy occasions. Both Sunnis and Shias respect the weeks of mourning in the memory of the martyrdom of Imam Hussein, the grandson of the Prophet, at Karbala in 680 A.D.[18] Shias, donning black clothes, walk in processions while beating their chests as they pay homage to Hussein and his family, whereas Sunnis hold somber meetings in the mosques or recite the Quran at home. Shias have their own mosques and, other than pilgrimage to Makkah, aspire to visit holy places in southern Iraq.

Academically, there are two views on the differences between Shias and Sunnis. According to one school of thought, these are not major doctrinal differences but over the years, a political issue of succession to the Prophet Muhammad 14 centuries back has been made into a huge divide. Many Muslim scholars, undoubtedly aggrieved over the chasm, would desire a greater dialogue and tolerance so as to bridge this fragmentation of the *ummah.* The contrary view, shared by some Sunni and Shia extremists along with a few foreign scholars, posits that the divide is real, multiple, and unbridgeable. Other than its political or doctrinal roots, the Shia-Sunni differences, also called the sectarian discord in Pakistan, are linked with the geopolitics of the southwestern and Middle Eastern regions. Shias and Sunnis have several doctrinal orientations on the issues, such as the intercession by saints and Sufis, although all of them would follow a local leader *(imam)* for daily prayers. These *imams* may vary in their overall educational qualifications but hold respectable positions within their local following. Senior Shia leaders are called Ayatollahs and Mujtahids, whereas some of them follow the Aga Khan as the spiritual head.

The Shias are mostly settled in the Punjab, with sizeable presence in Karachi, Quetta, Hyderabad, and Peshawar. In addition, in the tribal areas, Shias are a dominant majority among the Turis of the Kurram Agency, with a significant number from among the Bangash settled tribe. In Quetta there are Shias of Hazara (central Afghanistan) and Iranian background. Most of the Shias in Pakistan are called Twelvers,[19] whereas the Ismailis, Dawoodis, Bohras, and the Khojas account for smaller communities.[20] Excluding the Ismailis of Hunza, Gilgit, and Chitral, the rest of these latter Shia groups are urban communities engaged in business and other commercial enterprises. The Twelvers are almost evenly divided between rural and urban groups, although it is difficult to establish concrete figures. It is quite difficult to offer exact statistics on minorities given the emotional and political issues involved. In addition, many Muslim sects or denominations refuse to be characterized as minorities.

Within these two broad sects, there are several more denominations among Pakistani Muslims, although more so among the Sunnis, as they are the largest of the two. Although most of them would follow Sufi practices, several others may emphasize literalism. Through their mosques and attached seminaries—more like Sufi shrines and monasteries—the purists have their own networks and, in many cases, are immensely politicized. These literalist groups evolved in British India and were also influenced by similar movements in the Arab Middle East. To them, Muslims must purify their religion of all kinds of lateral innovations, as Islam can provide holistic and systemic solutions to all types of problems. To them, the Prophet Muhammad's own role as a messenger cum statesman has to be re-created even if it might imply more than persuasion. During the 1980s, such groups became quite vocal because of their involvement in the Afghan resistance against the former Soviet Union. Afghanistan became a center of political Islam, with powerful Sunni groups from across the Muslim world fighting alongside the Afghan holy warriors

(Mujahideen). The Western powers, Saudi Arabia, Pakistan, and several other nations supported this anti-Russian war, generally known as Jihad.

The emergence of the Taliban in 1994 and their conquest of most of Afghanistan two years later strengthened Sunni purist movements, which demanded similar systemic changes in other Muslim regions including Pakistan. The Taliban—literally meaning students—were the descendants of these Mujahideen and had studied in seminaries where a Saudi version of strict Islam deeply influenced them. They had the support of the Pakistani authorities as well as other orthodox Sunni groups, and it was only after September 11, 2001 that Islamabad took a strong stance against them.

The Iranian Revolution of 1979, led by Ayatollah Khomeini (d. 1989), not only symbolized the salience of Shia Islam in Iran but also reenergized Shia groups in the neighboring nations, including Pakistan, where 20 percent of the local population is Shia. Pakistan was being ruled by General Zia-ul-Haq (d. 1988), who was a fervent Sunni Muslim and very close to both the Saudis and the Americans. He helped facilitate the assistance to the Afghan Mujahideen, besides making Pakistan into a front-line state in the war against the Soviets. Zia-ul-Haq's imposition of certain strict Islamic laws—also known *Sharia*—showed a strong Sunni bias that further provoked Shia reaction. The differences between Pakistani Sunnis and Shias were soon translated into a full-fledged conflict, with secret armed groups selectively killing religious scholars and other professionals in major cities and towns across the country. Even after various restrictions and bans on such militant outfits by General Pervez Musharraf, the Shia-Sunni cleavages refused to heal and incidents of bomb blasts and well-planned murders have happened quite frequently.[21] The Sunni groups are not against Shias per se and vice versa, but powerful sections have certainly often made the situation volatile. Some Sunni extreme groups have been asking the government to declare the Shias as a minority because the Sunnis happen to be a majority; and some Shias have been demanding greater protection, as they remain a scattered minority all over the country. The lack of a sustained democracy and the complex geopolitics in West Asia have certainly contributed to these sectarian tensions.

The local religious scholar *(alim* or *mullah)* is an important figure for the Muslim community as he leads five-time prayers, offers special prayers at all the religious festivals, and also leads funerary prayers. These scholars have mostly memorized the entire Quran and several prophetic traditions, and they are thus deeply respected in their localities. They are usually linked with other clerics through a formal network, and some of them are well versed in traditional religious scholarship, as they have been trained at well-known seminaries *(madrassas)*. Like elsewhere, people may privately joke about these religious leaders in reference to their penchant for food, marriages, and verbosity, yet they also accord them a special deference at all occasions. Clerics, although dependent upon the local community for their own support and for the maintenance of the mosque, still can fire up emotions as well as diffuse disagreements and mediate other problems. These ecclesiasts impart religious instruction to the children and might take some of them to other villages for propagating religiosity among fellow Muslims. Such small forays are called *tabligh,* and the local mosques offer the visitors hospitality while they spend their own money on food and travel.

Broadly, there are three ideological categories of these clerics: first, those who simply lead prayers and offer religious instructions as they obtained it from their forefathers or mentors. The second group views shrines favorably and, in some cases, may be the only group to hold some spiritual claims. The third group involves clerics and their organizations who abhor Sufi Islam, and with a higher level of politicization, aim at converting the entire society in their own vision. These latter two groups have caused divided loyalties among Muslims in South Asia, and even in the diaspora such dissensions may often surface. Excepting some cases, most of the *ulama*—both from amongst the scripturalists and syncretists—have been working as the guardians of religious traditions.[22]

PLURALISM

Pakistan is an immensely pluralistic country characterized by religious, sectarian, and ethno-lingual diversities, which, in many cases, have engendered tensions and conflicts. It is an overwhelmingly Muslim community with more than 90 percent of its inhabitants adhering to Islam, yet they belong to quite a few doctrinal sects. In addition, there are several Christian denominations, Hindus, Sikhs, Parsis, Bahais, and Kalashas who are identified as non-Muslim Pakistanis. In 1974, the Pakistani National Assembly declared Ahmadis—also called Qadianis—a non-Muslim minority. They are a small community, which allocates a highly elevated religious status to the late Mirza Ghulam Ahmad (d. 1908), the founder of the movement in British India. Both the Sunni and Shia Muslims believe that Ahmad is projected by Ahmadis as the promised Messiah and a prophet refuting the finality of Muhammad's prophethood. Although a vast majority of Pakistanis converse in or understand Urdu—the national language—compared to various regional languages such as Punjabi, Pushto, Balochi, Sindhi, and others, Urdu remains the mother tongue of about 10 percent of the total population. The Urdu speakers are mainly the immigrants from India and their descendants who, at the time of Partition in 1947, opted for this predominantly Muslim homeland by leaving a Hindu majority India behind. The historic and more recent migrations have immensely contributed to Pakistan's sociocultural, religious, and ethnic pluralism.

In 1947, Pakistan's independence accompanied the greatest movement of people ever known in human history. As is generally accepted, more than 14 million people moved across the borders, with Pakistan receiving more than eight million Muslims from all over India. Most of them came to West Pakistan with 1.2 million moving into the then East Pakistan. Most of the Hindus and Sikhs who had earlier settled in West Pakistan left for India, whereas several Hindu communities in East Bengal remained intact until the subsequent events compelled their migration. East Bengal, Sindh, and Balochistan largely remained unaffected by riots accompanying the Partition and hence there were fewer incentives for non-Muslim Pakistanis to migrate. The Indo-Pakistan discord over the former princely state of Kashmir not only brought Kashmiri refugees into Pakistan but also made it difficult for many non-Muslims to stay on in Pakistan. The emigrations of individual Hindu families from East Pakistan into India continued even after the Liaquat-Nehru Pact of 1950, which had resulted in similar policies on refugees, migrations, and evacuee properties in both the countries. The pact virtually stopped the migrations but did not solve the problem.

Partition had left Muslims divided on all three sides—India, and East and West Pakistan—although Hindus and Sikhs largely remained concentrated in India. Another community to be seriously affected was the Christians, whose predominant concentration in Northern India was in the Punjab—religiously the most diverse of all the British provinces—where religion and language had played an important role in solidifying the divide between the communities. The year 1947 left Punjabis divided on both sides of the Indo-Pakistani borders, along with several radical changes in their political economy. East Punjab was largely cleansed of Muslims and likewise West Punjab of Hindus and Sikhs. The migrations and the concurrent killings involving Hindus, Muslims, and Sikhs, especially in Punjab, have seriously impacted the regional politics of both the countries. That is why, to many observers, the Kashmir conflict or Indo-Pakistani dissensions over water resources, among other factors, are symptomatic of this malaise. After the civil war between East and West Pakistan and India's intervention in 1971, East Pakistan became the new state of Bangladesh, which led to another series of transregional migrations. Whereas the East Bengalis left West Pakistan for Bangladesh, Pakistan accepted the repatriation of several Urdu-speaking East Pakistanis, also called Biharis.

Non-Muslim Pakistanis

As mentioned, Pakistan's population is generally known to be around 159 million, although according to the official census reports it is around 140 million. According to the census of 1981, out of a total of 84,253,644, Muslims accounted for 81,450,057, followed by 1,310,426 Christians and 1,276,116

Hindus. The Sikhs, Ahmadis, Buddhists, Parsis, and others accounted for 2,146, 104,244, 2,639, 7,007 and 101,009, respectively. With a de-emphasis on family planning and the millions of Afghan refugees and some Iranians, the population growth has been immense. The next census could not take place until 17 years later because of ethnic conflicts in Sindh, with the fear of exaggerated census numbers. However, in 1990, predicting based on the average growth rate of population at 3.1 percent, it was estimated that the minorities made up 3.1 percent of the total population. According to these estimates, there were 1,769,582 Christians in Pakistan followed by 1,723,251 Hindus. There were 2,898 Sikhs, 3,564 Buddhists, and 9,462 Parsis, whereas the others collectively were estimated to be 13,640. The total figures were around 3,663,167. Two years later, the aggregate figures stood at 4,267,463 with Christians and Hindus almost equal at 2,061,306 and 2,007,743, respectively. The Ahmadis, Sikhs, Buddhists, Parsis, and the others were estimated to be 163,982, 3,374, 4,150, 11,021 and 15,888, respectively. It is interesting to note that even the Parsis, despite some outward migration, had registered a slight increase.[23] The census of 1998 did not contest these figures, with the total number of the minorities nearing 11–13 million altogether. The Hindus, Christians, and Ahmadis all claimed to be 4 million each, which means that the ratio of non-Muslim minorities is higher than the official figures.

It is quite crucial, however, to note that given the disadvantages and stigmas, communities do not like to be identified as minorities. The minorities make up to eight percent of the total population (11–13 million) and except for Parsis most of them live in rural areas, which is in consonance with the general patterns of national demography. More than 65 percent of them are young people; the rate of literacy in just a few cases is certainly higher than the national average although the other denominators are not good. The Christians are predominantly in the Punjab and so are the Sikhs, whereas Hindus are mostly in Sindh with smaller communities elsewhere. Most of the Sikhs are again in upper Pakistan with a few families even in the Khyber Pass. Almost 50 percent of the Christians live in urban areas—predominantly in Punjab—while Ahmadis are scattered across small towns and big cities. The Christians have churches across the country, and their organization is similar to their counterparts elsewhere, although with specific South Asian characteristics. The churches and cathedrals built during the colonial era have a distinct red brick structure with spires or rotundas, while the newer ones are more modern in the cities and basic in the rural areas. Families use these churches for prayers, funerals, and for other social events. Both the Catholic and Protestant denominations celebrate Christmas and Easter through several congregational activities, mostly conducted in Urdu or Punjabi. The Christian names are usually a mixture of Muslim and European names.

The Bahais are also a total urban community that rather remains invisible because of the fear of a backlash, as nearly all of them are converts. The sect began in Iran (Persia) in the nineteenth century and spread to South Asia in the subsequent decades. Pakistan has a very small and almost totally invisible Bahai community, who prefer to keep a low-key profile. Pakistani Hindus celebrate their festivals such as Diwali, Holi, and Dusehra, although their outflow from the upper Indus Valley in 1947 has left many temples *(mandars)* deserted. Hindus, unlike Muslims and Christians, cremate their dead, while the Zoroastrians leave them in the Towers of Silence for vultures to consume human remains. Priests who keep the fire alight in the temples while reading from the holy book maintain these towers. Zoroastrians are called Parsis both in India and Pakistan, as they originated in old Persia. Their number is dwindling largely because of outward migrations and also because they do not accept conversions. Parsis are the wealthiest community, and they are well-respected and many of them have been involved in charitable activities.

There are several Sikh *gurdawaras* across Pakistan, although not all of them are in use as most of the Sikhs left for India in 1947. However, three of the holiest Sikhs shrines are in Pakistan. Nankana Sahib is the birthplace of Baba Guru Nanak (A.D. 1469–1533), the founder of Sikhism, and Hasan Abdal in upper Punjab has the Panja Sahib, another holy shrine. In Lahore, next to Badshahi Mosque, there is the Ranjeet Singh Marhi, dedicated to the Fourth Guru, which is also known as Dera Sahib. At these places, *Guru Granth Sahib*—the Holy Book—is recited all the time and free food *(langar)* is available to all. The Sikh *gurdawaras* allow women and children to pray and eat on the holy premises.

Gurdawara. Courtesy of the author.

Given its agrarian roots in Punjab, Sikhism celebrates festivals in the context of sowing and harvesting. Other than the birth and death anniversaries of all the Gurus, Baisakhi festival is the main occasion of celebration, which coincides with the harvest. Basant, another age-old agrarian festival of happiness, is celebrated by Pakistanis especially in Lahore as a special occasion to eat, dance, and fly colorful kites. Lahore has assumed a global profile because of its colorful celebration of Basant, which always occurs at the beginning of spring season. This is a unique case of folk culture being adopted by city dwellers. The annual village fairs *(melas)*, and annual gatherings at the Sufi shrines *(urs)*, form important features of a rich socioreligious heritage. In addition, religious shrines and places of worship have added to the country's architectural diversity while concurrently sharing some similar patterns in designs and utility. The Sufi shrines attract millions of people every year, where feasting and playing of *qawalli* music are the significant activities, allowing ordinary people an escape from the drudgeries of their life. Shrines and the festivals may have their spiritual origins, but their role as socializers and manifestations of a cross-ethnic folk culture allocate them a special status.

Pakistanis, in general, have never sought separate electorates or lower legal status for minorities, since the latter never posed any threat to the majority community.[24] It was, in fact, General Zia-ul-Haq who, through his selective laws, divided Pakistanis into Muslim and non-Muslim groups and, while appeasing the Sunni majority, ended up antagonizing Shias, non-Muslims, women, and reform-minded groups. The new system of separate electorates was implemented in the partyless elections conducted by Zia in 1985, although in 1983 the local bodies' elections had been held under the new system of separate constituencies.

The removal of separate electorates, as well as the reservation of some special seats in 2002 by General Musharraf augured well for minorities, although the backlash from the combined religious opposition (Muttahida Majlis-i-Ammal, United Action Forum [MMA]) remained unabated. However, it is to the credit of the civil society in the country that the demands for the repeal of separate electorates and other discriminatory practices remained high on the agenda of public debate. These civic groups strive to restrain statist unilateralism while trying to create a greater awareness amongst the masses about the sanctity and inviolability of equal citizenship. At another crucial level, through documentation and active lobbying, they organize civic groups to play an effective role at the local levels so as to safeguard the pluralistic nature of Pakistani society. Such a tridimensional strategy is understandable, as it offers a buffer against official unilateralism and societal nihilism. Groups such as the Human Rights Commission of Pakistan (HRCP) are nation-wide, nonsectarian, and non-profit think tanks, whereas each community may have its own respective safety networks.[25]

Similar textbooks, common ecology, a shared national ethos, lingual commonalities, an increased socioeconomic mobility, the evolution of an ambitious middle class, and the rise of modernist consumerism are influencing an overwhelmingly youthful society and move toward an interdependent destiny. However, the forces of underdevelopment, sectarian tension, and regional dissension have not only posed serious challenges to these consensual areas, they have also been visible in the pervasive problems of governance. Pakistan's own people—especially its minorities—are certainly its assets and have an undeniable right to fully enjoy security, equal rights, and human dignity. It has been borne out by several studies and opinion polls that a vast majority of Pakistanis are supportive of equal rights for minorities and all women and of building up a friendly relationship with India. They are equally abhorrent of the official or any other specific and sectarian use of religion that may veto equal citizenship, civic rights, and participatory politics.[26]

NOTES

1. Abdul Sattar Edhi, *An Autobiography*, narrated to Tehmina Durrani (Islamabad: National Bureau, 2000), 319.

2. Rahmat Ali (d. 1951) coined the word and subsequently it was adopted by Indian Muslim leaders like M. A. Jinnah and the All-India Muslim League. The P in Pakistan stood for Punjab province, A for Afghania or the Frontier, K for Kashmir, S for Sindh, and TAN for Balochistan. The I was added later for ease in pronunciation.

3. It is often interesting to see the ideological debate among Pakistanis about being Muslim first and then anything else. The orthodox elements, including the religio-political parties, demand and espouse the Muslim-first-and-anything-else-later dictum. However, it appears that for the educated post-1947 generations, this is not an obvious issue, although many of them, in a rather emotive way, may support the Islamization of Pakistan. But here Islamization would mean not merely more mosques for compulsory five-time prayers, but a systemic change that may allow full justice and accountability. In other words, Islam, to them, is a force that brings people together as well as a political alternative. Global events, such as in Palestine, Iraq, Afghanistan, Chechnya, and Bosnia have also fed into this Muslimness, although the separation of East Pakistan in 1971, despite a common Muslim identity, certainly pushes some skepticism about this sole defence of a common religion. In addition, the sectarian strife, especially between the Sunni majority and the Shia minority in recent years, has compelled many people to reflect on a presumed *given* oneness.

4. Given the demographic trends, it is safe to assume that the Christians and Hindus are almost equal in numbers, although the latter are less visible, unless one

counts the rural Sindh area. See Iftikhar H. Malik, *Religious Minorities in Pakistan* (London: Minority Rights Group, 2002).

5. One of the well-known Pakistani Christians was Justice A. R. Cornelius, a former and well-respected chief justice of Pakistan. One of the most senior bishops in the Anglican Church is a Pakistani. Michael Nazir-Ali, the bishop of Rochester, is from Punjab and a former bishop of Lahore. In 2003, he was one of the three finalists to be considered for the position of Archbishop of Canterbury. (But this is not to suggest that all the Pakistani Christians are privileged like Nazir-Ali.)

6. In the 1980s, the first Pakistani Nobel-Laureate, Abdus Salaam, a physicist, was a practicing Ahmadi. For many Orthodox elements, his Ahmadi connection was always irksome, although his followers were proud to identify him as the first-ever Muslim Nobel Laureate.

7. Cowasjee is a bold, popular, and contentious columnist who is never tired of challenging the mighty of the land. Bahram Avari is a hotelier and a well-known sportsman, and Sidhwa is a globally known novelist. Two former chief justices of Pakistan have been from the Parsi community. Justice Kaykaous and Justice Dorab Patel were the highest judges in a Muslim country, which also reveals some positive aspects of this religious pluralism. The latter was also the founder of the Pakistan Commission on Human Rights, a reputable think tank and research institute on human rights practices across the country.

8. For more on his life, see Karen Armstrong, *Muhammad: A Western Attempt to Understand Islam* (London: Victor Gollancz, 1992); Karen Armstrong, *Islam: A Short History* (London: Phoenix, 2001); Chris Horrie and Peter Chippendale, *What is Islam?* (New York: Virgin, 1990); and Michael Cook, *The Koran: A Very Short Introduction* (Oxford: Oxford University Press, 2002).

9. A well-known French scholar of Islam has especially highlighted these aspects of the Prophet Muhammad's life. See Maxime Rodinson, *Mohammed* (London: Penguin, 1979).

10. For a quick read on Islam, see Alfred Guillaume, *Islam* (London: Penguin, 1990) (reprint); and Muhammad Asad, *Islam at the Crossroads* (Gibraltar: Daral Andalus, 1982).

11. For more on Sufism, see A. J. Arberry, *Sufism: An Account of the Mystics of Islam* (London: Mandala, 1988).

12. This is not to suggest that Sufi Islam was totally apolitical, since in North Africa and Central Asia, Sufis put up strong resistance to foreign occupation. Algeria and Chechnya are the best examples of the active defiance to the French and Russian colonial control. There are several Web sites devoted to Sufi literature, customs, and shrines. For a Pakistan-based site, see: www.sufiwisdom.org.

13. Saudi Arabia, Iran, and a few other Muslim countries discourage this kind of *pir*-disciple relationship and pursue a literalist version of Islam, decrying the need for intermediaries. In Iran, some senior religious scholars hold these important spiritual positions.

14. There were some coastal regions of Balochistan already under Muslim Arab control, but A.D. 712 is considered to be the beginning of Muslim rule over India.

The conquest of Iran a few years earlier had made access to India easier for Muslim armies. Interestingly, it was in the same year that Islam conquered Central Asia as well as Spain, thus heralding the golden era of Muslim civilization.

15. For details, see Ishtiaq H. Qureshi, *Ulema in Politics: A Study Relating to the Political Activities of the Ulema in the South Asian Subcontinent from 1556 to 1947* (Karachi: Maaref, 1972).

16. Quite the contrary to many accusations of Muslim aggression and desecration of Hindu temples in southern India, the Muslim elite patronized Hindu and Christian cultures. See David Gilmartin and Bruce Lawrence (eds.) *Beyond Turk and Hindu: Rethinking Religious Identities in Islamicate South Asia* (New Delhi: Research Press, 2002).

17. To many people in British India, Hindi and Urdu were almost the same, although with different scripts, and they preferred a collective term, Hindustani, for them. With the evolution of nationalist struggle among the various communities, language became the bedrock of these identities. Indian Muslims as their national heritage adopted Urdu, whereas for Hindus, Hindi became the national expression.

18. Sunnis—or proponents of consensus—do not contend the issues of political and spiritual succession of the Prophet, whereas Shias (literally meaning companions) have always upheld Ali in higher esteem. To them, the Prophet's son-in-law and his future descendants deserved the politicospiritual succession, which was constantly denied to them.

19. They believe in the religious and spiritual succession, provided by the 12 of the Prophet's descendants. Following the occultation of the twelfth imam, the guidance is provided through mujtahids and ayatollahs, the senior-most clerics.

20. Like the Twelvers, they have their own spiritual heads, or living imams.

21. General Musharraf took over the control of the country through a coup on October 12, 1999. He dissolved the current political government and became the de facto ruler, until the country's judiciary upheld his coup. After September 11, 2001, Musharraf emerged as the major ally for the United States in the war on terror, which made him more controversial to his religious critics but also guaranteed him the external support. For details, see Owen Bennet-Jones, *Pakistan: the Eye of Storm* (New Haven, CT: Yale University Press, 2003).

22. Muhammad Qasim Zaman, *The Ulama in Contemporary Islam: Custodians of Change* (Karachi: Oxford University Press, 2004).

23. Government of Pakistan, *Pakistan Year Book 1994–5* (Karachi: Finance Division, 1996), pp. 5–6.

24. Separate electorates meant that the non-Muslims have their separate constituencies and representatives to the councils and assemblies. This thus signified politicosocial segregation.

25. The HRCP has not only published annual reports documenting the state of human rights in the country, it has defended several cases as well. In addition, its workers have trained several Pakistanis across the country on human rights issues. Their reports and workshop are the most influential and constructive arms of Pakistani civil society. See HRCP, *State of Human Rights in Pakistan in 2004* (Lahore:

HRCP, 2005). Also see the earlier yearly reports of 2003, 2002, 2001, 2000, 1998, 1997, and other Urdu publications.

26. For such a unique and little-known consensus, see "Fifty Years-Fifty Questions," *Monthly Herald* (Karachi), January 1998.

SUGGESTED READINGS

Armstrong, Karen. *Islam: A Short History.* London: Gollancz, 2001.

Cook, Michael. *The Koran: A Very Short Introduction.* Oxford: Oxford University Press, 2002.

Malik, Iftikhar H. *Religious Minorities in Pakistan.* London: Minority Rights Group, 2002.

Zaman, Muhammad Qasim. *The Ulama in Contemporary Islam: Custodians of Change.* Princeton, NJ: Princeton University Press, 2004.

3

Literature and Arts

I have nothing to do with poetry; it is sheer wordsmithery. In fact, I am
trying to rope in a camel, which has lost its caravan in the desert.
—Muhammad Iqbal, one of the leading philosophers and architects of
Pakistan (1873–1938)[1]

Pakistan's literary and artistic heritage spans numerous centuries and diverse
regional and pluralistic traditions and reflects the country's identity from the
ancient Indus Valley society to young statehood. Oral traditions, ancient seals
discovered from Mohenjodaro and Harrapa, the figurines and stone carvings from historic cities such as Taxila, Kattas, and Bhaun, and the elaborate
Greco-Buddhist artifacts from the Gandhara epochs offer solid foundations
for a culture that successively flourished under the Dravidians, Aryans, Persians, Greeks, Arabs, Afghans, Turks, and the Europeans.[2] The great religious
traditions of South and West Asian origins including Jainism, Hinduism,
Buddhism, Zoroastrianism, Christianity, Islam, and Sikhism interacted and
even competed to outdo one another across the Indus lands, which have been
the traditional crossroads for so many civilizations. Located close to the Great
Silk Route in the north and to the west, with its vast Makran and Sindh
coasts commercially and culturally linked with the Arab and African lands,
this region and its people have pioneered and synthesized unique literary and
cultural traditions of a historic subcontinent.

The classical ecclesiastic traditions—both oral and written—proved the
mainstay of all these religions, whereas prosaic and poetic epics, mystical
songs, folks ballads, medieval historical accounts, and traditional commentaries and travelogues in languages such as Sanskrit, Persian, Turkish, and Arabic

formed the early, high-brow literary heritage. Over the last three centuries, the interaction with the West, mass literacy, and technical innovations have led to the evolution of more modern genres such as novels, short stories, poetry, and plays, and a vast, multi-disciplinary literary corpus that has been reflective of pluralism, emerging nationhood, and concurrent ethnoregional manifestations. In the same vein, the arts such as sculpture, hieroglyphics, cave drawings, stone masonry, ceramics, coinage, textiles, wood carving, calligraphy, and garden designs provide a rich backdrop to subsequent encounters with other traditions, a process that has gone on more earnestly in the last three centuries.

The institutionalization of Urdu as a widely shared medium, along with the older languages such as Punjabi, Pushto, Hindko, Sindhi, Balti, Shina, Brohi, and others, has not only created a more cohesive national ethos but also mediates among diverse traditional expressions. Simultaneously, the unchallenged growth of English as the official language and also a symbol of power and globalization has offered Pakistani writers their own niche within a growing mainstream of non-Western literature in an international language. Still, the multiplicity of these lingual traditions has not been able to challenge the higher profile enjoyed by Arabic as the language of classical Islam, although Persian was a South Asian *lingua franca* for a thousand years. However, Arabic has been steadily losing ground to English and Urdu.

The periodization of Pakistan's literature and arts may appear to be straight forward but can be controversial as well. On the one hand, the available paradigms of "ancient," "medieval," "modern," and "contemporary" sound convenient, yet their characterization could be as problematic as defining the paradigms of "tradition" and "modernity." Certainly, civilizations rise and fall or merely decline, yet it is always difficult to delineate specific time scales, when every nationality bases its origin on some glorious past. These four "periods" may then be used as overarching categories rather loosely. Simultaneously, defining Pakistan's literary and cultural heritage only in terms of its Dravidian, Hindu, Buddhist, Muslim, Sikh, and Christian epochs could be immensely problematic and controversial, especially to those to whom history and culture are not totally religion-bound. Such essentializing may, to such analysts, only exacerbate communal tensions within any pluralistic society, and that is not unique to Pakistan or India.

However, culture—comprising literature and arts—can be more conveniently classified in terms of its origins, usage, and diffusion. For instance, Pakistan's Vedic Hindu past, the Gandhara epoch, and the Muslim period can be collectively defined as its classical heritage. The Bhikshu, Bhagat, Sufi, and Guru traditions are important manifestations of its mystical domain, whereas the European encounter marks the advent of modernity, where industrialization, urbanization, and certainly the powerful forces of Westernization usher in newer strains. Here cultural classification becomes more diverse and explicit. By the early twentieth-first century, while there are efforts to preserve classical heritage through a selective use of technology and innovation, South Asian cultures have also assumed popular and mass embodiments.[3] Other than these three forms—classical, popular, and mass—folk cultures also strive to persist, although they face modernity more as a foe rather than a preserver.

After 1947, defining national identity through conscious efforts in literature and arts, and experimentation with extra-regional, especially Western, traditions, both have not only added new forms and contents, they have equally intensified the divide between traditional and modernist forms. Issues such as seeing literature and arts merely aesthetically or as comments on the harsh realities of life become more intense. One can say that Pakistani literary and artistic pursuits concurrently reflect explicit periodization, thematic plurality, class-based divisions, and ideological disputes, and are dynamically influenced by the forces of nationalism, religion, region, class, and globalization. In the same way, questions of gender, caste, and global dichotomies, especially the issues of poverty, violence, and environmental degradation, find their presence within these creations. However, it would be fallacious to suggest that literature and arts remain static, aloof, or totally religion-centered, as secular and sacred, oral and written, high and low, classical and popular, mass and folk all manifest themselves in a plethora of forms and vicissitudes. This chapter focuses on Pakistan's literary heritage, followed by the country's various realms of arts and its current visual arts, as identified toward the end of this chapter.

ANCIENT HERITAGE

Pakistan's ancient literary and artistic heritage for a long time remained unknown, and it was only during the 1920s that the archaeological excavations led by Sir John Marshall and his successors unearthed the historic sites at Mohenjodaro and Harrapa.[4] These revolutionary discoveries established the subcontinent's own historicity and credentials as a cradle of one of the oldest civilizations.[5] Earlier, it was assumed that India lacked its own civilization and its cultures were derivatives from West Asian cultures. The further excavations at Taxila, Takhtbhai, and in Balochistan revealed the scale of a multidimensional civilization that was agrarian and well structured and was mostly run by the priest-kings. The study of Gandhara art in northwestern Pakistan and the discovery of cave paintings in the Northern Areas in the lower Karakorams dating from antiquity have further enriched the knowledge of ancient inhabitants who lived in well-planned cities with elaborate streets, efficient plumbing, extensive storage facilities, and organized religion-based hierarchies.[6] These ancient Pakistanis were soon overtaken by events from the north when Aryans invaded the region and gradually established Hinduism as the dominant force in northern India.[7] The archaeologists have not yet been able to decipher the language of the ancient Dravidian civilization, as thousands of seals remain untranscribed. However, figurative art depicted on tablets shows priest-kings, women dancers, and longhorn cattle, who have become the symbolic representation of this ancient culture.

The classical Hindu period, with Sanskrit as the main language, featured written works such as the *Ramayana, Bhagwad Gita,* and *Mahabharata,* which were soon joined by mystical literature recorded in *Puranas.* The emergence of Zoroastrianism and Buddhism in the pre-Christian millennium further added to scriptural literature. The Indo-European and Semitic languages competed with one another for space and followings and thus led to significant additions in the contemporary religious corpus. Overall, the sacred and secular forms of knowledge remained the monopoly of specific classes of religious teachers (the Brahmins and Pundits), whereas the regional languages—precursors of present-day Pakistani languages—not only were used in daily conversation as *bhashas* (full-fledged language) but also transmitted ballads and other folk traditions.[8]

The revival of the Indo-Buddhist cultures under the Maurya Dynasty (321–184 B.C.), especially under Ashoka (d. 232 B.C.), tried to energize literary traditions, although the emphasis remained mostly on Buddhist scriptures, sculptures, and architecture. The Buddhist stupas, built across Southwestern Asia during the rule of Ashoka, falling a few centuries before the Christian/ common era, revived Taxila, Mingora, Mankiyala, Takhtbhai, and other such places as the centers of academic pursuits. The university at Julian trained Buddhist monks, who took this Indian religion across the Silk Road into China and to further eastern and southern parts of Asia, and monasteries and magnificent stupas were built in these regions, signifying the salience of Buddhism.[9] Ashoka had also built the well-known Buddhas at Bamiyan in central Afghanistan, which, in fact, were carved from the hills, similar to the presidential memorials on Mount Rushmore in the United States. The Silk Route provided the tangible link for Buddhism with China and Tibet, a process that was soon repeated in the cases of Judaism, Christianity, and Islam in the subsequent centuries.[10] Some of the earliest sacred texts, drawings, utensils, handicrafts, carved prayers, and *mantras* on statues and sculptures, along with the travel accounts of some Chinese visitors, such as those in the Hindu epics and Greek histories, form a crucial past of this classical heritage of Pakistan.[11]

The legacy was continued for a while by the Gupta Dynasty, established by Chandra Gupta I in Bihar in A.D. 320, which revived some of the classical heritage besides attempting a cultural and political unity of the subcontinent. By the sixth century, this Hindu empire suffered from internal schisms and South Asia reverted to its segmentary patterns.

RELIGIO-CLASSICAL LITERATURE

The arrival of Islam in South Asia in the seventh century has left its lasting imprints on the literary and artistic heritage of Pakistan, and Islam continues to reverberate at different levels through powerful idioms and content. This region became overwhelmingly Muslim because of Sufis and other publicists and also underwent a major change in terms of skills and medium. Arabic and Persian emerged as the two powerful and permeating mediums of sacred and secular literature, respectively. As the classical Islamic heritage was in Arabic, South Asian Muslims became members of a transregional community. Despite a comparatively low rate of literacy, Pakistan's literary heritage, both written and oral, is quite extensive and spans several centuries, traditions, and languages. It ranges from religious to mundane and modern varieties, banking on high and low sides of the spectrum. The core religious literature in this predominantly Muslim country is in Arabic and is based on the Quran, traditions of the Prophet *(Hadith),* and other literature from the early—classical—period. It is mostly written, and a reading knowledge with some comfortable level of comprehension is expected of every Muslim youth. Some of this literature is equally oral, as it filters through homes, mosques, schools, friends, Sufi shrines, and the media.

At the time of birth, every Muslim child is supposed to hear the Quranic words first, which are usually recited by the father or some other elder, who announces the greatness of Almighty Allah into the ears of the infant. During childhood, a special tutor or the cleric of the local mosque is requested to teach basic Arabic to the child so that a reading knowledge of the Quran and its recitation can be obtained. Girls receive basic Islamic instruction at home either by the cleric's wife or some other elderly lady. Boys are sent to mosques to gain religious knowledge and learn to recite the Quran and the ways for offering prayers. Sometimes, younger girls also join boys at the mosques for basic religious instruction. Being able to read and recite all the 75,000 words of the Quran, divided into thirty books of several chapters, is considered to be an auspicious achievement.[12] Children born to Muslim families are viewed essentially as Muslim, although regular instruction and some other rituals may then lead them to formalize a commitment as practicing believers. Along with circumcision for boys, a formal initiation into becoming a Muslim, the method and the contents of offering five daily prayers as well as Friday's congregational prayers are also instilled at an early stage. Arabic prayers at funerals or for all other commemorative occasions are also learned during this phase. Both boys and girls also learn some basic traditions of the Prophet and a concise overview of the early Muslim history. Schools maintain basic curricula on Islamic studies where one may gain a closer understanding of Islamic law and the knowledge of basic Arabic and Muslim history besides an overview of jurisprudence *(Fiqah)*. Normally, a religious school *(madrassa),* attached with some main mosque, offers full-time religious instruction mostly for boys until some of them become imams, while the rest may pursue other occupations. The year-round religious ceremonies, doctrinal initiation, and other festivities further ingrain a continuum of religious knowledge, which may vary based on one's sectarian or denominational choice. Other than the holy texts in Arabic, students may be encouraged to read some classical Persian literature and a few prescribed books in Urdu. In Sindh and the Frontier, several books in Sindhi and Pushto also add to religious knowledge, mostly recapitulated in weekly Friday sermons by imams.

Another form of religious literature is Sufi writings, which have Persian, Urdu, or such other origins. The works of saints such as Data Gunj Bakhsh, Shahbaz Qalandar, Baba Farid, Amir Khusrow, Bulleh Shah, Rehman Baba, Shah Latif Bhitai, Waris Shah, and Mian Muhammad are not only recited in public meetings or in *qawallis,* they are also shared and discussed in common parlance, highlighting their strong moralism. Such classical works were written either in Persian—the literary language of the subcontinent until recent times—or in other traditional languages. Thus, other than Arabic sources and Persian classics by Firdausi, Al-Beruni, Shaikh Saadi, Fariduddin Attar, Hafiz Shirazi, Maulana Rumi, and Nizami Ganjwi, the third major area of religious literature comes from these South Asian Sufis who, other than Arabic, Persian, and Urdu, used Punjabi/Saraiki, Pushto, and Sindhi to transmit their knowledge and devotion. This type of literature is again mostly poetic and builds on folk stories, morals, and metaphysical legends aimed at teaching the insignificance of this world while urging a shared humanity and ethics as a universal heritage. Such literature, both in its printed and oral forms, is interspersed with humor and incidents from the lives of ordinary people and animals.

Persian has remained the basis of Perso-Indian Muslim culture, with transregional and multidisciplinary roots. After a brief Turkish period, Persian became the court language as well as the dominant literary expression across India, Afghanistan, and Central Asia and, of course, Persia (Iran). Indian Muslims were able to relate with their coreligionists and coethnics from these lands through Persian.[13] In fact, the Persian literature created from the time of the Mughal period until the early twentieth century, when English, Urdu, Hindi, Bengali, and such other languages replaced Persian, is itself massive and of high caliber compared with similar literary traditions elsewhere.[14]

Educated South Asians, for several centuries, conversed in Persian, which was the mode of both official and literary expression. Besides Masud Salman Lahori, Naziri Nishapuri, Abdul Qadir Baidal, Khan-i-Khannan, Emperor Jahangir, Abul Fazl, Faizi, Abdul Qadir Badayuni, Gulbadan Begum, Zaibunnissa, Noor Jahan, Dara Shikoh, Jahan Ara Begum, Bahadur Shah Zafar, Mirza Asadullah Ghalib, Mirza Sauda, Mir Taqi Mir, and Khawaja Dard, even Hindu writers and scripts used Persian until well into the nineteenth century. The last famous writer and intellectual to use Persian as a medium of expression was Sir Muhammad Iqbal (1873–1938), the former Cambridge University and Munich University graduate and an eminent poet-philosopher of the East, who also envisioned a Muslim state for the Indian Muslims. Other than three Urdu collections and his personal conversations in Punjabi, Iqbal mainly used Persian and English for his philosophical and poetical works.[15] By using three languages he wanted to reach a wider readership across the Muslim world. It is not uncommon to come across traditional scholars in Pakistan who can recite great Persian writers such as Rumi, Saadi, Khayyam, and Iqbal along with offering a thorough explanation of their ideas.

URDU AS THE NATIONAL LANGUAGE

Urdu is the main national language in Pakistan, which, like Hindi, evolved over the centuries when Muslims of various ethnosectarian backgrounds interacted with their Indian counterparts. Literally meaning army (lascar), it is a Turkish word that symbolizes the long rule of Muslim Turkic dynasties over India but also embodies an amalgam of various West and South Asian languages. Written from right to left in Arabo-Persian script, Urdu has an astounding amount of vocabulary from Indian and indigenous languages and, in its spoken form, was also referred to as Hindustani—the language of Hindustan or India. Its absorptive qualities spawn various accents and, most of all, even vocabulary from other tongues. Urdu evolved in several distinct phases. First, under the Mughals during the seventeenth century, it was a lingua franca in northern India when classical stories and poetry accounted for most of its literature. It remained a spoken language, although traces are found in Deccan as well. During the thirteenth century, the Sufi poet, Amir Khusrow of Delhi, used it for his lyrics. In Deccan or southern India, Wali Deccani is considered to be the earliest known poet with his own poetry collection, or Diwan, available since the seventeenth century.

The second phase in the evolution of Urdu coincides with the consolidation of the British East India Company's control when conscious efforts were made to push for a commonly shared language across the colonial possessions. Persian and other regional languages gradually began to lose out to English and Hindustani, whereas Hindi and Urdu found greater acceptance among the local elite. Urdu evolved as a common mode of expression in upper India, and by the late eighteenth century its elevated status as a literary expression coincided with the decline of the Mughal Empire (1720–1857) and the consolidation of British rule. By the late eighteenth century, Urdu, because of its simplicity and its resemblance both to Persian and Hindi, had emerged as the cherished expression of the Muslim elite in British India. Many non-Muslim Indians also found it convenient. It had the potential to emerge as the real lingua franca of the whole of India. It was also known as Raikhta, and some of the writers of this era included Mir Taqi Mir, Khawaja Dard, and Mir Sauda.

All through the British era, Delhi, Lucknow, Lahore, and Hyderabad (Deccan) and the surrounding regions of these metropolitan areas were the focal centers of serious literary works in Urdu. The princely states of Lucknow (Oudh) and Osmanli Hyderabad promoted Urdu as the court language, and at the behest of the Nizam (princely ruler) of Hyderabad, the first Muslim university using Urdu as a medium of higher education was opened and came to be known as Osmania University. The princely states of Kashmir, Bhopal, Pataudi, and Bahawalpur also promoted Urdu, although English remained the official and imperial language. By the mid-nineteenth century, Urdu began its second phase when it became the main medium of social, literary, and historical thought, especially among the North Indian Muslims. The schism between Hindi and Urdu, symbolizing two separate national and cultural expressions among Hindus and Muslims of India, occurred during this phase. The efforts by the eminent Muslim reformer, Sir Syed Ahmed Khan (1818–1898), gave a fillip to Urdu while poets such as Mirza Ghalib, Khawaja Zauk, Mirza Dabeer, and Mir Daaqh, through their masterpieces in prose and poetry, ensured its thematic diversity and literary vitality. Syed Ahmed Khan was a great reformer and modernist who introduced the Western form of education for Muslims in India. In his own writings as well through a variety of institutes, he attempted to present a simpler and more accessible form of Urdu expression. In addition, he encouraged writers such as Altaf Hussain Hali to compose poetry on the Muslim past so as to enthuse the community, as it suffered from a serious sense of loss.

The third period in the development of Urdu covers the pre-1947 decades when it became the main medium of expression for religious, political, literary, and historical literature. By the 1930s and 1940s, more than any other regional languages or even some other regional counterparts, Urdu obtained the center stage in the discourse on Muslim nationalism. Writers such as Muhammad Iqbal and several other poets, essayists, playwrights, politicians, and journalists widely used Urdu, until it became a symbol of Muslim nationalism.

The next phase in the evolution of Urdu began after independence when Urdu literature wrestled with the ideas of Pakistani identity within the purview of overarching Islamic and concurrent pluralistic identities. The young state adopted it as the national language, which only exacerbated the resentment in East Pakistan where Bengali had been the commonly subscribed language both among the masses and the elite. The role of the Pakistani state in encouraging Urdu as the national language, besides efforts to control any radical thoughts, led to two responses from the 1960s through the 1980s. At one level, several writers challenged the superimposition of uniformity and were uncomfortable with the dictums of literature for nationhood or Islam, whereas others opted to join state-run institutions to support the cause of a Muslim/Islamic Pakistan. The language riots in East Pakistan and then in Karachi reminded many that Urdu might have the overwhelming support of several public and private sectors across the country, but pluralistic and ideological aspirations had to be equally considered within the national discourse.

Urdu's decline in post-1947 India and its displacement by Hindi revealed similar trends on both sides of the borders, where uniformist official policies aimed to create a shared nationhood by fully promoting a common language. History, religion, and writing have received attention both in India and Pakistan so as to make Hindi and Urdu into the full-fledged embodiments of two "separate" nationalisms and statehood. The Pakistani state has nevertheless gone ahead by providing institutional support to promote Urdu at all levels. However, with a multi-tier educational system, English still persists at the apex of the hierarchy and elitism. Soon after independence in 1947, immigrants from India and the national elite joined to offer Urdu the vanguard role as the national language and to operate as a leveler. Karachi as the earliest capital saw the evolution of organizations including Maulvi Abdul Haq's Anjuman-i-Tarraqi-i-Urdu (the Association for the Promotion of Urdu). During the 1970s, after the trauma of a civil war and the resultant evolution of Bangladesh, the Modern Language Authority and Academy of Letters joined the erstwhile Iqbal Academy and such other organizations to promote Urdu as a national language. In fact, the constitution of 1973 promised the universal implementation of Urdu at all levels within two decades, although English-based elitism and pluralistic pulls have not allowed this to happen. Still, Urdu has certainly come a long way from a young regional tongue to the national expression of countless millions in South Asia as well as in the diaspora.

Historically speaking, Muslims in India brought with them an entire historiography to India. Their Perso-Arabic literary heritage transformed the entire literary scene. Other than Sufi and secular literature, the genre of longer fiction—*daastan nawaisi*—flourished in India with human and supernatural themes combined. The stories, incorporating humor, involved both humans and animals and ended with a strong moral. After the encounter with the Europeans, these long tales eventually turned into modern Urdu fiction, both in short stories and novels. The role of Fort William College in Calcutta in the 1800s under the headship of John Gilchrist provided an incentive to this transformation as some European colonials became interested in Indian literatures and religions. Enthused by the interest of philologists such as Sir William Jones and his pioneering research on the Indo-European languages, this college gathered Indian elites for translation purposes. Here, English, Persian, and Urdu literary traditions influenced one another within an imperial context. For a short while, the traditional genre of long stories remained in vogue. Some of the early Urdu fiction writers were Mir Amman, Rajab Beg Surur, and Pandit Ratan Nath Azad. Persian and English still dominated the literary and official parlance, and it was only in the last quarter of the nineteenth century that Deputy Nazeer Ahmad pioneered the modern Urdu novels. Most of the stories by this religious Muslim scholar were about women, emphasizing a more traditional and modest role for them as depicted in the heroines in the novels.

However, Abdul Halim Sharar—a younger contemporary of Nazeer Ahmad—could be called the pioneer of historical romance in Urdu, which further flourished under Mirza Muhammad Hadi Ruswa. Most of these writers came from Delhi and Lucknow, but Lahore had also begun to emerge as the center of an Urdu literary renaissance. Other than the poetic renditions by Hali, Daagh, and Iqbal, Maulana Muhammad Hussain Azad had also begun to contribute historical narratives while Maulana Shibli Nomani focused on Islamic history to counter the Orientalist attacks.[16] Maulana Nomani's Darul Musannifin, an institute devoted to research in Azam Garh, and Altaf Hussain Hali's long poem on the rise and decline of Muslims *(Mussadas)* were meant to create an Islamic regeneration through Urdu, which Iqbal picked up in his widely quoted works. Lahore, by the late nineteenth century, through its associations *(Anjumans)* and educational institutions played a vanguard role in creating a communitarian consciousness among Muslims.

By the early twentieth century, Urdu symbolized Muslim India, and with the efforts of poets and writers such as Muhammad Iqbal, Allama Yusuf Ali, Zafar Ali Khan, and Hasrat Mohani, it soon became the bedrock of Muslim cultural nationalism. By this time, the Urdu press across the subcontinent had become the mouthpiece of Muslim political and cultural aspirations.[17] Syed Mawdudi, the religiopolitical leader and founder of Jama'at-i-Islami (1941), used Urdu for his influential writings and even shifted to Lahore to establish his party and research institutes. Journalists such as Mahboob Alam, Muhammad Ali Johar, Abul Kalam Azad, Shorish Kashmiri, and Abdul Majid Salik used Urdu to reach a wider public, and all the Muslim political parties across South Asia used Urdu in their rallies and literature. The wide-reaching studies on Islamic exegesis such as *Bahishti Zewar* by Maulana Ashraf Ali Thanwi or similar other works by the Jamiat-i-Ulama-i-Hind and Tablighi Jama'at simply used Urdu for a mass of religious and political literature.

The issues of gender also received a varying degree of attention by political parties such as All-India Muslim League, and some cultural organizations and specific magazines began to debate the role of Muslim women within a changed cultural and historical milieu. Mumtaz Ali, Hijab Imtiaz Ali, Justice Shah Din, Sir Muhammad Shafi, Begum Jahan Ara Shahnawaz, Bi Amma, and Fatima Jinnah led reformative and educational efforts among Muslim women in pre-1947 India.[18]

In the decades preceding independence, stories by Prem Chand, Ghulam Abbas, and Saadat Hasan Manto in the tradition of the liberal left introduced progressive ideas into Urdu fiction, while clerics used Urdu in their sermons to redress the Muslim sense of loss over their political and cultural decline. Munshi Prem Chand, in particular, had introduced the issues of poverty and exploitation, especially of landless farmers, in his fiction. Such themes were being highlighted by the two major Urdu literary organizations—Halqa-i-Arbab-i-Zauq[19] and the Progressive Writers Association (PWA)—both of which had come into being during the 1930s.[20] Influenced by socialist thoughts, writers associated with these two major literary movements included activists such as Sajjad Zaheer, who had been one of the founders of the Communist Party. Ahmad Ali, the well-known author of *The Twilight in Delhi,* was another famous writer and founder of the PWA who interpreted literature as the major force for collective change and not as a mere luxury or pastime.[21] Krishan Chandar, Jannissar Akhtar, Saghir Ludhianwi, Quratulain Hyder, Mumtaz Mufti, Husein Raipuri, Saadat Hasan Manto, and Muhammad Hasan Askari are the other well-known names among liberal writers who espoused such progressive views from the platform of PWA, although Partition posed a serious ideological division within the group.[22] The Urdu poets of the pre-1947 era, other than Iqbal (d.1938) and his philosophical and political exhortation on the reconstruction of Muslim identity in India, focused on socioeconomic issues.

Several non-Muslim writers such as Prem Chand, Jadu Nath Sarshar, Rajinder Singh Bedi, and Krishan Chandar promoted Urdu short stories, although the growing communal divide in British India continued to exacerbate Urdu-Hindi differences. Their impressive fiction in Urdu tried to stem the gradual decline of Urdu in post-1947 India and mostly dwelt on the bitter experiences of the Partition.[23] Partition provided major themes of human displacement and agony to writers such as Bedi, Chandar, Manto, Ahmed Nadeem Qasimi, Abdullah Hussein, and Intizar Husain, whose poignant Urdu works have attained proverbial fame.[24] The other well-known writers with enduring impact on the successive generations of Urdu writers include names such as Qudratullah Shahab, Ashfaq Ahmad, Bano Qudsiya, Altaf Fatima, Nasim Hijazi, and Rais Ahmad Jaafari.[25] However, by the time Pakistan became independent, Urdu, despite being the mother tongue of people in northern India, was expected to be the unifying force for at least West Pakistan, whereas Bengali was the common language in East Pakistan. Three of the most famous Urdu poets of the twentieth century—other than Iqbal—were Josh Malihabadi, Faiz Ahmed Faiz, and Noon Meem Rashid, who reflected liberal and anti-imperial traditions in their verses.[26]

Malihabadi was a radical and anti-imperialist poet who was born in Lucknow and then migrated to Pakistan. Known for his powerful poetry and antiestablishment views, Malihabadi's compositions and autobiographical writings usually incited wrath from the official and clerical establishments. Faiz was a poet of ordinary people who defied exploitation and engaged himself in revolutionary movements outside Pakistan as well. In the early 1980s, he was based in Beirut during the civil war and edited *Lotus,* the Palestinian literary journal. Faiz was awarded the Lenin Prize for literature and remains the most influential and highly esteemed Urdu poet of the last century. Married to an English woman, Faiz, like Iqbal, had been born in Sialkot, and while growing up during the 1930s was deeply moved by socialism. The plight of the rural poor and urban workers, despair with the ruling elite and the entire tradition of resistance across the globe were Faiz's subjects, whose Persianized Urdu *ghazals* (a genre of romantic poetry) continue to inspire progressives and liberals all over South Asia. Like Iqbal's, his work has been translated into numerous languages. Faiz's revolutionary poetry is discussed in annual literary conferences and rallies in Lahore, London, and elsewhere and continues to enthrall his followers. Noted classical and semiclassical singers such as Nayyara Noor, Iqbal Bano, Noor Jahan, and Tina Sani have sung his poems. Noon Meem Rashid, also deeply influenced by progressive ideas, was more of an exponent of literary modernism and experimented with surrealism and prose poetry. Rashid mostly lived abroad serving international organizations, and his poetry collection, *Mawarra,* is widely read and respected.

Malihabadi, Faiz, and Rashid were followed by a generation of Urdu poets who generally used *ghazal* as a means of expression and tried to highlight dismay, misery, and exploitation through romantic metaphors. Ahmad Faraz, Nasir Kazimi, Mustafa Zaidi, Parveen Shakir, Kishwar Naheed, and Rashid Amjad are some of the well-known Urdu poets who have been influenced by the trio. Faraz, to many, is the most widely read and influential poet of this generation, while the late Parveen Shakir, in her poetry, tried to combine traditional romance with the harsh realities of existence. Ahmad Nadeem Qasimi, a journalist, poet, and novelist, has been quite influential among the younger generation and, like Shahab, has been associated with various official institutions. Hafeez Jallundhri was a poet of traditional values who dwelt on early Islamic history and was known for a melodious rendition of his own poems. His masterpiece, *Shahnama-i-Islam,* is patterned on the style of Firdausi's *Shahnama* and is widely sung in rallies. Hafeez also wrote Pakistan's national anthem, which again is highly Persianized and is sung daily across the land by millions.

Along with Iqbal and the other pre-1947 writers, Urdu literature in fiction, journalism, and religious realms had provided a major groundwork as an identity marker for Muslims in this part of South Asia. Syed Mawdudi, Shibli Nomani, Maulana Azad, Muhammad Ali Johar, Maulana Shaukat Ali, Maulana Muhammad Ilyas, Maulana Ashraf Thanwi, and several other leaders used Urdu for their political and religious works and speeches. However, the more mundane and rather secular form of Urdu literature owes itself to poets such as Faiz Ahmed Faiz, Josh Malihabadi, Ibn Insha, Ahmed Nadeem Qasimi, Ahmad Faraz, Nasir Kazimi, Mustafa Zaidi, Saaghir Siddiqui, Habib Jalab, Parveen Shakir, and many more who, through their *ghazals* and quartets *(rubayyaat),* focused on human feelings and experiences. Other than romance, drudgeries of life, personal loss, political dissent, and yearning for change are the subjects of Urdu *ghazal.* Jalab, in particular, was a poet of the masses who took on dictators, feudal landlords, and clerics. Intizar Husain, Shaikh Ayaz, Ibrahim Jalees, Hameed Akhtar, Anwar Sajjad, Muneer Niazi, Kishwar Naheed, Hijab Imtiaz Ali, Abdullah Yusufi, Hakeem Muhammad Saeed, and Haseena Moeen went beyond the traditional literary parameters by encompassing all kinds of social and political issues including gender in their literary works.[27]

In the realm of literary humor, interestingly, some military officials have published interesting collections of poetry and prose. Some of these writers are Zamir Jafari, Muhammad Khan, and Siddique Salik. Simultaneously, Urdu criticism *(tanqeed)* has become another major area of literary development, especially since the 1960s, when General Ayub Khan's military government tried to win over literary circles through the Literary Guild and some monetary inducements. Shahab played an important role in such official efforts, much to the ire of radical poets such as Muneer Niazi and Ibn Insha.

Presently, almost every university in Pakistan has a department of Urdu, although the earliest one is still called Oriental College at the University of Punjab in Lahore. Here, academics such as Ibaadat Brelvi, Viqar Azeem, Waheed Qureshi, Wazir Agha, Anwar Sadeed, and Muhammad Baqir have been promoting research on the historicity and diversity, as well as the adversity of Urdu literature. Independent writers such as Anwar Sajjad, Mumtaz Shireen, and Farman Fatehpuri and retired civil servants such as Jamil Jalibi have produced excellent and composite books on Urdu criticism, while in the diaspora scholars such as C. M. Naim and Umar Memon have brought out their valuable commentaries on varying traditions and genres within the ever-increasing domains of Urdu.

Urdu's ascension in Pakistan as the main medium of instruction and journalism, its multidisciplinary literature, and its powerful role as a common bond across regional loyalties is a significant development. Thousands of schools, colleges, *madrassas,* television programs, numerous newspapers and magazines, digests, movies, plays, religious works, and political commentaries offer a wide variety of literature for everyone. Agha Hashar, Imtiaz Ali Taj, Mustansir Tarar, Asghar Nadeem Sayed, Noorul Hudaa Shah, Arif Waqar, Surayya Bijia, Anwar Maqsood, Amjad Islam Amjad, Munoo Bhai, and Haseena Moeen are some of the well-known Urdu playwrights whose television serials have created deeper awareness of intricate socioeconomic issues. Pakistanis in the diaspora have equally tried to organize poetry recitals in Urdu and other regional languages besides publishing their books. Poets such as Faiz, Faraz, Ataulhaq Qasimi, and prose writers such as Munoo Bhai have always enjoyed major followings in Europe and North America. The pre-eminent Urdu poets in Britain have included Hyder Akbarabadi, Khalid Yusuf, Faizan Arif in addition to quite a few Punjabi, Pothowari, Sindhi, Pushto, and Saraiki writers. The Urdu classes at the University of London under scholars such as David Matthews, Ralph Russell, and Christopher Shackle and translations of Iqbal and Faiz by eminent writers such as Victor Kiernan have introduced Urdu literature to an outside readership.[28] The work of several organizations such as the Iqbal Academy, and periodic poetry recitals— *musha'airas*—besides the numerous newspapers and Urdu television channels have kept the literary scene alive.[29]

ENGLISH LITERATURE OR ELITISM

Other than Urdu, English remains the official and favored language for the Pakistani elite. The earliest work in English by a non-Westerner was the travel account by Sake Dean Mahomet (1758–1851), who had lived in Calcutta, Cork, London, and Brighton.[30] His books appeared from Ireland and London during the 1790s. But it was Syed Ahmed Khan who undertook special efforts to popularize English among the South Asian Muslim elite, whereas contemporary Muslim scholars such as Allama Yusuf Ali, Syed Ameer Ali, and Abdul Latif mainly wrote in English. Iqbal's doctoral research in Germany was on Persian metaphysics but in English. M. A. Jinnah was more fluent in English than in Urdu or his native Sindhi/Gujarati. Two known pre-1947 works were novels by Ahmed Ali and Mumtaz Shahnawaz. Shahnawaz was a talented young Muslim woman from Lahore who died in an air crash in Ireland.

After independence, English has remained the language of power and the ruling elite, and with increasing mobility and newer universities it has grown in its significance. Several Pakistanis—both in the country and abroad—have adopted English for their writings, and thus there is an impressive amount of English literature in areas such as fiction, journalism, history, politics, and law. Some who write in English are Bapsi Sidhwa, Nadeem Aslam, Sara Suleri, Daud Kamal, Taufiq Riffat, Alamgir Hashmi, Mohsin Hamid, Rustom Kayani, Muneeza Shamsie, Athar Tahir, Irfan Husain, Anwer Mooraj, Mahir Ali, and Kamila Shamsie.[31] In recent years, a multidisciplinary literature in English by Pakistani writers, both in the country and the diaspora, reveals the greater involvement of a younger generation in which women writers seem to be outnumbering men.[32] Diaspora writers such as Salman Rushdie, Tariq Ali, Hanif Kureishi, Ziauddin Sardar, Sara Suleri, Zulfikar Ghose, and Ayub Khan Din have personal links with Pakistan. Journalists such as Omar Kureishi, Ardsher Cowasjee, I. A. Rahman, Razia Bhatti, Zamir Niazi, Najam Sethi, Ahmed Rashid, and Munoo Bhai, or jurists such as Hina Jilani and Asma Jahangir, and historians such as K. K. Aziz, I. H. Qureshi, Aziz Ahmad, A. H. Dani, and Mubarak Ali all have used English for their extensive writings. Several Pakistani academics including K. B. Sayeed, Anwar Syed, Hafeez Malik, Samuel Burke, Asma Barlas, Ayesha Jalal, Riffat Hasan, Salim Qureshi, and many more have made valuable contributions in disciplines including politics, history, history, gender, and Islamic law.

REGIONAL EXPRESSIONS OR BASTIONS OF TRADITIONS

Other than Urdu and English as the bastions of national and elitist aspirations, numerous enduring regional expressions have remained the repositories of centuries of folk wisdom besides operating as mother tongues for almost 85 to 90 percent of Pakistanis. Certainly, Sindhi, Balochi, Brohi, Punjabi, Saraiki, Pothowari, Pushto, Hindko, and Shina are not mere regional languages; they are full-fledged identity markers and account for a significant place in Pakistan's traditional and folk heritage. Khushal Khan Khattak, Rahman Baba, Shah Latif Bhitai, Sachal Sarmast, Baba Farid, Mian Muhammad, Waris Shah, Shah Muhammad, Khawaja Farid, Sultan Baho, and Bulleh Shah are luminaries of this heritage whose songs, epics *(vars)*, poems, duets *(doahas)*, and witty proverbs *(tappas)* are often recited and quoted across the Indus Valley.[33]

Punjabi jokes, Saraiki Sufi literature, Shia elegies, folk romances across the Indus land, and ballads of fabled heroes and heroines are the major shared themes of this traditional literature, creating a wider sense of belonging. The River Chenab is the heartland of numerous romances, although some of them may also have West Asian locations. For instance, Layla-Majnoon is a widely quoted love story between an Arabian prince—Qais—and his African beloved. From being used in the daily parlance to serious fiction to highlight the symbolism of devotional love, the epic is widely used across the country as a folk tale. Shirin-Farhad is the love story between an artisan and an Iranian princess. Treachery, in the form of misinformation, leads to Farhad's suicide. Within Pakistan, the romances of Heer-Ranjah, Mirza-Sahiban, Sassi-Punnon, and Sohni-Mianwaal have engendered a vast spectrum of literature, folk tales, and dances. Ranjah falls in love with a Punjabi woman. Mirza is a Turk seeking the hand of a Punjabi maiden, Sahiban. Mianwaal is from an upper caste but is madly in love with the potter-girl, Sohni (literally meaning beautiful), who meets him secretly in the night while swimming across the Chenab. She floats on an earthen pitcher and, on one occasion, a family member supplies her with a flimsy pitcher, which dissolves so she drowns. Punnon is a Baloch from Makran (Kech) whose love is reciprocated by the Sindhi girl, Sassi, but their love ends in tragedy as in all other stories. These tales—both in Punjabi/Saraiki and Sindhi and in their poetic forms— are widely understood and sung across the country during festivals, fairs, and marriages. This literature is also quite popular among the Sikhs, to whom Punjabi is more than a literary expression and rather has a sanctified position because of its status as the language of their holy book, *Guru Granth Sahib.*

Many of these epics, *doahas, tappas, and vars,* are sung during special ceremonies such as marriages or *urs* at shrines.[34] Rural bards and gypsy musicians sing them on these occasions and are joined by people of all ages. Since the 1960s, musicologists and experts on folk heritage have recorded many of these ballads and songs.[35] The Sindhi, Balochi, Pushto, and Punjabi ballads, Sufi narratives, renditions of romances, and even the unlimited supply of Punjabi jokes have not only ensured their longevity, they are now being shared by all across various boundaries.[36] Poets and writers such as Ahmed Rahi, Faquir Husain, Israel Ashnaa, Shaikh Ayaz, Gul Khan Naseer, and Rashid Rana have been experimenting with traditional as well as modern themes and constructions, while radio and television programs also ensure regional representation in their broadcasts. During the marriage ceremonies, men and women often compete in relating jokes or singing these traditional songs in their own individual and duet styles. For instance, *Hir* has its own unique pattern of singing, while Mian Muhammad's *Saiful Muluk* retains its own distinct melodic variations. In the same vein, Bulleh Shah's poetry requires a special skill and style, while *vars* necessitate a specific rendition.

The death ceremonies are also characterized by some traditional elegies, generally known as *bain,* where women remember the dead with all his/her deeds in quite a moving way. It is not mere wailing; rather it is a sentimental tradition inherited from past generations. Some women assume special significance within the locality because of their rendition of *bain* and are widely respected and invited to funerals to sing. In the same vein, Sunni and Shia clerics offering special sermons *(waz, majlis)* retain their own eloquent styles and are often helped by one or two singers whose moving rendition may, in fact, win the cleric many fans at such open assemblies. Shia clerics are defined by their capability in making their audience cry over the tragic narratives of Karbala in Iraq, where the Prophet's grandson was martyred in A.D. 680.

The official patronage for these regional languages in academies in Lahore, Peshawar, Quetta, and Jamshoro and the introduction of postgraduate programs at the universities have tried to inculcate an inclusive image, although the emphasis certainly remains on Urdu and English.[37] The intermixing of languages and epics reveals a great sense of adaptability and an extra-regional shared heritage. Such commonalities, whether in the name of sacred rituals or sheerly for mundane purposes, strengthen Pakistani identity, enliven folk culture, and allow Pakistanis to contextualize their experiences in a larger regional sense where Western and South Asian traditions converge to enhance an enduring versatility. Pakistan's greater integration in the global and dominant extra-regional institutions may diminish the use of some of its older and mostly oral expressions, with English and Urdu ascending, yet given their established past and a greater usage among the various strata still offer some hope for their future.

ARTS AND CREATIVITY

Pakistani arts offer a wide spectrum of diversity and creativity as well as an interesting encounter between tradition and modernity. The ancient cave drawings, hieroglyphics, and sculptures have, over the centuries, given way to sophisticated paintings, palatial buildings, elaborate ceramics, and the various other forms of visual arts. The Islamic, Indian, West Asian, and modern

Western influences have deeply influenced Pakistani arts, which have their elite, national, and regional embodiments. Whereas the Mughal Arts have been the high-brow culture for the whole of South Asia, for Pakistan this remains the major art heritage. The regional themes and modernist techniques continue to merge to offer the young country its own unique profile. The traditional arts and handicrafts including leather goods, carpets, rugs, embroidery, ceramics, woodwork, tiles, jewelry, costumes, furnishings, and related decorative arts have been equally influenced by the forces of modernity, nationalism, and pluralistic religious ethos.

Even before independence, Lahore had become the center of classical and modern arts because of its Mughal and British traditions and the presence of the oldest teaching institute in South Asia. The Mayo School of Arts was established in 1875 in the vicinity of the Lahore Museum and in front of the Punjab University, where the famous Zamzama gun of English novelist Rudyard Kipling's fame heralded the start of the Mall. At the time of independence, Anna Molka Ahmed, a known artist, established the Department of Fine Arts at the Punjab University. Partition and ensuing migrations and tragedies energized the quest for national identity in the young country.[38] Two contemporary doyens of neoclassical arts heralded the revival of Pakistan's Indus Valley and Mughal heritage in their paintings. Abdur Rahman Chughtai (1897–1975), known for his figurative arts, now fully concentrated on the Mughal traditions and combined colors, lines, and native subjects in captivating styles.[39] His lyrical, historical, and romantic themes offered a profusion of penetrating colors and allocated to him the enviable position of the pioneer of the Perso-Indian art of Pakistan.[40]

Ustaad Allah Buksh, another contemporary and resident of Lahore, focused on landscapes and Punjabi epics, combining local and modern traditions. His oil portraits decorated offices and private mansions.[41] In addition to these two master artists, Shakir Ali's contributions in establishing the early traditions of modern Pakistani art and a lifetime devotion to preserving a synthesized heritage merit special attention.[42] Trained in England and after having worked in India, he came to Lahore to head the Mayo School of Arts, now known as the National College of Arts (NCA).[43] Here, Ali experimented with Cubism for a while but gradually came to dwell on prehistory, myths, and calligraphic representations. His long and creative career ensured a resilient generation of Pakistani artists trained at the NCA. Ali, in his later years, designed a brick house, incorporative of traditional and modern architectural designs, and housed his collections therein. Not far from the Chughtai Museum, Shakir Ali's home, studios, works, and belongings are now a national heritage, as he donated them to Pakistan.[44]

The other notable contemporaries and pioneer painters included Zubeida
Agha, A. J. Shemza, Ahmad Parvez, and Ali Imam, who mostly focused on
modernist themes, owing to their own cross-cultural experiences and interaction with Western counterparts. Three well-known Pakistani artists obtained
global fame for their paintings and calligraphy. Zainul Abedin (1914–1976)
was born in Bengal and made his name by painting the shocking images of
the victims of the Bengal Famine of 1943. After living and working in Karachi he shifted to Dhaka in East Pakistan in 1948 and established a pioneering Arts Institute there. His works represented traditional rural life and, like
those of Goya, focused on human sufferings.[45] Sadequain (d. 1987), while
based in Karachi, decorated various national landmarks with his exceptionally dexterous Quranic calligraphy and portraits. Ismail Guljee, also based
in Karachi, went beyond portraits and calligraphy and experimented in several other realms including free pen sketches and intricate lapis lazuli. His
son, Amin, has been concentrating more on metallic sculpture and jewelry in
recent years.[46]

During the 1980s, the NCA and liberal Pakistani artists came under strong
official pressure to "Islamicise" their works and were even dissuaded from rais-
ing political issues. Some religiopolitical forces and their student supporters
tried to denigrate the creative works at the NCA by labeling them as heretical,

Quranic calligraphy inside the Shah
Jahan mosque. Courtesy of the author.

yet artists continued with their works. Several women artists found themselves in the forefront of protecting civil society, and thus arts became a major area of dissent and debate. Some other Pakistani painters and calligraphers include Zahoorul Akhlaq, Ozzir Zuby, Ghulam Rasul, Hanif Ramay, Jamil Naksh, Bashir Mirza, A.R. Nagori, Ijaz Anwar, Khalid Iqbal, Ahmad Saeed Nagi, Ahmad Pervaiz, Salima Hashmi, Sumayya Durrani, Quddus Mirza, Athar Tahir, Saba Hussain, and Changez Sultan.

Although Karachi, Lahore, and Islamabad are the main art centers with numerous galleries and teaching departments, individual artists all across the country have been creating interesting and valuable artwork.[47] From the truck and bus painters to billboards and cinema poster designers and the small-town artists focusing on the portraits of heroes and villains, or rural and mountainous landscapes, Pakistani arts remain quite diverse, participatory, and vibrant.[48] Some non-Pakistani artists have also used Pakistani themes, locales, and portraits in their own works. For instance, Lin Yong and Su Hua, two Chinese artists, have exhaustively depicted landscape through sketches and figurative forms.[49]

The other domains of visual arts, such as calligraphy, films, and architecture have equally witnessed a steady growth in volume as well as diversity, although a greater emphasis on uniformity, especially under General Zia-ul-Haq, made it difficult for some art forms to develop fully. Sculpture is such an area, which has suffered the worst because of the official and ideological strictures, although its various forms have also provided outlets for political and pluralistic dissent. Calligraphy is an exceptional art genre, one of the oldest art forms in a predominantly Muslim society such as Pakistan and has duly benefited from its traditional mainstream as well as from modernist innovations. Muslims always beautified the Quranic texts in all the calligraphic scripts such as Kufic, Nasta'alique, Naskh, Khat-i-Maghrabi, Andlusi, Babri, Alique, and Riqqa, using floral patterns on special paper in addition to ornamenting the script with gold and multiplicity of colors.[50] The Quranic verses, the tradition of the Prophet *(Hadith),* and Persian, Turkish, and Urdu quartets have been sketched and carved on Muslim miniatures, architectural monuments, household walls, arches, and on the tombs and graves. Calligraphy is a major art form all across the Muslim world, which incorporates the sacred with the purely aesthetic. Miniature art, which flourished all across the Muslim regions for centuries, reached its zenith under the Great Mughals, when masterpieces such as *Hamzanama, Humayunama, Akbarnama, Kaleelao Damna, Tuzk-i-Jahangiri,* and *Padshahnama* and such other rare manuscripts took decades to complete. The poetry collections, history volumes, autobiographies, religious literature, and travelogues all were enhanced by mosaic calligraphy. The traditional calligraphers, known as *naqaash,* kept this art form alive in Muslim South Asia, and Pakistan inherited some of the

Visitors to Muhammad Iqbal's tomb, next to the Badshahi
mosque, Lahore. Courtesy of the author.

naqaash families. Like poets, these scribes and calligraphers have pen names,
which symbolize their calligraphic skills. These traditional *naqaash* are often
respected as Sufis because of their creative efforts and lifetime devotion to
highlighting and beautifying the holy names and sacred literatures. Thus,
the profession is considered to be prestigious and highly respectable. Some
of the foremost Pakistani calligraphers—trained in traditional ways and also
belonging to noted families—include Sufi Abdul Majeed Parveen Raqam,
Tajud Din Zareen Raqam, Munshi Mohammad Siddique, Almas Raqam,
Hafiz Yusuf Sadidi, Abdur Rashid Rustam-i-Qalam, M.M. Sharif and his
son, Aftab Ahmad and, of course, Sadequain.[51]

PERFORMING ARTS

At independence, Lahore had the Parsee Theatre, besides a nascent film
industry consisting of two studios, which soon began producing Urdu and
Punjabi films. With Calcutta now in India, East Pakistan had to start anew in
the various realms of visual arts including theaters and films, and writers such
as Qazi Nazrul Islam assumed a primary role in defining the Muslim Bengali
arts and letters. The Government College Lahore's Dramatic Club, since its
inception in the pre-1947 era, had been training generation of artists and per-
formers, many of who were destined to play key roles in Pakistan's performing
arts. Zia Mohyuddin, Shoaib Hashmi, Sarmad Sehbai, Kamal Ahmad Rizvi,
and Madeeah Gohar are some of those familiar names who have enriched
Pakistan's performing arts. In 1948, noted intellectuals including Faiz, Rafi
Peer, Imtiaz Ali Taj, M.D. Taseer, and Agha Hameed established the Lahore
Arts Council, which included a small theater and a gallery but soon assumed
a mainstream role in promoting arts.

During the 1970s, Zulfikar Ali Bhutto, eager to promote Pakistani cultural identity, led the foundation of a number of institutes and councils to recognize, preserve, and diffuse the various forms of Pakistani arts. Under the guidance of Faiz, the Pakistan National Council of Arts came into being in Islamabad with branches in all the major provincial capitals. Additionally and quite significantly, the National Institute of Folk Heritage (subsequently renamed Lok Virsa) was established in Islamabad to collect and promote Pakistani folk and traditional arts. Other than gallery and archival repositories, Lok Virsa promotes workshops of artisans and artists and publishes and records their works. Over the last several decades, this institution has established an impressive collection of Pakistan's rich folk cultural heritage and, in some cases, has facilitated the recording and preservation of traditional arts, crafts, and oral narratives. Its annual folk festival, known as Lok Mela, brings in scores of Pakistani artists from around the country to the scenic Shakarparian Hills, where their live performances and masterly ingenuity are widely appreciated by large audiences.

While commissioning a new cabinet division called the Ministry of Culture, Bhutto also founded the National Dance Academy and the National Film Development Corporation, which somewhat declined during the 1980s because of strong official restrictions. During this period, Pakistan lost several of its artists, such as Naheed Siddiqui, a legend in performing Kathak and other such classical dances, who sought exile in England. With the dance totally banned by the Zia-ul-Haq regime, dancers such as Seema Kirmani, Nighat Chaudhary, and Tehreema Mitha would perform only at private residences.[52] However, the vocalization of religious hymns such as *hamad* (poem praising God), *na'at* (composition praising the Prophet) and the *qawalli* music became more pronounced under a military regime, which propounded a literalist version of Islam and frowned upon all other forms of visual and recreational arts. In the rural areas, however, people continued to seek entertainment from the local professionals *(mirathis)*, while the minstrels/bards *(bhands)* would entertain gatherings during wedding ceremonies and rural sports. These entertainers and musicians, along with the traditional transvestite artists *(heejras)* and impersonators *(behroopias)* continue entertaining millions of Pakistanis across the towns, villages, and tribal settlements. The forces of globalization, technology, and mobility pose challenges as well as exciting opportunities to such parallel and multiple forms of literature and arts across the country.

CRAFTS

Pakistan has several handicrafts to represent its cross-cultural traditions and historic epochs. The Mughal period remains a major reference when it comes to decorative art such as jewelry, textiles, calligraphy, ceramics, and miniatures. The British period, as reflected through modernist influences in architecture and utility-oriented structures, is equally visible in furniture, housing, upholstery, fibers, glass, and cutlery. Pakistan's classical handicrafts are made with metal, wood, textiles, marble, and leather. Pakistani rugs and carpets—both old and new—and decorative items made of glass, ivory, onyx, and metal have a large national following. Other than gold jewelry, silver has staged a comeback with its emphasis on traditional patterns using sapphire, ruby, and other stones ingrained in ornaments and also inlaid in other handicrafts. Lampshades made from camel skin, swords with extensive handiwork, vases, wooden chairs, carved wooden pillars, and panels (especially from Chiniot), metallic utility items from Wazirabad and Gujranwala, and extensive sports and clinical goods (such as surgical instruments), and kilts from Sialkot are well-known products with an increasing domestic and international market. Pakistani metal plates, samovars, decorative trays, knives, footwear, and clinical implements support a major home-based industry, which combines old techniques with modern technologies. Musical instruments including the Highlander's bagpipes are produced in Sialkot. The big cities across the country and tourist resorts such as Murree, Swat, Mohenjodaro and the Northern Areas have shops devoted to Pakistani handicrafts.

NOTES

1. Muhammad Iqbal, *Kulliyat-i-Iqbal Farsi* (Complete Persian Works), Lahore Academy, 1973.

2. The Museums in Peshawar, Lahore, and at Taxila offer a wide range of artifacts excavated from these historic sites. See also Jonathan Mark Kenoyer, *Ancient Cities of the Indus Valley Civilization* (Karachi: Oxford University Press, 2000).

3. The valuable studies by Emile Durkheim, Max Weber, and Margaret Mead have been quite helpful in a greater understanding of the evolution of various forms of culture and their relationship with the forces of society and state at large. In recent times, the roles of technology, globalization, media, and mobility have spawned further debate on the evolution, diversification, and diffusion of cultures. The works by Geertz, Nye, and MacLuhan merit special attention and have to be studied in conjunction with a Saidian critique of power-centricity, where hegemonic cultures could even deny equal space to some of their counterparts. See Clifford Geertz, *The Interpretation of Cultures: Selected Essays* (New York: Basic Books, 2000); Russel Nye, *The Unembarrassed Muse: The Popular Arts in America* (New York: Dial,1970); Marshal MacLuhan, *Verbal-Voco-Visual Explorations* (New York: Something Else Press, 1976); and, Edward Said, *Orientalism* (London: Penguin, 2003) (reprint).

4. Bridget Allchin and Raymond Allchin, *The Rise of Civilisation in India and Pakistan* (Cambridge: Cambridge University Press, 1982).

5. Bridget Allchin and Raymond Allchin, "Discovering and Preserving the Cultural Past," in *Old Roads, New Highways: Fifty Years of Pakistan,* ed. Victoria Schofield (Karachi: Oxford University Press, 1997). Also see F. R. Allchin, *The Archaeology of Early Historic South Asia* (Cambridge: Cambridge University Press,1995).

6. J. Marshall, *The Buddhist Art of Gandhara* (Cambridge: Cambridge University Press, 1960); Mortimer Wheeler, *Five Thousand Years of Pakistan* (London: Royal Society, 1953).

7. For more on this, see Romila Thapar, *A History of India,* vol. 1 (London: Penguin, 1979); and A. L. Basham, *The Wonder That Was India. A Survey of the Culture of the Indian Sub-continent before the Coming of the Muslims* (London: Sedgwick, 1954).

8. That is partly the reason that Sanskrit gradually died out, as it had become selectively elitist.

9. For further details on these historic towns, see A. H. Dani, *The History of Taxila* (Tokyo and Paris: UNESCO, 1986); and A. H. Dani, *Chilas: The City of Nanga Parvat* (Islamabad: A. H. Dani, 1983).

10. A. H. Dani, *History of Northern Areas of Pakistan* (Islamabad: National Institute, 1989); also A. H. Dani, *Human Records on Karakoram Highway* (Islamabad: A. H. Dani, 1983); and Irfan Husain, *Pakistan* (London: Stacey, 1997). The explorations and excavations by Sir Aurel Stein, the famous Hungarian-British scholar during the colonial era, unearthed multiple significance of the Silk Road in reference to religions, migrations, trade, and arts. Hundreds of artifacts including ancient manuscripts, sketches, household goods, and other buried items highlighted the role of this major ancient artery used by a wide variety of people across the centuries. A special exhibition on the historic Silk Road at the British Library in 2004 and an ever-increasing literature on the subject have been quite crucial in our understanding of a historic yet lesser-known globalism.

11. More recently, there has been a growing celebration of this pre-Muslim past, and intellectuals seek Pakistan's evolution from the earliest human habitation across the Indus region. For instance, see Aitzaz Ahsan, *The Indus Saga and the Making of Pakistan* (Karachi: Oxford University Press, 1996).

12. Thousands of Pakistani children even memorize the sacred text and are known as *Huffaz,* which is the plural of *Hafiz.* They recite the holy book in the mosques and on special occasions. The evening prayers during the month of fasting *(Ramadan)* are devoted to reciting the entire text.

13. For an excellent work in the realm of intellectual history, see Aziz Ahmad, *An Intellectual History of Islam in India* (Edinburgh: Edinburgh University Press, 1969); and Muzaffar Alam, *The Languages of Political Islam in India, 1200–1800* (London: Hurst, 2004).

14. For a well-informed research work on the Mughal empire and its political economy, see Irfan Habib, *The Agrarian System of Mughal India, 1556–1707* (New Delhi: Oxford University Press, 2000); and Muzaffar Alam, *The Crisis of Empire in Mughal North India: Awadh and the Punjab, 1707–48* (Delhi: Oxford University Press, 1986).

15. For a competent selection of Iqbal's Urdu poetry, see Victor Kiernan, *Poems from Iqbal: Renderings in English Verse with Comparative Urdu Text* (Karachi: Oxford University Press, 1999) (reprint).

16. As aptly defined by Edward Said, Orientalism was the cultural and intellectual legacy of European imperialism, which defined the East as inherently inferior, weak, and emotional, needing reforms by a rational, superior, and predominant West. See Said, *Orientalism*.

17. Some of the newspapers of the era included *Paisa Akhbar, Hamdard, Inqilab,* and *Ehsan*.

18. For a historical work on the politicization of middle-class Muslim women, see Dushka Saiyid, *Muslim Women of the British Punjab: From Seclusion to Politics* (Basingstoke: Macmillan, 1998).

19. In English, it would mean the circle of people with literary taste. It met in several cities at specific places and its sessions attracted and promoted generations of writers, both men and women. In Lahore, Halqa would hold its weekly sessions at two tea/coffee places, which continue to symbolize the quality debates and poetry recitals.

20. Halqa was established in Lahore. At its weekly meetings in cafes and private homes, essays, poems, and other writings were read. The Progressive Writers Association (PWA) was established in London and soon moved back to India. In the early 1950s, the Pakistani regime banned the PWA, accusing it of communist ideas, whereas Halqa continued its work and opened branches in Karachi, Peshawar, Quetta, and Rawalpindi.

21. Their collection of ten stories, *Angaray* (Red-hot embers), focusing on human misery and exploitation, became a manifesto for a generation of progressive writers. Ahmed Ali, et al., *Angaray* (Lucknow: Sajjad Zaheer, 1932).

22. After 1947, Sajjad Zaheer, the founder of the Pakistan Communist Party, came under official scrutiny and eventually left for India. Quratulain Hyder, also disappointed with military rule, left for India, where she published her masterpiece, *Aag Ka Daryaa* (Lahore: Sang-e-Meel, 1994) an allegorical novel of immense significance. A Pakistani writer, Fahmida Riaz, also spent quite a few years in self-exile in India and only returned after General Zia's death (1988).

23. Muhammad Umar Memon, ed., *The Colour of Nothingness: Modern Urdu Short Stories* (Karachi: Oxford University Press, 1998).

24. Manto has been usually viewed as the greatest fiction writer in contemporary Urdu literature, and his biting realism on communal and individual issues has transformed him into almost a cult figure. Bedi was unhappy with Partition, while Chandar dwelt on higher themes. Intizar Husain produced his novel, *Basti* (Lahore: Sang-e-Meel, 1983), which is viewed as a masterpiece in nostalgia and realism on the tragic experiences of migration and new national identity. Ahmad Ali, after his migration to Pakistan, mostly lived a reclusive life in Karachi, and Abdullah Hussein penned his masterwork, *Udaas Naslain* ([Sad Generations] Lahore: Qausain, 1978), which remains a powerful account of migration and accompanying personal tragedies.

25. Shahab, Ahmad, and Mufti were quite a well-knit group who espoused an Islamic identity for Pakistan. Bano Qudsiya, Hajra Masroor, and Altaf Fatima are well-known women novelists, whereas Hijazi wrote impressive and widely read novels on Muslim Spain and the decline of Muslim rule in India. Jaafari was a poet as well as a noted fiction writer who focused on historical themes. Interested in astrology, his quartets *(Rubayyaat)* were known for wit and satire.

26. For details, see M. H. Askari, "Urdu Literature," in Schofield, *Old Roads, New Highways.*

27. Kishwar Naheed is herself a noted feminist and activist whose Urdu works are widely read and critiqued.

28. Several universities, including those at Berkeley; Beijing; Philadelphia; Chicago; Madison, Wisconsin; London; and New York offer courses in Urdu, although, like South Asian studies, it is not a major recruiting area.

29. Bollywood films have popularized Hindi across South Asia as a dominant cultural expression, whereas Pakistani television plays and Urdu music have tried to maintain a simultaneous niche for Urdu, although the Urdu film industry in Pakistan remains marginalized.

30. Michael H. Fisher, *The First Indian Author in English: Dean Mahomed (1759–1851)* (Delhi: Oxford University Press, 1996); Sake Dean Mahomet, *The Travels of Dean Mahomet* (Berkeley: University of California Press, 1997) (reprint).

31. For representative collections of works by a growing list of Pakistani writers using English as a medium, see Muneeza Shamsie, ed., *A Dragonfly in the Sun: An Anthology of Pakistani Writings in English* (Karachi: Oxford University Press, 1997); and Muneeza Shamsie, ed., *Leaving Home: A Collection of English Prose by Pakistani Writers* (Karachi: Oxford University Press, 2001).

32. For a survey of some of the recent works in fiction, poetry, and other literary and academic domains, see Muneeza Shamsie, "Rich Offerings—Pakistani English Literature, 2004," *Dawn,* 6 February 2005.

33. For a flavor of one such poet, see Athar Tahir, *Qadir Yar: A Critical Introduction* (Lahore: Adabi Board, 1988); and Athar Tahir, *Punjab Portraits* (Lahore: Sang-e-Meel, 1992).

34. Marriage ceremonies go on for days and in the evening, besides local minstrels, boys and girls share singing and dancing of some popular folk songs. Songs may vary given the occasion, especially when the bride leaves her home or when the groom riding a horse heads toward her home.

35. The Islamabad-based Institute of Folk Heritage has done an excellent job of preserving, promoting, and publishing this vast area of oral traditions besides the folk crafts. Its written works, archives, and audiovisual productions have inspired several serious multidisciplinary studies inside the country. The preservation of a vast and diverse folk culture has been a major achievement, and its celebration through annual fairs has greatly strengthened Pakistani identity.

36. There are Web sites devoted to Sufi music, Punjabi jokes, and other such shared oral materials.

37. Critics may bemoan the general indifference to these languages by the natives, who are more eager to learn Urdu and English. However, many writers are seriously devoted to the promotion of these languages. For instance, just in Pushto, during 2004, among several writers, three women made their mark. They included: Rabia Mumtaz, Wagma Saba Aaamir, and Sorayya Hawa, and all of them came from literary families. For details, see Sher Zaman Taizi, "A Whiff of Fresh Air: Pushto Books in 2004," *Dawn,* 16 January 2005.

Since the 1990s, literature and journalism in Sindhi have impressively flourished because of an increased politicization in the province. Sindhi authors such as Amar Jaleel, Tanvir Ansari, Abdul Wahid Aresar, and Husain Bakhsh Narejo have focused on political issues, gender empowerment, and reforms in the province, while Amar Leghari's works focus on environmental degradation. Noted Sindhi intellectual Nabi Bakhsh Baloch has kept up with his comprehensive research on literary and mystical heritage, whereas journalism and travelogues feature in the works of authors like Abdul Hayee Palijo, Anwar Hakro, and Khalil Moryani. Mazhar Jamil's *Jadid Sindhi Adab* (2004) is a holistic study of contemporary Sindhi literature in Urdu. For details, see Abbas Jalbani, "Breaking New Ground: Sindhi Books of 2004," *Dawn,* 6 February 2005.

Concurrently, the demand for the introduction of Punjabi at the primary education level was reinvigorated, and quite a few new magazines and newspapers came into being. The international Punjabi conferences and the vigorous linkages between the Pakistani and Indian Punjabs turned 2004 into a memorable year. Several noted Indian and Pakistani writers of Punjabi origins held joint seminars and conferences where nostalgia, curiosity, and affection underpinned well-publicized literary gatherings. Newspapers and television channels carried exhaustive reports on these literary efforts, and even the politicians and bureaucrats on both sides vied to outdo each other in the promotion of such events. Pakistani writers such as Najm Hossein Syed and Illyas Ghuman received prestigious Indian literary prizes, and dozens of books in Punjabi made their entry on the literary scene. Other than fiction, commentaries on classical mystical works, poetry collections, and literary critique, Punjabi literature in Britain and the United States also received increased attention among the Punjabi circles in Lahore. In addition, the Masud Khadarposh Trust carried on with its two-decade-old tradition of awarding prizes for the best Punjabi books. For more details, see Safir Rammah, "A Dream Year: Punjabi Literature in 2004," *Dawn,* 30 January 2005.

38. For more on her, see Miriam Habib, *Painter-Teacher, Anna Molka* (Lahore: Habib, 1984).

39. Arif Rahman Chughtai. ed., *The Story-Teller: M. A. Rahman Chughtai* (Lahore: Chughtai Trust, 1997). Arif Chughtai is the son of the late master artist and looks after the Chughtai Museum in Lahore.

40. His museum is in the suburbs of Lahore and houses his own works and commemorative photographs. Chughtai, to a great extent, became a perfect representative of Pakistani art in its neoclassical styles.

41. For more details, see Salima Hashmi, "The Visual Arts," in Schofield, *Old Roads, New Highways*.

42. Haji Muhammad Sharif was another early Pakistani artist who dwelt on traditional themes and techniques. For more on these early master artists, see M. Yusuf Abbasi, *Pakistani Culture: A Profile* (Islamabad: National Institute, 1992), pp. 269–95.

43. For first-hand information on the NCA, see Tehnyat Majeed, "1997 at the NCA," *Arts and the Islamic World* (50 Years of Art in Pakistan) 32, 97–101. Also Abbasi, *Pakistani Culture*, pp. 305–310.

44. Akbar Naqvi, "Transfer of Power and Perception: Four Pakistani Artists," *Arts and the Islamic World*, 9–15; also Akbar Naqvi, *Image and Identity: Fifty Years of Painting and Sculpture in Pakistan* (Karachi: Oxford University Press, 1998).

45. For a brief biography and the reproductions of his works, see Jalal Uddin Ahmed, ed., *Zainul Abedin* (Karachi: Pakistan Publications, 2004) (reprinted from the 1958 edition).

46. See Muhammad Sadequain, *Chronological Biodata and World Opinions* (Islamabad: National Institute, 1981); and S. Amjad Ali, *Gulgee-Versatile Artist* (Islamabad: National Institute, 1984), cited in Abbasi.

47. The Sadequain in Islamabad, Abasin in Peshawar, Alhamra in Lahore, and the Frere Hall in Karachi are some of the well-known galleries in addition to several arts councils, private galleries, and Western cultural centers that also help organize special exhibitions.

48. See Marcella Sirhandi, "Paintings in Pakistan: 1947–1997"; S. Amjad Ali, "Forward Looking Art: Years before and after Independence"; Nilofur Farrukh, "Echoes of Socio-Political History"; and Marjorie Hussain, "Pakistan's Art World Celebrated a Golden Jubilee," in *Arts and the Islamic World*, 32 (1997). Also see Marcella Sirhandi, *Contemporary Paintings in Pakistan* (Lahore: Ferozsons, 1992); Athar Tahir, *Lahore Colours* (Karachi: Oxford University Press, 1997). After some lull due to ethnic unrest, Karachi has also begun to revive its arts scene. The formation of the Foundation for Museum of Modern Art (FOMMA) in 2002 is an encouraging development. A few well-publicized events have also aimed at establishing teaching facilities and a modern museum in Pakistan's largest city. See, Salwat Ali, "Mapping the Change," *Dawn*, 4 December 2004; and Asif Noorani, "An Art Affair to Remember," *Star Weekend*, 4 December 2004.

49. Lin Yong and Su Hua, *Pakistan* (Beijing,: Pakistan Embassy, 1985).

50. Many of these rare manuscripts, including the earliest copies of handwritten Quran and Hadith collections, are held in special museums and libraries across Europe. For instance, the British Queen Elizabeth has some of the immensely unique miniatures and manuscripts in her personal collections, and they are occasionally put on display in different galleries. Dublin's Beatty Collection boasts the world's largest collection of diverse Muslim manuscripts including the Quran; however, the British Library has the claim to have some of the oldest Quranic scripts. Istanbul's Topkapi Museum also possesses a few of the earliest Quranic manuscripts including that of Caliph Usman, a companion and political successor of the Prophet.

51. *Raqam* means a scribe while *Qalam* means a pen. Both these words are Arabic in origin. For more on this see Aftab Ahmad, *Islamic Calligraphy* (Rawalpindi: Ahmad, 1984).

52. Curiously, the puppet theater was revived during this decade, although mostly on television programs such as Farooq Qaisar's "Uncle Sargam." Simultaneously, stage shows, usually mixing satire in songs and dialogues, also became quite popular, with artists such as Moeen Akhtar. The Faiz Mela in the late 1980s also assumed a vanguard role by bringing in literary elite and folk artists to Lahore. The Basant festival, characterized by colorful kite flying contests, has offered another popular pursuit.

SUGGESTED READINGS

Abbasi, M. Yusuf. *Pakistani Culture: A Profile.* Islamabad: National Institute of History and Culture, 1992.

Memon, Muhammad Umar, ed. *The Colour of Nothingness: Modern Urdu Short Stories.* Karachi: Oxford University Press, 1998.

Schofield, Victoria, ed. *Old Roads, New Highways: Fifty Years of Pakistan.* Karachi: Oxford University Press, 1997.

Shamsie, Muneeza, ed. *A Dragonfly in the Sun: An Anthology of Pakistani Writings in English.* Karachi: Oxford University Press, 1997.

———. *Leaving Home: A Collection of English Prose by Pakistani Writers.* Karachi: Oxford University Press, 2001.

Tahir, Athar. *Lahore Colours.* Karachi: Oxford University Press, 1997.

4

Architecture and Housing

I have built a house next to the mosque and thus a lowly person has entered Allah's neighbourhood.
—Mirza Ghalib, preeminent Urdu poet

A Westerner imagining Pakistan might think of a country where cities are bursting at their seams or villages surrounded by stinking water pools infested with tropical insects where water buffaloes float around lazily fighting off thousands of flies, while an army of half-clad children chases a few stray dogs. Or one might imagine the Mughal monuments, rugged mountains, sleepy villages, and comfortable suburbia of Islamabad and Lahore, often depicted on the country's currency, post cards, and stamps. Another image may be of symmetrical rows of Chaukhandi tombs in Sindh and Balochistan, and glazed Sufi shrines with their blue or green domes shimmering in the sun all across this vast, largely tropical Muslim land. The marble and mud, much like palatial bungalows and basic huts, certainly juxtapose the two contrasting realities of Pakistan and for that matter of the developing world, where tradition and modernity as well as poverty and prosperity and likewise this worldliness contrasted with an ascetic otherworldliness coexist. Across the labyrinthine habitations of this Indus land, climate, religion, and economy may underpin the old and new architectural vistas, but a host of other equally important factors account for versatility and plurality. History, religion, extended family systems, patriarchy, individual choices, cross-cultural tastes, modernist and post-modernist influences, neotraditionalism, honor, security, regional conventions, and sensitivity to aesthetics or even the lack of them have continued to fashion Pakistani attitudes toward housing.

Chaukhandi tomb. Courtesy of the
author.

The most important factors in the evolution of architecture and housing in
Pakistan, other than politics, money, and technology, have been the environment and religion. In a land without thick forests yet not totally arid either,
architecture in this part of South Asia, both in its forms and techniques, presents an interesting interface with the environment. The hot climate, visibility
of the sun most of the year, moonlit nights, hillocks, and even rivers prone
to flooding during the Monsoons have all fashioned the long march in the
epochal history of building houses as well as monuments. Such a landscape
allows a greater visibility of temples, mosques, shrines, palaces, forts, and even
hamlets that dot this land. Until the nineteenth century, traditional architecture emphasized grandeur to exude a sense of authority, yet it did not sacrifice
interior beauty and utilitarianism to meet community needs.[1]

In the early years of Pakistan, the conscious emphasis, both at the official and academic levels, was to highlight the country's cultural distinctness
from everything *Indian,* yet the fact remains that architectural traditions
have been based on diffusion and invention. Comparatively recent borders
of the nation-states are not helpful guides in ascertaining the roots and shared
norms across centuries and diverse lands. There are areas where one can easily discern individual characteristics highlighting certain specific official or
religious symbols, but in most cases it is the story of human needs and visions
being realized through available technology and resources. Whether inher-

ited as ancestral craft or shared as a global pursuit because of an overriding technology and instruction, architecture is one of those rare human activities that reveals an astounding degree of human sharing. According to one of the leading Pakistani architects, who admits to having gone back from being a committed "modernist" to embracing "traditional wisdom," the "building industry has made little advance since Mohenjo-daro. The only progress in plumbing since the Romans has been the introduction of the water sealed trap."[2]

Architecture is a cherished human activity that has certainly been conscious of history and aesthetics, and style has always remained a major preoccupation for builders and designers. Most of the material used in construction remains the same as in the past, although plastics and steel are more recent addition to mortar, stones, and bricks. The Pharaohs, ancient Mesopotamians, and Dravidians of the Indus Valley were the pioneers in building temples, palaces, tombs, castles, granaries, canals, and bridges. The Greeks, like other preceding and contemporary cultures such as Hindus, added male and female statues on their columnar and geometrical structures. Clay, baked bricks, plaster and ornamentation soon joined stone, mud, and wood.

The modern architectural tradition that came into the developing world after its Europeanization has significantly overshadowed the erstwhile traditional forms and patterns, and countries such as Pakistan have been deeply impacted by it. Especially in the early years of its nationhood, Pakistan tried to incorporate Western traditions ambitiously, because like other Third World countries it desired to be considered "modern." From instruction to implementation, the building sector bypassed climatic, historical, and traditional considerations. It is only in recent decades that efforts by several intellectuals and planners have turned once again toward respecting tradition with the objective of finding a synthesis. Some of these architects and designers are themselves the products of Western institutions and are not against modern technology per se, yet they are increasingly sensitive about its annihilative and hegemonic portents. From private houses to official buildings and utilitarian buildings to galleries, one notices a conscious back-to-roots effort that has equally encouraged the movement toward the preservations of historical monuments, *havelis* (traditional South Asian houses), worship places, shrines, and forts. Pakistan's burgeoning population, its economic limitations, and greater desire on the part of the *nouveau riches* to look modern all hamper preservation efforts. The desire to build palatial houses and multi-story plazas and construct dams, industries, and highways all have been threatening these historic buildings, accentuating the environmental imbalances. The conservationists and modernist-traditionalists such as Kamil Mumtaz are not only trying to restore old patterns and skills, they are increasingly uncomfortable with a Eurocentric classification of architecture to merely three categories: secular, materialist, and temporal. This classification has not only simplified a centuries-old heritage but has engendered a serious inferiority complex across the non-Western world. While focusing even on Islamic architecture, these critics accept the preceding cross-cultural additions into it but refuse to accept it as the only and authentic Pakistani tradition. Thus, the material and representations of Pakistani architecture will be surveyed here from the ancient Indus towns to traditional hamlets and present-day suburbia.

HISTORIC MONUMENTS

As the home to the ancient Indus Valley civilization, Pakistan has some of the most unique and oldest ruins of the earliest human habitations. The pre-historic Dravidian and the early Aryan dwellings at ancient cities such as Mohenjodaro, Kot Diji, and Harrapa are quite revealing and instructive on the urban lifestyles of ancient Pakistan. Dating from the third millennium B.C., these elaborate cities had geometrically organized broad streets with the temples, storage buildings and official buildings located in the town centers. The use of properly designed and baked bricks, pavements, wells, and an efficient underground drainage system were prominent features of these pioneering Indus cities. They reveal beauty, majesty and originality at an early stage.[3] These cities held economic, political, and religious significance and were closely linked with villages and towns across the region and elsewhere.

The professionalization of different population groups under the tutelage of ancient priest-kings allowed an interesting mixture of sacred and mundane. While warriors and agriculturalists looked after the needs of the community including defense, the artisans ensured proper and hygienic dwellings and sanitation. Carpenters, masons, blacksmiths, and ordinary laborers built towns, canals, and roads, while traders operated caravans to other lands, including an efficient connection with the great Silk Road. The priests, in their roles as managers and religious overlords, ensured distribution of labor and produce and built huge granaries to meet the needs during emergencies such as invasions, pestilence, and floods. The city of Mohenjodaro was built six times on the same spot, as the floods in the Indus would often wipe out the dwellings. The river was, however, the lifeline for the purposes of navigation, agriculture, commerce, and fishing. The nearby lakes would also sustain fishing communities such as present-day Mohanas in Sindh, where lifestyles have changed very little over the centuries and are currently threatened by pollution and other encroachments. These fishermen live on Manchar and Keenjhar Lakes like their Dravidian ancestors, and their boats are used as homes for themselves as well as for their cattle. The ancient Indus Valley civilization disappeared because of ecological changes and largely because of the Aryan invasions into the subcontinent from the north during the second millennium B.C.. The Aryans were nomadic Central Asians, yet the vanquished cultures were able to acculturate them into settled communities.

During the classical Hindu period, elaborate temples were constructed as tributes to various gods and goddesses. It is not unusual to find some old Hindu temples across Pakistan, although it might be difficult to determine their age because they have suffered from disrepair since 1947, when most Hindus left for India. Some of the oldest Hindu temples are to be found in the Salt Range, but they might date from the post-Buddhist era when Hinduism reemerged as the dominant religion of India and Taxila became the capital of Muraya Empire. The fifth century B.C. is certainly a turning point in South Asian history when Buddhist, Zoroastrian and Jain faiths started adding to the religious and cultural complexity of this region, with Persian political influences making present-day Pakistan the part of a Greater Persia. The Zoroastrian as well as Jain influences on the native architecture are hard to trace, but the Buddhist influence reflects a bridgehead between Hindu, Persian, and Greek traits, which were soon to mature into the Gandhara civilization in the upper reaches of the Punjab, Frontier, and Northern Areas.

Alexander, in his campaign to annex the outer reaches of the Persian Empire, traversed through Chitral, Swat, the Salt Range, central Punjab, and lower regions, and introduced Greek influences, although only the remains of a temple at Taxila survive. The statues of Buddha, in plaster, stone, or metal, visibly reveal Greek features—contrasted with the images of Siddhartha found in rest of India and Sri Lanka. The pinnacle of Greco-Buddhist traditions was through a multitude of stupas, monasteries, libraries, and residential quarters for the monks. Other than Taxila and Takhtbhai, these monuments are found in several places in the upper reaches of the Indus Valley. Emperor Ashoka, who had converted to Buddhism by renouncing violence and ensured the construction of some of the unique architectural monuments, built most of the stupas. These were constructed all the way from western Afghanistan to Orissa, and the Buddhist monuments prominently featured in the valleys of Bamiyan, Peshawar, and Pothowar. The largest and the oldest stupa in South Asia is at Mankiyala, about 25 miles outside Rawalpindi on the way to Lahore. There are stupas all around Swat and a prominent stupa stands by the Grand Trunk Road (GT Road) near the town of Landi Kotal in the historic Khyber Pass. These magnificent, circular structures rise like a dome and, in some cases, still have Buddhist carvings and motifs on them. Traditionally, surrounding these structures would be residential facilities for monks and prayer halls, although they disappeared long ago. The Mankiyala Stupa is almost 300 feet high and has a narrow gap over the top. It was repaired during the British era. It is believed that it held some holy relics.[4] Interestingly, some of the domes of the old mosques and shrines both in South and Central Asia closely resemble these stupas.

The Buddhist influences in northern Pakistan are evident in elaborate buildings at Julian, the Buddhist hill town outside the ruins of Taxila, where a bustling university existed in ancient times to train monks. The square buildings with courtyards, prayer rooms, residences, and solid thick stone walls featuring a uniquely built pattern—found in some ancient buildings in Greece—are the highlights of these structures, which served both sacred and mundane purposes. Various alcoves contained smaller stupas with elaborate carvings showing Buddha in several positions along with his early followers. The secluded monastery near Julian appears to have been the seat of religious significance and even after centuries, its location within the sides of the Margalla Hills reveals the proverbial Buddhist quest for tranquility. Some of the statues are headless because of some subsequent fanaticism, yet their massive sizes only reflect a great sense of proportion and aesthetics. Buddha is mostly shown seated in the usual Indian style with an upright back, curly hair, and his eyes transfixed in meditation. He is always shown wearing a loin cloth, which looks more like a Roman toga.

The city of Taxila symbolized urbane culture and sophisticated technology and was itself a city of temples and universities. Like Mohenjodaro and Harrapa, the city was divided into several geometrical sections with a broad street passing through the middle. Stone and mortar were extensively used in buildings, with numerous decorative and sacred carvings on the walls. The Buddhist influences seemed to dominate these buildings, although remains of an early Greek temple with its massive columns affirm multiplicity of cultures coexisting at Taxila. Taxila might have been still younger than some of the ancient rural settlements with Hindu temples, which were strewn across the Indus Valley until Emperor Ashoka made Buddhism the official religion of his empire. Buddhism did not wipe out Hindu traditions and instead synthesized them with the Greek and West Asian influences, an experiment ultimately resulting in the flowering of a classical heritage, known as the Gandhara Art. The statues of Buddha—both in his Indian and Greek incarnations—his various moods and positions, the scenes of worship and even of wars characterized the wall carvings in the houses, public buildings, and temples across the Peshawar valley and in the adjoining regions.

The city of Taxila, like Mohenjodaro, is a multi-layered town, showing its various reincarnations after fires or invasions. Its straight lanes, central boulevard, well-located temples with carvings, such as of twin-headed eagles and snakes, and well-proportioned official buildings and private houses, all built in geometrical designs, always seem to outshine the work of city planners in Islamabad, the modern capital of contemporary Pakistan. A boundary wall and suburbs surrounded Taxila's main city while the monasteries and ancient universities were perched high on the hills and comparatively secluded from the city itself.

The ancient designers who ensured security and water supply as well as enough land-based resources for essential supplies thoughtfully selected the location of Taxila, Takhtbhai, Mingora, and Peshawar—on one side of the Hindu Kush. The rivers such as Indus, Swat, Gilgit, and Kabul, and various seasonal streams allowed sufficient water while the weather was generally temperate. The fabulous Gandhara culture developed here. All the ancient religious and commercial activities coexisted, including some of the earliest Jewish and Christian communities. The Peshawar Museum holds some of the rare specimens of statues (including those of a fasting Buddha and of Hindu deities), figurines, trinkets, coins, jewelry, ceramics, and other utensils of daily use, which show the urban, cosmopolitan, and multilayered political economy of this ancient culture. It appears that the historic Indus cities were well planned and diverse and combined several architectural traditions. Stones, wood, and plaster were used by the traditional artisans to build dwellings that were suitable to the environment as well as to human taste.

The resurgence of Hinduism under the Mauryas and Guptas stipulated a golden age where arts, literature, and architecture flourished across the subcontinent. Other than townships, emphasis was on building temples and the decorations both within and external. The complex structures made of stones and bricks but usually plastered white were horizontal, often topped by a small, circular canopy. These temples revealed continuity with the preceding traditions; and they were built by the streams, rivers, or on the hillocks overlooking the towns below. Without a courtyard, the inner sanctum, accessible through a narrow passage, would usually contain deities on a platform with space for offerings. The exteriors of these square buildings, often built on a raised platform, had carved statutes of humans, animals, and chariots, occasionally with Greek columns added to the main entrance. One of the holiest and the earliest Hindu temple in the Salt Range, locally known as Pir Kattas, is spread over a huge area between two hills. It sits on both sides of the stream —*chashma*—that is attributed to the tears of Vishnu, the chief god. The main temple site behind the bathing space has its pre-Mughal and Mughal features of arches and a red stone exterior. Consisting of many buildings for numerous purposes, the area has several caves where holy ascetics—*sadhus*—used to reside. The structure above the main sanctum is white, multilayered, and in an oblong shape.[5]

The subsequent historic periods, as witnessed in the ruins at Taxila and Takhtbhai, show a further diversification in architectural patterns, with an intermixing of Central Asian and even Greek styles. In the town of Malot, visited by Alexander in the fourth century B.C., are some of the earliest Hindu temples, which predate the Greek influences, yet reflect West Asian features. In the town of Bhaun—another historic village of great significance in Hindu traditions—one finds several temples and places reserved for funerary rituals. Just outside the town, there are igloo-type structures with colorful decorations on their walls and Sanskrit scriptures, where holy men meditated and built pyres for the dead bodies.

In the early Christian era, St. Thomas purportedly visited Taxila, but it is certainly impossible to locate the ruins of any old churches, although in southwestern India, Syrian Christians always maintained a steady presence. Given the traces of Christian amulets, crosses, sketches of priests, and even an early synagogue excavated on the Silk Road, it is possible that the Christians and Jews added some new features to the existing patterns in the Indus regions. However, the dissolution of central Hindu authority at Taxila because of invasions from the north and the earlier disappearance of Buddhism allowed the emergence of regional potentates. Across Sindh and Balochistan, the local influential rajas established their dynastic rule, while upper Punjab and the Salt Range came under the tutelage of the Hindu Shahis. These monarchs built temples, which, by that time, revealed a multiplicity of traditions and also the salience of Hinduism in the region. The Hindu Shahiya temples in Malot with all the usual features and detailed niches and other ornate patterns on the oblong structures, reveal artistic achievements of the local artisans. Built on the square and solid platforms and using mortar and other local materials, these temples have multilayered sidewalls, windows, carvings, and other geometrical designs. Although smaller in size, the temples reveal complex decoration and dexterous construction. The temple at Sassi Da Kallar was built using red baked bricks for walls and also for exterior designs and ornamentation. The walls are buttressed by oblong additional support structures that are integrated in the design, whereas at the top, the exterior looks more like a huge yet proportional chimney, as found on Victorian English homes. The temple and adjacent complex at Tilla Jogian, located on the lower reaches of the Salt Range, looks like an isolated spot today, but in its heyday it was a bustling religious center. It overlooked the valleys, yet was not too far from the old route into India. Tilla Jogian, like Pir Kattas, was a Brahammincal seminary with extensive residences around, and had been visited by Emperor Akbar. It is a short distance from Sher Shah Suri's gigantic fort at Rohtas, which sits halfway between the GT Road and Tilla Jogian.[6]

Among several other vital innovations, the most important thing that the Hindu architecture gave to South Asia was the introduction of *bawali,* or the staired well. Given the emphasis on purity and early morning bath *(ashnaan),* Hindus made the water wells accessible through winding stairs so as to reach the underground water. These brick wells would be mostly located next to the temples to be used by the community before offering prayers *(puja).* They thus added a new dimension to the old Persian wells, which were meant both for irrigation and domestic purposes. Persian wells were and are still operated in and around Pothowar region by a moving bull or even a camel, who are blindfolded so as not to be detracted from their circular movements.

THE MUSLIM PERIOD

The revival of Hinduism under the Guptas during the early Christian period eclipsed the Greco-Buddhist phase, although migrations and invasions from the northwest continued for quite some time. Most of these new adventurers were tribal and nomadic groups who were gradually indianized until the arrival of Islam in the early eighth century. The Muslim conquest in A.D. 712 of Sindh, Punjab, and Balochistan—the major regions of the Indus Valley—significantly impacted the civilization. Earlier on, the Sufis and publicists had been filtering into the subcontinent from West Asia and had built up their monasteries and mosques, and with the advent of a formalized Muslim political control Islam emerged as a dominant cultural factor in the region. Several dynasties formed what is collectively known as the Delhi Sultanate, which was followed by the Mughals in the sixteenth century. After the invasions by Sultan Mahmud of Ghazni in the eleventh century, Sultan Muhammad Ghauri (d. 1206), in fact, completed the conquest of northern India. However, it was his successor, Sultan Iltutmash (1211–1236), who formally established the institutional framework of the Delhi Sultanate. Cities such as Delhi, Lahore, Peshawar, Kabul, Ghazni, Multan, Qanauj, Attock, Jaunpur, Ferozepur, Sikandarbad, and Agra soon boasted new secular and sacred buildings, which reflected Indian and Central Asian influences. The Mughal rule began in 1526 and formally ended in 1857 when the British Crown formally took over the control of India, yet 1557–1707 (the period beginning with the Emperor Akbar and ending with Emperor Aurengzeb's death) is viewed as the era of the Great Mughals. This era marks the highest point in the development of a unique Islamo-Indian architecture and is also known for various cultural, literary, and artistic accomplishments.

During the first five centuries of the Muslim rule, the domed mosques with rising minarets and similarly designed tombs joined the Buddhist, Jain,

and Hindu temples, and all across the Indus regions and in the Gangetic valleys, the Sufi shrines displayed arches and huge round structures and glazed
tiles—a few of the pioneering traditions. While ordinary Muslims adopted
local rural and urban housing patterns, the elite made a conscious effort to
introduce West Asian patterns. The Arab, Persian, and Central Asian styles
and techniques with a greater emphasis on *jali* work (perforated stone slabs),
tiles, minarets, domes, and arches soon dominated the South Asian architectural horizons.[7] While Muslim architecture, and to some extent entire South
Asian architecture has become synonymous with the Mughal embodiment,
its predecessors and other transregional influences are important. The establishment of a sultanate in Delhi from the eleventh century onward reveals
Muslim and Hindu artisans working together to create shared patterns and
designs. The mosques, shrines, new townships, seminaries, cemeteries, and
forts were some of the buildings found in old cities such as Lahore, Delhi,
and Multan.

The earliest Muslim monument of this pre-Mughal era is the mosque in
Delhi, called Quawatull Islam, which has prominent Hindu and West Asian
features from its stone slabs to pillars and carvings on the walls. The nearby
Qutb Minar appears West Asian, but its contours are quite Indian as well. In
the same vein, the tombs of the Tughlaq, Khilji, and Lodhi kings in the Lodhi
Gardens of Delhi reveal indianization of West Asian traditions. Gardens,
open spaces, onion-like domes, Quranic calligraphy, arched corridors, and
the square boundary walls with rooms for prayers and clerics made their entry
into Indian architecture. The tomb in Lahore of Qutbuddin Aibak—one of
the founders of the Delhi Sultanate—and those of other kings including Sher
Shah Suri in Bihar reveal a dominant Muslim feature of the buildings, since
pre-Islamic religious traditions in India did not have cemeteries; cremation
was used instead, and ashes were either taken to the Ganges or were strewn
around. In the case of Zoroastrians, dead bodies were not allowed to "pollute"
the earth and thus were disposed of over the surface. Thus, with the advent
of Islam, India underwent a major change. Now it had mosques with their
unique characteristics in addition to shrines, gardens, calligraphy, and cemeteries dotting the entire subcontinent. The mosques boasting at least four
minarets, several arches, corridors, courtyards with spouting fountains, and
green or blue domed shrines testified to the presence of Muslims in towns,
and especially when the mosques resounded with the calls for prayers *(azaan)*
five times a day.

Muslim half-domes presented a synthesis of Buddhist stupas and Central Asian massive domes, canopying the shrines and mosques. These domes
would be decorated with tiles—or plastered in solid blue, white, or green—
whereas inside the square building the *mihrab* (place for imam to lead the

prayers), always facing Makkah, would be adorned with the Quranic calligraphy and floral patterns displayed on the arches. Because of the requirement to face toward Makkah and the fact that worshippers stand shoulder to shoulder in straight lines, the interiors of the mosques have to be alike—airy, open, and geometrical. Because Islam prohibits portraying human forms especially at the places of worship, the Quranic calligraphy was used to decorate the walls and arches.[8] For easy movement of worshippers and to have cooler air, mosques would have several doors, verandas, and side windows. In the hilly and cold climate, mosques would retain their basic features but with lower ceilings and fewer doors. Still, they would have ample courtyards for ablution as well as for praying in the sun. The mosques thus had pillars, arches, carved doors, calligraphic patterns, vast courtyards, water tanks, sculptured fountains, and ornate wooden ceilings with elaborate motifs. A few extra adjacent rooms for the clerics and their students meant that mosques were busy places. They also emerged as social centers, fostering communal solidarity.[9]

Shrines were raised either adjacent to the mosques or out in the open and they would gradually be surrounded by an ever-growing number of graves, again a pioneering tradition. Muslims are only supposed to bow before God, so shrines with the saints and Sufis buried in them could not substitute for prayers. Thus, smaller mosques adjacent to these tombs evolved, where imams held prayers and gave religious instruction to students. Shrines would usually comprise a single structure of square building with a green, white, or blue dome. The wooden entrance would always be quite small. Inside, a raised grave always covered in green or an embroidered cloth would be the centerpiece where the visitors would mill around reciting the Quran. Sometimes, a living Sufi would be on hand, not only for the upkeep of the shrine but also to offer charms and blessings to the rural visitors retaining a strong belief in spiritual healings. On saints' anniversaries, special festivals *(urs)* will take place with people thronging the shrine and *qawallis* being sung by the artists. Many of these shrines are of the Sufi orders *(silsilahs)* that had roots in different regions, so this devotional tradition and its accompanying cultural traits and architecture linked India with the entire Muslim world in Asia, Africa, and Europe.

Under the Islamic influence, the tombs, shrines, graves, mosques, gardens, and open houses across India heavily added to the existing traditions, and the use of bricks, marble, carved wood, calligraphy, red stone, and fountains enhanced the spiritual and aesthetic attributes. The Islamic gardens featuring four terraced sections and resplendent with fountains and queues of cypresses, jasmine, and roses were pivotal innovations, which reached their climax under the Great Mughals (1526–1707). Delhi, Lahore, Multan, Surat, and Agra were soon different cities, more akin to their counterparts to the

West. Other than thousands of splendid and ordinary mosques, elaborate orchards, columns, roads, sarais, bridges, graveyards, and fortresses heralded a massive Muslim tradition, and these architectural novelties further enriched South Asia.[10]

Under the Delhi Sultans and then under the Mughals—from the eleventh century to the mid-nineteenth century—the South Asian urban landscape changed radically. Delhi, Lahore, Rohtas, Rawat, Multan, Sheikhupura, Hasan Abdal, Hyderabad, Thatta, Attock, Agra, and towns across Kashmir and Deccan soon boasted splendid buildings, although most of the Indians still lived in rural areas. However, it would be unfair to squeeze the entire Indian architecture into a single Muslim embodiment and similarly unjust to consider the Mughal architecture as the only archetype for the entire Muslim tradition. Certainly, under the Mughals, synthesizing processes and novel techniques in ornamentation and aesthetics reached their zenith and India obtained some of the most unique monuments. The Mughal emperors and princesses patronized visual arts and literature and indulged in leisurely activities. Vast resources at their disposal made them experiment with music, letters, brush, mortar, and metal. The Mughals built forts, roads, mosques, bridges, canals, gardens, residential quarters, mausoleums, and palaces. They also patronized saints and *sadhus* (Hindu ascetics) and built their shrines and monasteries while simultaneously encouraging calligraphy, miniature arts, paintings, and jewelry.

The roads connected the Mughal Empire from Kabul to Murshidabad in Bengal. The Taj Mahal, Red Fort in Delhi, the Thatta Mosque, Lahore's Badshahi Mosque, Delhi's Jamia Mosque, the Attock Fort, several beautiful buildings within the Lahore and Delhi Forts, Fatehpur Sikri, Shahdara, and well-designed lovely gardens all over the subcontinent further popularized the image of a fabulous India. The Shalimar Gardens in Lahore and Srinagar, the Wah Gardens, Hiran Minar in Sheikhupura, numerous mosques and palaces within the forts, and the royal courts all were prioritized by the Mughal planners and masons. The forts at Agra and Delhi received special attention, while Lahore's Fort was used as the capital under Akbar and then his son, Jahangir. Inside these forts, several mosques, women's rooms, royal bedrooms, secret pathways, and servants' quarters all were built with the elaborate use of marble, red stone, and carved wood.

The best and most visible Mughal monument is, of course, the Taj Mahal, which is the tomb of Emperor Shahjahan's wife, Mumtaz. In the shrine-like structure all made of white marble with black calligraphic details, the emperor is buried next to the queen. The mausoleum is on a raised plaza accessible from all sides by marble stairs while an extensive and equally exquisite garden surrounds it on two sides, and a beautiful mosque and the River

Jumna border on the other two. Despite its age and industrial pollution, the Taj has continued to amaze visitors with its serenity, delicacy, and grandeur, the work of thousands of Hindu and Muslim artisans who labored on it for two decades.[11]

The Lahore Fort, like the Attock Fort, is a massive structure, which housed armies, offices, courts, private palaces, servant quarters, and stables for horses, mules, and elephants besides being a storage place for munitions. Its Sheesh Mahal is the royal residence where thousands of mirrors and pieces of glass offered a soothing space for the royalty to relax. The slim arches and airy corridors, all made of marble, remind one of the interiors of Granada's Alhambra. The royal tombs in Shahdara outside Lahore are spacious mausoleums with extensive gardens, water tanks, and running fountains where trees and plants were planted in a symmetrical manner. The architecture here combines Indian, Persian, and Central Asian features, and the Quranic calligraphy and majestic floral patterns on tiles beautify the walls immediately surrounding the grave of the Emperor Jahangir and that of Queen Noor Jahan. The Queen had willed a simple final abode for herself, but her husband's tomb is grand and resembles Humayun's Tomb in Delhi, where his grandfather is buried. Between the two royal tombs in Shahdara lies the Central Asian-style tomb of Asif Khan, who was Noor Jahan's brother and the father of Queen Mumtaz.

The mosques built during the Mughal era reveal grandeur, beauty, and majesty. For instance, the Badshahi Mosque in Lahore, built by Emperor Aurengzeb, has several minarets reaching hundreds of feet high, and numerous proportionate domes of white marble over the main red structure dominate the skyline. The mosque itself, covering a vast area, is built on a raised

Main entrance to the Lahore Fort. Courtesy of the author.

plaza and is entered through a massive red stone door. The courtyard leads
to the prayer area in the front while all around there are corridors and rooms
for clerics and theology students. Just by the entrance to the main gate, there
are special rooms where relics from the Prophet, including his hair and sandals, are kept for general viewing. The mosque was the biggest of its kind in
the entire Muslim world until the twentieth century. The Badshahi Mosque
certainly exudes beauty and serenity and its grandeur never overpowers the
solemnity.

In Lahore, the Mosque of Wazir Khan, also built during the Mughal era
and still in use, has all the unique Indo-Muslim characteristics seen in other
similar mosques in every other major city. The geometrical designs on the
entrance to Masjid Wazir Khan—bordered by balconies—and the elaborate
frescos of trees, plants, and cypresses and floral details on its interior walls,
are a rare artistic synthesis. The calligraphy is in Arabic, yet Persian verses and
quartets abound. The entrance also celebrates the reign of Emperor Shahjahan. Both the mihrab and the dome have fascinating frescos, while delicate
arches blend the ornate ceiling with the walls and floor. The details on its
minaret and kiosks and the honeycomb patterns on the central portion of the
ceiling *(Eewaan)* again resemble the style of the Alhambra. Like the Mughal
emperors, their provincial governors and generals also vied with one another
in building monuments, and thus the Mughal architecture became an India-
wide universality.[12]

In Peshawar, the Mahabat Khan Mosque, situated right in the old city, and
the Saadullah Khan Mosque in Chiniot are some of the exceptional specimens
of this high Mughal art. The Shahjahan Mosque in Thatta continues to attract
visitors—other than regular worshippers—to this part of rural Sindh, where
its simplicity and blue tiles and white exterior blend with the balmy sun of
the desert. To reach the prayer area, one treads a lovely passage across the well-
designed gardens where roses, jasmine, and cypresses queue along the water
tanks and spouting fountains. The prayer area has open brick-laid arches,
which not only keep the inner areas cool but also are also quite enchanting
to look at. The four boundary walls also retain several proportionate arches,
which blend artistically with the main prayer areas. The Moti Mosque inside
the Lahore Fort and similar mosques in the forts at Agra, Delhi, and Attock
reveal unity in patterns with a vivid Mughal imprint intermixing red and
white stones with black calligraphy, adding to the exquisite beauty of the
borders of the arches and other interiors. In the dry heat of the subcontinent,
the appearance of these magnificent buildings itself is soothing. The marble
and a generous use of tiles and airy passages, arches and double ceilings, open
courtyards and fountains keep the temperature down. Visiting these mosques
during a moonlit night, like a visit to the Taj on the 14th of the lunar month,

is certainly a rewarding and exhilarating experience, which is duly enhanced by the cooler and fragrant breeze from tropical plants such as jasmine and roses. The Mughal fascination for gardens, trees, flowers, fountains, and birds such as peacocks, nightingales, and eagles is evident from such monuments. Increased population and a gnawing pollution endanger them, but they have rendered immortality to countless cities and hamlets.

The tradition of Islamic gardens, shared all over the Muslim world, both for aesthetic reasons and also purported as a worldly reincarnation of heaven, has been a favorite pursuit among rulers and nobility across three continents. In India, the forts, graveyards, seminaries, and palaces would have gardens as an important section, while separate gardens in the form of architectural monuments emerged under Emperor Jahangir and his son, Emperor Shahjahan. The Shalimar Gardens in Lahore and Srinagar and the Wah Gardens have been visited by millions of people, although they have equally suffered from civil wars, invasions, and now pollution. Yet their basic designs, structures, and extensive use of water for cascades and fountains, bordered by well-designed cypresses and further supplemented by elaborate lawns and shadowy trees all reveal a revolutionary innovation. The water tanks, spouts, and fountains, mixed with colorful lights and marble plazas right in the middle of a water tank and only accessible through slender pathways, present the dexterity of the Indian artists, who might have benefited from the input of their Persian and Turkish counterparts.

As mentioned, the evolution of shrines and graveyards for burial and spiritual reasons has been a pioneering Muslim tradition in the subcontinent and

Mughal Emperor Jahangir's tomb, Shahdara. Courtesy of the author.

has led to a unique, enriching and diverse architecture. While kings, sultans, and nobility might have used special spots for their graves, the religious and environmental factors also played a crucial role in the evolution of tombs and cemeteries. Many of the Delhi Sultans, Mughal emperors, and other members of these royalties are buried in cities such as Delhi, Agra, and Lahore, but there are places such as Aurengabad, Fatehpur Sikri, Malwa, Ahmadnagar, Kabul, and Patna with individual royal graves. Like their palaces and gardens, Mughals preferred elaborate tombs, surrounded by waterways, well-designed gardens, tall trees, and seminaries devoted to Quranic scholarship. The earlier patterns in tomb building heavily reflected Persian and Central Asian styles. Bigger domes over bricked walls of usually square shape featuring glazed blue or white tiles stood over the grave itself. In Balochistan, the earliest tombs had borrowed heavily from the Zoroastrian fire temples of the Sassanid era, which depended heavily on bricks, with arches featured on the outside for ornamental purposes and also to buttress the rising walls. Here, bricks would be of varying sizes, patterns, and hues to exude complexity as well as simplicity. Such buildings, like the other subsequent funerary monuments, were not meant to show power, arrogance, and control, but rather were meant to reveal mortality as well as some replica of a heavenly space. These early patterns were extensively used in shrines built later across the Indus region, as they came in through Balochistan and Afghanistan.[13]

THE CHAUKHANDI TOMBS

Any discussion of the Indo-Muslim culture is incomplete without mention of some rare specimens of architecture across the region. A unique human heritage, which has attained an international recognition is known as the Chaukhandi Tombs. Named as "the Jewel of Sindh," the yellow sandstone tombs and graves in the province of Sindh and neighboring Balochistan and Gujarat continue to impress tourists and scholars alike with their variety, architectural techniques, calligraphic and formal details, and, most of all, sheer number over an extensive area.[14] They are the "most enigmatic" funerary monuments in the world, and "have given rise to folkloristic legends and speculation regarding their origins."[15]

Many people are surprised to learn that the world's largest and some of the oldest graveyards happen to be in Sindh. For instance, spread over several miles, the graveyard at Makli is a heritage site with several thousand graves, tombs, and mausoleums dating from the medieval era. This graveyard, like its other smaller counterparts in the province, was purportedly built on a higher plateau and hills to avoid the annual Indus floods, which also explains why successive Muslim dynasties and ordinary citizens selected this largest necropolis for burials. The dynasties such as Tarkhans, Sammas, Turks, Afghans, Kalhorahs, and Talpurs often buried their dead here and most of the family graves can be identified because of their location and the inscriptions and dates. Many of them have carved Quranic inscriptions and lunar dates.

The graves first came to the attention of the Western scholars in the early twentieth century and were named as Chaukhandi Tombs because of the location of a cemetery in the town of Chaukhandi. As these graves and tombs both at Makli and Chaukhandi and around the region look like a cot *(charpoy)* with four corners, the form turned into a generic identification for all of them. One other explanation for the name Chaukhandi could be the square canopy structure *(chattri)* on many of these graves that was originally built for beautification and prominence.[16] Chaukhandi is about eighteen miles east of Karachi, and its historic cemetery has 400 tombs built between the fifteenth and eighteenth centuries. Hindian, Karpasan, Mangho Pir, Malir, and Goth Khattu Khan Brohi also lie within Karachi metropolitan area. The Chaukhandi-style tombs are found all the way between Karachi and Thatta, between Thatta and Badin, and between Thatta and Hala in upper Sindh. In addition, Bhagwana in central Balochistan—situated between the towns of Kalat and Khuzdar—has Chaukhandi-style tombs. More than 50 other Sindhi towns such as Saidpur, Jerruck, Sonda, Jungshahi, Pir Pathao, Gujjo, Pipri, Goth Haji Allahdino, Bhawani Serai, Hassan Sirhani, and Goth Raj Malik also retain scores of these old tombs, uniquely representing a lower Indus region tradition in architecture.[17]

Most of these graves and tombs are made of carefully sculpted stone slabs with occasional decorations added by the stonemasons. From afar they all look like symmetrical boxes with the top, made of several layers of horizontal slabs, usually rising like a pyramid. The earliest tombs were flat—a few layers of slabs hewn together. These layers would vary from three to six rising into a small pyramid. In the next phase in their evolution plinths were added and the scales became larger. These fifteenth-century specimens display occasional rosettes with star-like points and circular patterns carved on their slabs. More complex and multipatterned carvings and Arabic calligraphy emerged, often giving biographical information on the deceased individuals—both men and women. Some of the tombs have corridor-like designs right above the main plinths, while the slabs over the arches and further up have several cosmological patterns carved on them. For instance, the tomb of Jam Nizamuddin at Makli has patterns of mihrab, stars, *jali*, and other floral details on all the outer slabs.

At Makli, two or three tombs may share a single but bigger plinth. The number of rising pyramids above tells the number of individuals buried underneath. Also, at Makli some graves have two minarets rising from above the pyramids on both the ends, often culminating in a floral shape. Such tombs date from the sixteenth century and are unique to the Tarkhan dynasty, which might be the next phase in the evolution of this form of masonry. The tombs at Lakho Sheikh's graveyard in Malir and Goth Haji Allahdino all rise to a prominent height and, from afar, resemble the Jain and Hindu temples. Similarly, the parallel tombs at Chaukhandi itself, dating from the seventeenth century, reflect the influences from the neighboring Gujarat. On several early tombs, there are a number of carvings of horses, warriors, and their weapons, and geometrical patterns, something that is quite unique as Muslims usually avoid sculpting human forms, especially on the graves.

The canopy structures, which largely symbolize the Chaukhandi style, stand over several graves and are predominantly circular half-domes supported on several round columns. They all occur in strict geometrical patterns because of the Muslim tradition of burying the dead with their faces toward Makkah. Their domes are also made of yellow sandstone, but the roofs are plastered in white. The ceilings might consist of several smaller bricks joined together in circles. Many of these tombs have funerary enclosures denoting the entire exclusive burial plot belonging to one family with its several members buried therein. The entrances to some of these enclosures also reveal complex patterns and certainly the Quranic calligraphy, all in sandstone.

Earlier mistakenly called the Baluch tombs by European scholars, Makli and all the other graveyards of Sindh represent different epochs, dynasties, and varying masonry techniques of the Muslim past. The traditional structures in Sindh have been built both from sandstone and baked bricks, as found in the ruins of Mohenjodaro, but at Makli most of the graves, especially dating from the early era, are made of stone slabs featuring floral patterns and Quranic inscriptions. There are slim graves, which have domed structures built on them not only to provide shade to the grave itself but to reveal the prominence of the deceased. Here, the domes are symmetrical with an extensive use of blue tiles. The interiors have calligraphic and floral patterns on elaborate tiles. The domes, arched entrances, cooler interior, and wooden doors, as seen in the tomb of Sultan Ibrahim, highlight the early Central Asian styles and Persian patterns and may appear very akin to the counterparts in Isfahan, Herat, and Samarkand. The Indian influences came in from Gujarat and Kathiawar where Hindu temples and Buddhist Mandalas were built of sandstone. The tomb of Jam Nizamuddin at Makli, for instance, represents influences from the east instead of Perso-Turkic counterparts. The elaborate tomb of Isa Khan Tarkhan is a unique blend of arches, corridors, windows, terraces, *jali* work, and multicornered domes, all on a raised plinth. Several of these traditions were continued by the Kalhorah and Talpur dynasties that ruled Sindh until its annexation by the British in 1843. Their tombs at Hyderabad, Khudabad,

Isa Khan's tomb at Makli. Courtesy of the author.

and Chittori have pre-Mughal elements of pavilions, parapets, turrets, and perforated slabs *(jalis)*. These *jalis* are found on the railings surrounding the tombs and display floral and geometrical motifs.[18]

SHRINES AND FORTS

The graveyards in Multan, Uchh, Ajudhan (Pakpattan), Sehwan Sharif, Bhit Shah, and in other regions of southwestern Punjab and upper Sindh all reveal uniformity as well as a gradual trend toward more blended styles. These historic towns possess some of the earliest surviving structures of the Muslim era in Pakistan. For instance, the tomb of Saddan Shaheed in the Thal is a brown structure, which combines the traditions of Hindu temple, Zoroastrian tower of silence, and Buddhist stupa, with extensive Quranic inscription carved on the windows and on the outer borders. The tomb of Shah Rukn-i-Alam in Multan is considered to be one of the most enchanting buildings in the world. The tomb itself is a square structure of colorful—mostly yellow—bricks, which form an explicitly defined double-storied structure, topped by a white dome with a small minaret rising upward. All the entrances to the edifice are geometrically designed with calligraphy pronouncing the Islamic beliefs of the noted Sufi, and farther up, the lower edge of the dome is decorated with several geometrical forms, which look like metallic pitchers and samovars. The boundary wall is also made of more narrow bricks, and two circular multistoried towers again topped by narrow and elegant domes border the main entrance to the compound. The interior is characterized by arches and calligraphy on the walls, with the grave itself in the middle on the floor with open space for visitors. This shrine, characterized by extensive *jali* work and a fascinating mix of colorful bricks, tiles, and plaster, received the prestigious Aga Khan award in the early 1980s and dates from the Sultanate period.

The tomb of Shah Shams Sabzwari is smaller and displays structural similarities to the other shrines. It has impressive minarets on its multilayered form, which seems to have influenced the designers of Mohammad Ali Jinnah's tomb in Karachi.[19] All these shrines have 99 names of Allah and the Prophet each inscribed on their interiors and exteriors and embody a charming mix of colorful tiles, plaster, and marble. In the tomb of Bahaud Din Zakaria in Multan, built during the Tughlaq period of the Sultanate, palm forms and Central Asian-style massive domes are built with a dexterous use of bricks.

The Tombs of Abu Hanifa and Bibi Jawindi (a woman saint) at Uchh and the Tomb of Shah Yusaf Gardez in Multan embody intricate floral patterns on the walls as they mingle with a dexterous tile work. The Tomb of Bibi Jawindi shares close resemblance with that of Shah Rukn-i-Alam with palm forms providing beauty as well as support to the main structures, although in the former's case the minarets are heavily replaced by palm-like structures. The Tomb of Makhdoom Jahanian Jahangasht at Uchh has trees and several additional circular structures in its courtyards, meant for visitors to escape the summer sun. Unlike the shrines and tombs in cities, such as Data Durbar and Mian Mir in Lahore, these shrines in lower Punjab and Sindh have escaped innovations and even after centuries reveal freshness and spirituality.

Some shrines even in bigger cities, such as Musa Ahangar's Tomb in Lahore and Bari Imam's busy shrine in Islamabad are constantly threatened by urbanization yet have escaped radical renovation. The Mughal royalty and nobility also supervised the construction of several massive gates with four domical towers—*chauburjis*—built on square plinths and which opened into gardens, or, in some cases, were the entrance to special cemeteries. These huge entrances, although many of them are in disrepair, are very similar to their counterparts in West Asia and embody the structure built with the uniquely thin yet sturdy Mughal bricks. The usage of several arches, plaster, and colorful tiles makes these multidimensional edifices quite visible from afar because of their height. They were further beautified by a dexterous combination of Quranic calligraphy and Persian poetry. Lahore and Attock both have these square structures, although roads and pollution are threatening their existence, unless some preservation efforts are undertaken.

The Sher Shah Suri interregnum during the 1540s and 1550s represents a unique phase in Muslim architecture in India, because this Afghan king, after defeating and banishing Humayun, the Mughal Emperor, embarked on a rapid and impressive course of reconstruction of India. Not only did he give India a unifying revenue system to be followed up by the Mughals and the British—he also gave India the GT Road, then known as the Jarnaili Shahrah. This highway connected Kabul with Sunargaon in Bengal and passed through important towns in upper India and had sarais (rest houses), mail posts, and police guards every few miles. This road, further made famous by Rudyard Kipling in his novel, *Kim,* was improvised during the British era and since then remains the major artery for the two republics. The GT Road passes by a number of important forts, some of which are considered to be the marvels of an architecture that predominantly appeared to be Central Asian in form yet incorporated Indian elements.

One of these historic monuments is the Rohtas Fort near the town of Dina, which has 12 massive gates, a giant stone wall with buttresses and turrets covering several miles in circumference, and an inside compound that not only houses a town but has a *bawali*, palaces, mosques, and temples, all constructed to meet the religiocultural requirements of the Suri armies.[20] The gates, the boundary walls, and the remains of the palaces offer a unique glimpse of stone masonry where certainly defense and security were the main purposes. Some of the later buildings within the Fort, such as the Mansingh's palace, have a clear Mughal imprint. Just outside the main entrance—Sohaili Gate—one can still see the remnants of Sher Shah's old GT Road.[21] About 50 miles further up is the small but well-kept fort at Rawat, which was a Gakhar township and had sided with Humayun against Sher Shah. The mosque in the Rawat Fort is still in use. Its big semi-circular domes and high walls, all made of Pothowari stone, are characteristic of Central Asia. Within the courtyard of this fort are several old graves, including that of Khawas Khan, a Gakhar chieftain who, along with his sons, had fought Sher Shah and was killed.

By the River Soan, farther up toward Murree Hills, one comes across another Gakhar Fort, perched on the hills and strategically located. There is a village inside the Pharwala Fort, located on the old route to Kashmir. The forts at Lahore and Attock were certainly constructed during the reign of Akbar and despite their huge circumference and several boundary walls and other defense structures were also used for residential purposes. The palaces have the unique Mughal features of exquisite quarters made of marble and red stone and feature private water tanks, fountains, and mirrored bedrooms. Corridors and palatial pathways located on some altitude were meant to offer views of the Ravi and Indus. They also ensured private areas for the royals, especially during hot summer months. The successive Sikh, British, and Pakistani governments converted them into cantonments, with military supervising their maintenance. The Attock Fort is under the sole control of the Pakistani Army, whereas the Lahore Fort is accessible to visitors. Like the development of Makli's expansive graveyard, several forts were built in lower Punjab, Sindh, and Balochistan and offer a unique mix of local architectural techniques with extraregional influences. These forts were owned by regional rulers and tribal chieftains and were usually in good shape. Given the terrain, most of these forts used bricks and were located on comparatively high ground. The forts at Islamgarh and Derawar are quite unique in their construction and, unlike the Rohtas Fort, the boundary walls have several circular and barrel-like buttresses. The Balahissar Fort at Peshawar houses Frontier Constabulary and like its counterparts in the Khyber Pass and Malakand Pass was rebuilt during the British era and is solely used by the defense forces.

THE RAJ AND THE MODERN ERA

The British ascension to power in India since the late eighteenth century but especially during the second half of the nineteenth century added significantly to varied forms of architecture in India. In the areas making up present-day Pakistan, irrigation projects and town planning were carried out in the wake of early industrialization. The evolution of modern schools such as the Mayo School of Arts in Lahore, adjacent to the Lahore Museum and the Punjab University, displayed the changed realities of this region. The Old

Mansion with shops on the Mall, Lahore. Courtesy of the author.

City with its narrow lanes, warrens of *mohallahs* (urban localities or wards) and the places of worship and artisanry, was left to its own fate, whereas new suburbs and cantonments emerged to express the imperial power. Buildings such as the Government College in Lahore, with its immensely complex and beautiful neogothic-style spires, the monumental Lahore Cathedral, the domed St. Anthony's School, and several others were made from a mixture of brick and red stones with a generous use of marble. As seen in the buildings of the High Courts, Municipality, General Post Office and Aitchison College in Lahore, the British Victorian style accepted the domes, verandas, and arches from the existing Muslim traditions, although Lawrence Hall, the Governor's House, and Gymkhana were strictly European in their neo-Roman style. All these buildings stood by a new, tree-lined, and exclusive boulevard, called the Mall. The Customs House, Frere Hall, and Mohatta Palace in Karachi, Edward's College, Victoria Hall (now the Peshawar Museum), and Balahissar Fort in Peshawar, and similar provincial buildings across the region display the prowess of the Raj through magnificent buildings.

Some of the architects of the British buildings were local Indians who, imbued with old and new, worked with the Public Works Department (PWD). In fact, Bhai Ram Singh, a resident of Sialkot, was the doyen of these blended traditions and designed the buildings of the Punjab University in 1880, collaborating with Lockwood Kipling in designing the Lahore Museum, which face each other on the Mall. The Mughal *havelis* (traditional houses) within the old cities, characterized by narrow lanes, multistoried structures, and impressive wooden facades, held their grounds while modern malls, schools, hospitals, and other official buildings ushered in modern architecture. The Mayo Hospital, King Edward's Medical College, Punjab

Restored haveli in the Old City, Lahore. Courtesy of the author.

Screen work (jali) on an old house (haveli), Sethi Locality,
Peshawar. Courtesy of the author.

Public Library, and New Hostel near the historic Anarkali and other Mughal
monuments in Lahore retain their own characteristics. The malls in Lahore,
Rawalpindi, Peshawar, and Quetta, the eight bazaars converging at the Clock
Tower (locally known as Ghanta Ghar) in Faisalabad (formerly Lyallpur) and
the Sukkur Barrage on the Indus are powerful reminders of the Raj, which
engineered a wide variety of utilitarian buildings.[22] The Governor's House,
the Punjab Assembly, and the Falletti's Hotel in Lahore, Governor's House
in Nathiagali, the Cecil's Hotel in Murree, Hotel Flashman's, Gordon College, and the Rawalpindi Cathedral and the Residency at Ziarat are grand
monuments dating from the colonial era and carry powerful and impressive
European imprints.

Surely, the British edifices and traditions had their mixed impact on the
local artisanry and psyche and continue to influence contemporary architecture in a developing country such as Pakistan. However, it would be unfair
to suggest that "the British destroyed more and built less," although it is true
that the parallel evolution of modern cities resulted in the neglect and even
denigration of traditional architecture.[23]

During the British era, the irrigation canals and relocation of people in
new colonies in West Punjab with well-designed villages concurrently revived
the old rural traditions in the Punjab. While cities such as Lahore, Karachi,
Rawalpindi, Murree, Quetta, and Peshawar boasted of the malls, cathedrals,
schools, hotels, cantonments, colonial residences, and officer's messes situated
in the leafy suburbs, their rural counterparts showed the divergence between
canal-fed and rain-fed components. The tribal regions both on the Frontier
and Balochistan maintained their traditions rather more faithfully, yet the

Old Peshawar. Courtesy of the author.

profusion of transport, schools, and hospitals led to a gradual change, which eventually led to migrations, especially during the 1960s. While Muslims and Sikhs traditionally remained land-based and less attuned to modern education, Hindus, during the colonial era, fully adopted themselves to the changed realities. Soon they became the emerging middle class in the Indus heartland, with a higher rate of literacy, mobility, and commerce, fully reflected in their residential preferences. In the towns and cities across the Muslim-majority regions in the Indus Valley, Hindu localities with beautifully built brick houses *(maris)* with a proper ventilation system and secure quarters for women witnessed the synthesis of several traditions. These houses, such as in Peshawar's Sethi area or in Old Lahore and the Gwalmandi district, are fascinating structures located in narrow lanes and streets. Some of them have begun to attract national and global attention and are being used as art galleries.

CONTEMPORARY DIVERSITY: OLD AND NEW

Since independence, the Pakistani architectural scene has gone through several phases. For the first 30 years the emphasis was on modernist architecture and utility-oriented buildings to house migrants and offices. Suburbs such as Gulberg, Clifton, and University Towns emerged in Lahore, Karachi, and Peshawar, respectively. The need for a new capital led to the evolution of Islamabad, mostly designed by Western architects such as Le Corbusier, although since the 1980s, Pakistani architects have themselves assumed the task. Here, the apartment complexes, secretariat blocks (official administration buildings in the capital), parliament houses, president's residence, prime minister's house, national library, court buildings, private residences divided into grid-based sectors, hotels, commercial markets, and plazas are the most expensive in the country. The Quaid-i-Azam University, designed by E. D. Stone, was patterned on the ancient Buddhist stupas, although its critics do not like its gray cement structures, which rather block the scenic view of the Margalla Hills and the Rawal Lake. The Faisal Mosque, supposedly the largest mosque in the world, is another landmark, designed by a Turkish architect, and can be seen from afar.

Many people have complained of the abundance of modernist architecture, particularly commercial plazas and other multistoried buildings. However, in some recent cases, efforts to further indigenize architecture in the national capital and elsewhere are under way.[24] In this context, the role of the NCA—erstwhile Mayo School of Arts—has been noteworthy both in instruction as well as in the preservation of architectural traditions. Many Pakistani architects, especially those with higher degrees from abroad, have well-established practices, and their assignments include official, private, and foreign contracts for a wide variety of buildings. A greater emphasis on blending the past traditions along with modern comforts has already created a competitive atmosphere among these practitioners. Still, the forces of modernity prevail in every aspect of the Pakistani urban landscape, and the few efforts in the name of "nativity" and indigenization have to go a long way to make a substantive mark. Some of the Pakistani architects have been able to make their mark abroad. Fazlur R. Khan, a former East Pakistani architect, studied in the United States. After some work in Karachi and Dhaka, he returned to Chicago and played an important role in designing some landmarks, including the Sears Tower.[25]

A discussion of Pakistani architecture would be incomplete without acknowledging the role of traditional artisans, locally known *mistries* or *mimars,* in building mosques and shrines. Like the folk musicians, bards, and other artists, they have inherited the skills of designing mosques and shrines from their ancestors, and armed with rudimentary education and modern paraphernalia, they simultaneously operate as designers, architects, budget directors, and masons. Defined as "indigenous" and "vernacular" by Kamil Mumtaz, himself a practitioner of hybridity with greater emphasis on tradition, these masons draw up plans and use local unskilled labor and some artisans to construct the buildings, all complete with arches, high ceilings, balconies, courtyards, minarets, and canopies with floral decorations and calligraphy.[26] The Mosques, with their green and white minarets, in the mohallas, by the roadsides, and in the small towns, reflect a transregional unity within this age-old tradition.

As far as the housing and architectural traditions are concerned, Pakistan is still divided into tribal, rural, mountainous, and urban sections, showing the complex class-based variations. The tribal dwellings are the most traditional of their type. They are clustered together and serve two purposes: security and interdependence. Mostly made of mud and stone with a generous use of wood, the houses are surrounded by high walls with one corner sporting a special observation and defense post. Here the tribal people would sit night after night during emergencies to ward off any surprise attack. These watch posts and towers have small turrets, and likewise the outer wall is meant to afford greater maneuverability for weapons. The Pushtuns in settled areas would not have such specific defense arrangements, but all along the tribal belt there are row after row of fortress-like houses. Women are always within the compound while men meet and socialize in a separate section called *hujjra*.

Rural houses reveal simplicity and salience of tradition, where sections for cattle are added to the dwellings. The white mud houses of the Salt Range present a beautiful spectacle during early spring, with mustard fields growing all around. As in the cities and elsewhere, mosques, shrines, and the brick buildings of the relatively affluent people dot the rural scene. Many of the rural people in upper Punjab and Kashmir have been able to transform the rural scene largely because of their work abroad. Since the 1970s, billions of rupees earned by the Pakistani expatriates have gone into rebuilding modernist dwellings across these hamlets. With their elaborate furnishings and gadgets, there has been more pressure on public services and energy supply along with a rise in consumerism.

Rural dwelling built of stones and mud. Courtesy of the author.

Pakistan's hilly and mountainous areas retain unique features in their architecture. They are mostly made of stones with a generous addition of wood. At developed hill resorts such as Murree, Ziarat, and Swat they are more modern, while in the Northern Areas they still predominantly reflect traditional Tibetan and Central Asian styles. Wood, mortar, and low ceilings characterize these houses where centuries of experiences of living in an earthquake-prone region have disallowed any elaborate construction. The Hunza inhabitants are comparatively well off and may have some added luxuries and modern amenities in their homes although the 700-year-old Palace of the Mir of Hunza at Baltit is a unique piece of traditional architecture. In Chitral especially in the Kalasha Valley, the houses are simple with a fireplace right in the middle of the cubical room. Cold climate and the supply of wood determine the mode of dwelling here.

In Pakistan, in general, other than economy, demography has played a major role in changing the physical and sociological contours of the society. After partition in 1947, settlement of about 10 million homeless refugees was the highest priority. The property from those who left was divided among the newcomers and new haphazard settlements began to dot the urban horizons. The wars over Kashmir and Bangladesh, and the significant developments in Afghanistan and Iran brought in more refugees with mud and tent villages emerging on the Frontier and in Balochistan.

Six decades after independence, Pakistan has congested old cities and inner towns with overstrained civic facilities and infrastructure. Given the limited resources, their maintenance is proving difficult. In new cities such as Islamabad and models towns and suburbia, an ever-growing urban population unleashes more pressure. Karachi, Faisalabad, Lahore, Rawalpindi, Peshawar, and Quetta still have old quarters with rings and grids of more contemporary and recent buildings. The posh suburbs have large and impressive houses displaying wealth and status, whereas the small towns and villages across the country may still need basic facilities. The water supply, electricity, street maintenance, drainage, and other infrastructure remain a major challenge in the cities but especially in rural and tribal regions. In recent years, the military has been obtaining generous portions of rural and urban property allotments, and almost every major town and city has a "Defence Housing Scheme" displaying the most expensive, well-designed, and luxurious modern dwellings.

While the cities confront serious issues of overpopulation and pollution, the rural settlements, in many cases, are still fighting poverty. A visit to any city in Pakistan can afford a simultaneous view of old and new, with modernity and tradition locked in an unending contest, which is further underpinned by affluence or sheer poverty. The old Indus Valley-style one-room mud hut is the average dwelling of many rural poor, with the gypsies and nomads living in tents and reed cottages on the fringes. In cities, multimillion-rupee palatial houses coexist with the old Mughal buildings, pre-1947 *havelis,* and more recent opulent bungalows—not too far from the urban poor who may spend their evenings under a bridge or at a Sufi shrine.

Notes

1. For an early interesting work highlighting the individuality of Muslim Pakistani architecture, see Ishtiaq H. Qureshi, "Architecture," in *The Cultural Heritage of Pakistan,* ed. S.M. Ikram and Percival Spear (London: Oxford University Press, 1955).

2. Kamil Khan Mumtaz, *Modernity and Tradition: Contemporary Architecture in Pakistan* (Karachi: Oxford University Press, 1999), pp. x, 3.

3. Many of these ancient cities were destroyed again and again by floods or pestilence or disappeared due to some massive invasion. However, they would reemerge a few decades later with further elaborate planning. For instance, Mohenjodaro, the oldest city excavated in Sindh, had been populated and destroyed six times, and layers of six cities have been found one upon the other. Taxila, Takhtbhai, Harrapa, and several other cities also reveal similar patterns. See Mark Kenoyer, *Ancient Cities of the Indus Valley Civilization* (Karachi: Oxford University Press, 1998). Some places in the mountainous regions of the Northern Areas would succumb to earthquakes but reemerge subsequently. The invaders routinely decimated the Frontier hamlets, yet the traditional love for one's own ancestral land would lead to reconstruction.

4. Emperor Ashoka built several Buddhist monuments across his vast empire. In 2001, the Taliban destroyed the Buddhas of Bamiyan, the two massive carved figures of Buddha in the hills of central Afghanistan, dating from the ancient era. Other than such visible Buddhist monuments there are numerous stupas across the Indus Valley affirming the salience of this unique Buddhist art.

5. Here near the village of Jalalpur Alexander had defeated the armies of Porus and a few miles on this side of the River Jhelum, and famous medieval scholar, Al-Beruni (d. 1050) had completed his work, *Kitabul Hind.* The noted Muslim scholar had come into India with the armies of Mahmud of Ghazna (998–1030) and had settled in this area to complete his anthropological and geographical research on India.

6. Near the historic city of Kalar Kahar, the temple was a bustling place until 1947, when the last group of Hindus left the region for India. It is only in recent years that some pilgrims—*yatris*—have been allowed back to worship.

7. It may literally mean a woven net, but in an architectural sense it stands for perforated marble or wooden screens with several openings, both for beauty and cross-ventilation. These patterns are found either in fences or on some interior decorations.

8. For further discussion, see R.A. Jairazbhoy, *An Outline of Islamic Architecture* (Karachi: Oxford University Press, 2003) (reprint).

9. For the historical and technical details of this new era in South Asian architecture, see Ahmad Nabi Khan, *Islamic Architecture in South Asia: Pakistan, India, Bangladesh* (Karachi: Oxford University Press, 2003) (reprint).

10. These are the wayside rest houses built across the medieval Muslim world for travelers and traders, with stables and yards for horses, donkeys, and camels. Muslim forts were mostly of West Asian style with mosques and temples built inside. The forts in Punjab such as at Attock, Lahore, Rohtas, and Multan are massive structures with wells, palaces, courts, ammunition depots, and gardens. The forts in Cholistan and Sindh were usually of mud and clay.

11. Some writers in their enthusiasm for nationalism may focus on *Islamic* credentials of such buildings and would appear indifferent to hybridity. For instance, see Qureshi, "Architecture."

12. For more details, see Kamil Khan Mumtaz, "Reading Masjid Wazir Khan," in *Studies in Tradition* 2, no. 2 (1993): 68–79.

13. For an excellent book on these monuments, see Robert Byron, *The Road to Oxiana* (London: Pimlico, 2004) (reprint).

14. Suhail Z. Lari and Yasmeen Lari, *The Jewel of Sindh: Samma Monuments on Makli Hills* (Karachi: Oxford University Press, 2002).

15. Salome Zajadacz-Hastenrath, *Chaukhandi Tombs: Funerary Art in Sind and Baluchistan* (Karachi: Oxford University Press, 2003) (reprint). The Hungarian author (d.1998) wrote this archaeological work in German while residing in Karachi in the early 1970s, and Oxford University Press, Karachi, has recently published its English version. Like the detailed research undertaken by the Laris, this slim volume contains interesting technical details on forms and sites, and it has a useful collection of sketches and pictures.

16. On the adoption of this name, see Shaikh Khurshid Hasan, *Chaukhandi Tombs in Pakistan* (Karachi: Archaeology Department, 1996).

17. According to some narratives, Jinnah was born in the town of Jerruk—also written as Jhirak, though the consensus is on Karachi being his birthplace.

18. Shaikh Khurshid Hasan, "Talpurs and their Tomb Architecture," *Daily Star,* 15 January 2000.

19. Jinnah (1876–1948), the founder of Pakistan, is buried in Karachi and is generally called the Quaid-i-Azam or the Great Leader.

20. Sher Shah built another Rohtas Fort in present-day Bihar, and it is here that he died after catching fire during the victory celebrations. His tomb lies nearby in the village of Sahsaram.

21. This gate and the others look like some of the gates of the Attock Fort and Lahore Fort and is a gigantic structure with a huge wooden entrance and turrets above guarding the traffic.

22. The towns would have bricked and yellow painted police stations *(thanas)* and offices for local revenue officials *(tehsils)*. The district collector, who would always be British, would have elaborate offices and residence because he was the seniormost colonial official in the county. Not only did he administer revenues, he would also run the local judiciary and ensured law and order. The superintendent of the

police—again British who was head of the police stations in the county, would assist him. The police barracks were built in the district headquarters and, like the military cantonments, were intentionally located away from the locality.

23. M. Yusuf Abbasi, *Pakistani Culture: A Profile* (Islamabad: National Institute, 1992), p. 401.

24. Orestes Yakas, *Islamabad: The Birth of a Capital* (Karachi: Oxford University Press, 2001).

25. A street is named after Khan, who died at a comparatively early age. A recent biography by his daughter, herself an architect, focuses on his personality and profession. See Yasmin Sabina Khan, *Engineering Architecture: The Vision of Fazlur R. Khan* (New York: Norton, 2004).

26. See, Mumtaz, *Modernity and Tradition*, pp. 35 and 71. His volume includes some representative pictures and sketches of these buildings.

SUGGESTED READINGS

Khan, Ahmad Nabi. *Islamic Architecture in South Asia: Pakistan, India, Bangladesh.* Karachi: Oxford University Press, 2003.

Lari, Suhail Z., and Yasmeen Lari. *The Jewel of Sindh: Samma Monuments on Makli Hills.* Karachi: Oxford University Press, 2002.

Mumtaz, Kamil Khan. *Modernity and Tradition: Contemporary Architecture in Pakistan.* Karachi: Oxford University Press, 1999.

Zajadacz-Hastenrath, Salome. *Chaukhandi Tombs: Funerary Art in Sind and Baluchistan.* Karachi: Oxford University Press, 2003.

5

Cuisine and Traditional Dress

> You eat for yourself, but dress for others
> —traditional Pakistani proverb

As in any other country, the traditional Pakistani food and clothes are diverse and reflect historical, regional, climatic, and class variations. Certainly, food is the major and even the most significant component of all celebrations as friends, families, and communities socialize together. In a strictly traditional sense, depending on financial and social stature, the expanse of hospitality goes a long way in determining one's status in the family, community, or even in the tribe. While most people in a developing society such as Pakistan may be struggling to make ends meet, still they will be tempted to occasionally serve as hosts, which may prove costly. Pakistan is a largely traditional society with strong rural and tribal underpinnings, and Pakistanis pride themselves on entertaining guests, relatives, and colleagues. Sumptuous dinners costing thousands of rupees per person at parties held at banquet halls or five-star hotels certainly reveal a traditional core of this pluralistic society.

Pakistani cuisine is a synthesis of indigenous Indus valley dietary traditions with a strong Mughal imprint, and it has itself been internationalized by an active diaspora. All over the world South Asian food has become almost mainstream. In the United Kingdom and also on the Continent, no supermarket is complete without a generously supplied curry/Indian section. Numerous parties with South Asian savories such as *pakoras* (also known as *bhajis*) (deep-fried vegetable pieces coated in chickpea flour and herbs and spices), *tikkas* (chicken pieces cooked on skewers with herb seasoning), *papadoms* and *samosas* (pastries filled with meat or vegetables). The curry industry, both in terms of human and financial resources, has already surpassed the combined resources of the shipping, steel, and mining industries in the United Kingdom, with Britain becoming a nation of "curryholics." South Asian recipes, chefs, and cookbooks have assumed a mainstream significance in Britain, and annual competitions are held to choose the chef and curry house of the year.[1]

Rich Pakistanis may have more cosmopolitan taste and diverse menus to choose from, but the average people do not have such luxuries. To them, clean water, a few glasses per day of milky tea or green tea *(qahwa)* and bread with some curry, or rice with some toppings are all that they can hope for. Breakfast in the villages or towns typically consists of unleavened bread, which goes by different names, but essentially is baked in the oven or on a hot plate *(tawwa)* and eaten with some butter, jam, or honey on the top, or some spicy soup-like curry of meat or chickpeas. A farmer may have bread with some buttermilk *(lassi)* churned by the housewife. Urbanites may have eggs—either boiled or as spicy omelettes—to be followed by a few cups of milky sweet tea.

Farmers and shepherds may take their lunch and an earthen water flask with them, or at midday, somebody from the household may bring them buttered bread with some vegetable curry, chutney, and more buttermilk. The early afternoon tea for a Pakistani farmer or laborer may include more home-made bread or a few sweets, whereas the supper may be bread and curries with an occasional rice dish. Soft drinks, regular salad dishes, or yogurt followed by desserts are not eaten frequently, and even meat—chicken or mutton—is an occasional delicacy. The farmers eat to their fill and, like their compatriots in the towns, followed by smoking a water pipe *(huqqa),* for relaxation, and socializing. The farmers and shepherds may gather in the early evening at someone's compound or at a local tea stall where discussion may vary from the day's work to national politics and local gossip. The village menials may also join such social sessions to fill the huqqa at the proper intervals.

In the inner cities of Lahore, Karachi, Multan, Faisalabad, Gujranwala, Bahawalpuur, Rawalpindi, Jhelum, Hyderabad, Peshawar, and Quetta, people mill around the bakery ovens where they buy freshly baked bread *(kulcha)* for breakfast to eat with spicy curry and lassi. This curry is made from trotters or chickpeas sprinkled with coriander, ginger, and garlic. *Halwah* (sweet pudding) balances this spicy variety. These people overwhelmingly prefer traditional food and breakfast is a habit inherited from ancestors and has to be performed after morning prayers in the local mosque. Rich Pakistanis have servants to serve them tea with toast, a wide variety of jams, and occasional egg dishes. On occasion, they may also try traditional *kulcha* and *halwah* dishes, but within the confines of their homes, and if they ever venture out to the inner cities it will be in the company of friends.

The authentic traditional dishes are found in the older parts of these cities. Gwalmandi in Lahore is famous for its Food Street, while Luxumi Chowk, and Shahi Mohallah are also located in older parts of Lahore. The Raja Bazaar in Rawalpindi, and Namak Mandi and Qissa Khawani in Peshawar have become synonymous with the traditional dishes. Some new restaurants such as the Bundu Khan, located in the posh suburbs of the Gulberg, Defence and Fortress Stadium have won acclaim for their traditional ambience and local dishes. The Sajji House and Dera, located next to each other in Lahore's Qadhaffi Stadium, and the Village with its branches both in Lahore and Karachi, are modern restaurants but strictly specialize in traditional cuisine with a native rural ambience. Using the authentic recipes, the traditional cooks from the various regions of Pakistan prepare food right in front of their clientele.

The Frontier, always known for kabob dishes, naans (leavened bread), and meat specialties such as *karahi* and *balti* has a chain of traditional restaurants all over the tribal areas and in the cities where locals and visitors savor them. The world-known mutton and chicken pieces *(tikkas)*, skewered kabobs *(seekh)*, Peshawari naans, and karahi dishes, in fact, originated in the trans-Indus regions of the Frontier.[2]

The Pushtuns have a special way of making green tea *(qahwa)* in little teapots. The tea is digestive besides providing an excuse for socialization. Pushtuns prefer to sit on the carpeted floors with *qahwa* samovars, and a bit of snuff also going around, while the discussion may vary from neighboring Afghanistan to the latest guns and the currency rates in Barra, Darra Adam Khel, and Landi Kotal. Men prefer to eat on the carpeted floors or on cots *(charpoys)*, which are usually strewn around in the open. It is an all-male affair, as Pushtuns, especially in the tribal regions, would not allow their

Food Street, Old Lahore. Courtesy of the author.

women to eat out and be seen by other men. In posh restaurants and hotels, some urban Pushtun families can be found; otherwise, across the rural and tribal regions women remains indoors. Urban Pakistanis take their lunch to work. It may consist of bread and curries, while tea may be had from a tea stall. The health conscious among them will prefer sandwiches and more salad and fruit. Dinner is a more elaborate activity as a main socializing event at home or at some exclusive restaurant. Other than the three daily meals, Pakistanis may have special meals on the weekends, on the national holidays, and for religious festivals. Ceremonies such as the birth of a baby, circumcision of male children, successful completion of the first Quranic recitation, engagements, marriages, and death anniversaries all are other social events where food becomes a symbol of affection and hospitality. Women in the families mostly do the cooking, but on festive occasions or other major ceremonies, male cooks prepare meals, out in the open. In villages and tribal regions, barbers, who are important figures in the local life, prepare these communal meals. Barbers inherit the art of cooking from their ancestors and strictly follow their traditions. Other than giving haircuts, they almost run the households of their patrons during marital or funerary ceremonies. While male barbers cook, convey messages to other villages, and prepare *huqqa*, their women clean and run errands for their patron families. Both men and women receive special clothes, money, and even harvests from their patrons for their yearlong services to the family. A farmer, like his Indus Valley ancestors, duly shares his produce with these rural menials.

However, in the cities, there are professional hoteliers, cooks, and caterers who have set rates for varying menus and other related services. Such caterers serve at marriage halls and at the Sufi shrines where believers make special offerings to the deceased saint. Thursdays are usually the busy days at the shrines with the local cooks and caterers preparing *pulao* (spicy tender rice often mixed with meat and herbs) and sweet rice *(zarda)* in massive metallic pots out in the open and then distribute this food among the needy.[3]

A Diverse Cuisine

Pakistani cuisine is heavily dominated by meat dishes with various types of chutney, bread, and rice for accompaniment. Pakistani food still offers a wealth of vegetarian options. Feasts are monopolized by spicy meat dishes. Some dishes such as *balti* and *karahi*—meat dishes cooked in open, deep metallic pans—*pulao*, several kinds of curry, kabobs, *halwa*, and *zarda*, have obtained an international reputation. Pakistanis, like other Muslim peoples, prefer mutton and chicken to beef, although beef is widely used for flat kabobs and minced beef is found in unleavened bread, called *paratha*. The minced beef as well as minced mutton or lamb, after having been cooked in

Vendor selling chaat masalah and other savories outside the Lahore Museum. Courtesy of the author.

spices and mixed with lentils and other such ingredients, is also used for *kofta* dishes, which are meat balls in a curry, often mixed with potatoes or boiled eggs. If the boiled egg is put inside the steamy and spicy kofta, it is called a Nargissi type.[4]

The use of spices is an age-old component of a cuisine that may require professional skill. Pakistani food is decidedly on the hotter side, although not as spicy as it is in southern India or Sri Lanka. Rice is a major food component, but Pakistanis use more breads such as *chappatis, rotis, naans,* or *parathas* to scoop up curries.[5] In some traditional families and especially among the Marwat Pushtuns in Bannu, men like to eat with their hands from one huge open dish. This special *pulao* is called *sohbat,* which literally means company and contains cooked rice with generous mixing of tender mutton and spices. The *pulao* is put in on a big metallic tray. Family and friends sit around it on the carpet and help themselves. Another kind of *pulao* made of rice, herbs, and *daals* is called Kedgeree *(khichri),* which is popular across the subcontinent; it does not have meat and is considered highly digestive. *Khichri* is served to people with an ulcer or an upset stomach, and with yogurt added, it is both nourishing and mild. Such *pulao* dishes are garnished with coriander leaves, thin slices of fresh garlic, and some additional butter-fried onions. They are slightly different from the Afghani and Iranian *pulao* varieties, which are sweeter.

HISTORICAL AND REGIONAL ORIGINS

Pakistan's location as a crossroads between Southern, Central, and Western Asia has, over the successive centuries, resulted in a cuisine that is a synthesis of several dietary traditions. In the heartland of the historic Indus Valley civilization, the indigenous rural and agrarian characteristics of the cuisine have been paramount. From the major food items to eating styles and even meal times, the Indus Valley traditions and environment predominate the Pakistani eating experience. The food has been simple and digestive. Milk, butter, and buttermilk *(lassi)* along with wheat, greens such as spinach, and mutton are age-old standards.

Since cows and bulls have always been prized animals for agriculture and transportation until recent times, they were not slaughtered so often for food unless the supply of sheep and goats ran too low. In addition, the respect for the cow—as understandable from Hindu traditions—did not encourage beef dishes for quite some time. Even now, in some Pakistani villages one can find a taboo on eating beef because of the potential to annoy some goddesses. Bulls, especially of Dhani breed, in upper Punjab are valued for their beauty and swiftness and thus become prized possessions to be paraded at village fairs. Even after thousands of years, a bull operating a Persian well symbolizes the realities of Indus Valley societies. Because cattle were scarce in the West Asian and Central Asian regions, mutton dishes remained popular and influenced the cuisine. After 1947, with the departure of Hindus and Sikhs from the Pakistani regions of the Indus valley, beef dishes are much more prevalent, used especially in minced kabobs *(chappal, shami, seekh,* or *tikkas).*

In the former East Pakistan—now Bangladesh—beef and mutton both have been in short supply. The Bay of Bengal and several rivers supply fish for the abundant fish-based dishes. The fertile Bengal delta is suitable for paddy fields, so rice is the staple . Only in recent times has bread made its way into Bengali homes. However, it is the cuisine from the Northern subcontinent—mainly the Muslim regions of the Indus Valley, which has become the mainstream in the diaspora, with places such as Britain and the Gulf overwhelmingly absorbed in the curry culture.

The Indus Valley has provided its inhabitants with a wide variety of vegetables, herbs, beans, spices, and fish. Poultry, for a long time, remained a luxury. Unlike nomadic Arabs, people in the Indus Valley usually avoided eating camel or horse meat, although camel or horse milk was occasionally used for medicinal purposes. Camels and horses are found all across the Indus regions, but their value as beasts of burden precluded the possibility of their being slaughtered for food, unless, in the past, when there was some emergency such as famines or natural disasters. Fowl, rabbits, and deer have always been luxuries, and partridges and pheasants are reserved for formal occasions. Quails are often eaten either in a curried form or roasted like other fowls. Several types of sauces—chutneys—and pickles have their origins in South Asia where green chilies, tomatoes, onions, coriander, mint, cumin, cloves, and other tropical vegetables and herbs grow in large quantities. Because of their popularity in cosmopolitan cuisine, many Western companies now manufacture chutney products. The Central Asian influences have equally added to the existing curry dishes, which have been found in the Indus Valley for centuries. Here *pulao* with tender meat, carrots, or raisins, emerged as a compulsory Pakistani dish. The *pulao* mixed with cooked meat and potatoes is also known as *biriyani* and is a total food unto itself. In addition, roast chicken, or the roast leg of lamb, besides several kinds of skewered or flat kabobs, came in with the meat-eating Central Asians, Persians, and Arabs, who had been migrating into this region for centuries.[6] The Indus Valley and river deltas have always been plentiful with fowl, deer, and pigs, which were periodically hunted by the early inhabitants. However, since the advent of Islam in the region, pigs are routinely hunted as a pastime but not for dietary purposes, as like Jews, Muslims strictly avoid pork, ham, and bacon dishes. In addition, Muslims are supposed to slaughter animals and birds in a specific way, called *hallal,* cutting the main artery with a sharp knife. Hallal is similar to kosher, and Muslims try to be strict when it comes to eating meat. While slaughtering these animals and birds, it is imperative to recite the Quranic verses, which further brings religion into dietary practices.

The Muslim penchant for meat in the Indus Valley reached its zenith during the 1960s when, at one stage, it was feared that the goats would totally disappear from the region thanks to meat dishes and a growing demand. The crossbreeding in the mutton industry and, most of all, the emergence of the poultry industry, relieved the situation and now, no Pakistani gathering is complete without a vast array of meat and vegetable dishes. Meat is also the

Preparing chappal kabobs. Courtesy of the author.

symbol of prosperity and generosity, so on festive occasions one sees fewer vegetable and daal dishes, although yogurt, rice, kabobs, and salads have become necessary accompaniments, allowing more health-conscious people to eat less meat and more vegetables.

Strict Muslims also avoid alcohol, and thus most of the Muslim countries including Pakistan remain "dry." Non-Muslim Pakistanis and visitors can buy alcohol form special outlets, but alcohol consumption in the open is strictly prohibited. Other than the regular breweries since the British times, illegal plants are run by underworld types. The quality of such alcohol—commonly known as *tharra*—is quite poor and could be harmful. Given the religio-social taboo on alcohol, drinkers are commonly viewed as a social nuisance. Generations grow up internalizing the contempt for and distrust of alcoholics. Other than illegal sales and hoarding, foreign companies and missions are allowed to import drinks. Alcohol is also smuggled into the cities from India, Dubai, and China. South Asia has a wide variety of daals, which are used not only for kabobs but also for various other mixed dishes. Daal dishes are often made with a sizzling sauce of butter, garlic, ginger, and onions, which is known as *tarraka*. Daals can be added to a rice dish or can be eaten with the naan or chapatti. A special Pakistani dish, which originated around Delhi and Lucknow during the Mughal period, is called *Haleem*. It is a combination of various kinds of meat, daals, and herbs cooked on a slow flame for a day or two. It is served with a sprinkling of garlic, green chilies, coriander, and ginger and served with bread, or it is used as a sauce for rice.

Raita consists of mild yogurt mixed with herbs and is served with spicy dishes to take the heat off the tongue. According to the traditional wisdom, *lassi* and *raita* are considered digestive.

Chapatti, the unleavened bread baked in clay ovens, is an age-old Indus Valley food item. A wide variety of naans were brought in from West Asia by Muslims. For instance, unlike the round Peshawari naan, the Afghani naan is long and has furrows on it. The latter became more popular with the influx of Afghan refugees since 1979. Earlier it was available only near the Pakistan-Afghanistan borders . With the arrival of eight million refugees from India in 1947 and then millions of Kashmiri, Afghan, and Iranian refugees, several new dishes and recipes have found their way into Pakistani cuisine. The Afghani restaurants all over Pakistan are noted for their tender kabobs, *challo pulao* (a mild form of rice with mutton, raisins, and carrots) and rectangular naans, all followed by a delicious *qahwa*. The increased mobility and closer contacts with the West have also resulted in the evolution of several Western restaurants where pasta, a wide variety of salads, sandwiches, pizza, fried dishes, and steaks, favored by the upper middle-class Pakistanis, are served. The arrival of fast food chains in the bigger cities has made hamburgers and

pizzas quite popular among families and especially the urban youth. In addition to the traditional and Western specialties, available from specialized restaurants such as Café Zouk or luxury hotels, all major Pakistani cities have Chinese and Thai restaurants many of them owned by Pakistani Chinese.[7] Tea remains the main beverage in Pakistan. However, freshly churned lassi is also a popular drink across the country, especially in the rural and traditional parts. Tea leaves are usually brewed in a deep pot and then the liquid is mixed with sugar and milk until boiling. Pakistanis like their tea with milk and sugar, although one could also ask for *separate tea,* which means that sugar and milk are supplied separately.

Until the mid-1960s, a Pakistani soda water industry flourished, and given the hot climate, towns and cities all had their own privately run ice factories. During that era, Pakistanis would visit specific soda water shops where they would be served sherbet—a mixture of soda, vermicelli, milk, and ice—sweet-tasting and exuding a pleasant fragrance from rose or jasmine essence. The soda water shops went out of business the moment Coca Cola, Fanta, Sprite, Pepsi Cola, and such other Western soft drinks flooded the markets.

In recent years, *qahwa* has become a national hot drink, especially after an elaborate dinner. It is mixed with cardamom seeds with a dash of mint and it is thought to have various digestive qualities. Like the *balti* dishes, naans, and kabobs, *qahwa* is another major influence from the Frontier on the rest of the country. During the winter months, the tea stalls in towns and cities offer sweet Kashmiri tea, which is pink in color, and other than milk has raisins and coconuts sprinkled on it. It is quite thick and steamy and is usually accompanied with warm carrot pudding *(gajraila).* Coffee remains an urban, upper middle-class luxury, but green tea has broken all such class distinctions and thus has become a Pakistan-wide beverage, with its patrons enamored of its digestive attributes. Pakistanis enjoy a wide variety of desserts. These traditional dishes include vermicelli, sweet rice, or zarda with a mix of coconuts and raisins, milky rice *(kheer),* and sweet cream *(firni),* the last being a traditional form of ice cream made of ground rice, milk, sugar, and some natural scent. Another form of traditional cold dessert is called *kulfi,* which is made from flour, milk, and sugar often mixed with some dried fruit and made in a big earthen pitcher. Lately, this colorful dessert has become popular in Britain where it is available in bakeries and can be purchased frozen from South Asian stores.

While modern bakeries all across Pakistan offer numerous kinds of sliced breads, naans, croissants, sandwiches, rusk, biscuits, and cakes, the local traditional bakers *(nanbais)* continue with their traditional specialties. For instance, other than *gajraila,* boiled full-cream milk is used in various dishes such as *burfi, khoyaa,* or spaghetti-like *jualaibis,* which are fried in the purified butter *(ghee)*. *Nanbais* also produce *sheermaals,* which are round sweet bread eaten with hot milk or tea in the morning. The local *nanbai* shop is a social institution. Late at night, youths gather to drink milk and even hold competitions to see who can consume the most sweetened and fragrant milk served in big cups. Some *nanbais* are wrestlers *(pehlawaans)* and thus are role models for the local youngsters who might be interested in bodybuilding. Milk and exercise are considered to be important ingredients of becoming a good wrestler with enough stamina to defeat a rival at the specially designed inner-city arenas *(akharaas)*.

The *nanbai* shop is usually near a tea stall where local residents may gather to listen to music or share daily gossip. Adjacent to such stalls and restaurants are small tobacco shops, mostly specializing in *paans*—betel leaves—which are skillfully prepared by mixing spices and herbs, and the patrons chew on their *paans* while sharing small talk.

NATIONALIZATION TO GLOBALIZATION

The introduction of European and other East Asian dishes took place only in the recent past. With arrival of Chinese immigrants, many cities have restaurants offering a Pakistani-style Chinese cuisine. In the United Kingdom, where the South Asian Muslim food has become the largest food industry, the predominantly meat and wheat dishes dominate the South Asian cuisine. Bangladeshis, followed by a sizeable number of Pakistanis, own most of the Indian restaurants in Britain and very few Indian expatriates are in the restaurant business, although some noted Indian firms in the diaspora provide the wholesale supply of rice, vegetable oil, pickles, jams, beers, dried fish, and herbs. Otherwise the food industry, through its thousands of outlets, is dominated by Bangladeshis and Pakistanis. The grocery stores supplying *hallal* meat, rice, vegetables, and other provisions are mostly owned by Pakistanis. The Indians may handle production and supply and publish several glossy food magazines. This is a huge sector, employing hundreds of thousands of people and catering to almost one-half of the British population, and accounts for billions of pounds. It is a unique, recent, and immensely significant crosscultural exchange. There are a number of books, magazines, festivals, and competitions to select the best chef and restaurants.

CLOTHING

With its various regions and climates Pakistan is largely a tropical country with some arctic weather in the extreme north. There is a diversity of traditional dress styles, which have absorbed several local and regional influences over the centuries, and clothing is practical for the climate. In a rather basic sense, it is a land of cotton and wool and certainly of tunic and trousers. Clothing may have several patterns and designs, depending upon one's taste and economic standing and the nature of the occasion. Given the abundance of various household rituals and religio-national festivals, appearance both for men and women of all age groups assume a special significance. In addition, the weather and time of day play crucial role, in determining the choice of clothes and color patterns. Generally, in the evening Pakistanis dress up in their best clothes for special occasions Age and social standing plus religious festivals, travel, work, school, or leisure determine the dress choice.[8] The essential unit of Pakistani dress for both men and women across the country and also with the neighbors to the west and east is the tunic or upper garment *(kamees)*, with all its variations in texture, color, and tailoring. Trousers *(shalwar)* are worn by a vast majority of Pakistani men and women, irrespective of age and class, and are of some solid color.[9] The preference is mostly for white or gray cloth when it comes to baggy—rather pleated—*shalwar*, yet *kamees* (a tunic or long shirt) may have flowery and sequined patterns.

The *kamees* has two varieties: one with an open and circular collar, also known as *kurta,* and one with a regular shirt collar that is slightly longer. Younger men prefer silver-threaded knots is place of buttons or even opt for special embroidered sections on the front and arms. Middle-aged and elderly men and women prefer plain and mostly white *kurtas* (tunic). Some men and women always wear a *kurta-shalwar* or shirt-*shalwar* combination in the same color as a tradition, whereas others may try different color combinations. The Pushtun men prefer collared *kamees*, whereas Punjabis and Sindhis prefer *kurtas*, especially during the hot months of summer when cotton and muslin are preferred. The Baloch wear a tunic that usually combines the features of a *kurta* and *kamees* with round collars and buttons at the wrist, whereas Sindhis strictly wear heavily pleated and gathered *shalwars*.[10] Sindhis may alternate between a *kamees* and a *kurta.* The Urdu-speaking Pakistanis or Muhajireen—the descendants of the immigrants from India since 1947—very rarely wear *shalwar* and instead prefer pyjamas. These pyjamas originated in upper India, unlike *shalwar*, which originated in Western and Central Asian regions.[11]

Pyjamas are usually made of cotton and occasionally of satin, but they remain strictly plain. There are two styles of pyjamas: those that are loose around the legs with a straight-cut pattern, generally referred to as pyjamas, and the tighter ones called *chooridar,* which look more like jodhpurs.[12] Both varieties are tied at the waist with a knitted, circular belt, or *naara.* Not all Pakistani men wear a *shalwar* or pyjama; many in Punjabi villages still wear a loin cloth, called *chaadar.*[13] This loose cloth is tightly knotted around the waist and sometimes also fastened with a leather belt. There are two patterns of a typical *chaadar*. The first is a basic one with usual white or other solid-color cotton, which farmers wear during their work in the fields. The second type is again made of cotton or even of silk with quite a bit of ornamentation and embroidery added to it. In its formal incarnation it is called *lungi*, which has affinity with the Southeast Asian sarong. The *lungi* is for formal and festive occasions, but the *chaadar* or *dhoti* (a loose wrap-around) is more for field work as it is suitable for the hot weather and is inexpensive. When the farmers irrigate or plough their fields, especially those of rice, a *dhoti* comes is handy as, unlike *shalwar* or trousers, it can be easily tied up without muddying its ends. The cotton has its own cooling effect. Undoubtedly, *dhoti* and *kurta* are the ancient Indus Valley heritage, shared with its counterparts in the Gangetic plains. For holidays, such as the Eids, and for marriages and village fairs, affluent and younger men will don *lungi* while the rest will content themselves with a clean *dhoti* or a generously longer and well-ironed *chaadar*. *Dhoti* can also have various colors, patterns, and stripes.

Rural women may now prefer a *shalwar*, yet the *dhoti*, for a long time, has been their main clothing. Given the nature of their work, they would carry a loose wraparound *(dupatta)* not only to shield them from hot sun but also to cover their heads in front of strangers. The rural Pakistani women, especially in Southern Punjab and Sindh, mostly wear *shalwar*, which may have red and black patterns or are white. The *dupatta*, again depending upon age and economic background, could have some colorful borders or even some embroidered patterns. Women prefer loose clothes and avoid wearing skintight shirts. In addition, they adorn their ears and occasionally the nose with some traditional jewelry. Until very recently, rural women wore heavy bangles and earrings made of silver, but now only the gypsy women wear elaborate jewelry. The Kalasha women in the interiors of Chitral and bordering Afghanistan wear long, dark-colored dresses and cover their braided hair with specially designed headgears locally known as *bashalini*. They consist of beads, ivory, old coins, and other smaller items all sewn on to a longish hat.

The urban women in Pakistan prefer *shalwars*, which may have usually a slimmer fit. Some may wear bell-bottom trousers, whereas younger women may prefer more skin-tight costumes and even skirts for private parties. They take extra care in matching as well as contrasting the colors of the tunic and *shalwar* and one frequently comes across a lovely combination of regional traditions. For instance, the traditional flowery Sindhi *chaadar* called *ajrak* can be used for a *shalwar* or for adding borders to the tunic, whereas Swati textile patterns are found on the fronts of usually light-colored tunics. *Dupatta* in summer and a Kashmiri shawl in winter also constitute normal wear, although the colors, texture, and embroidered designs may vary by occasion and age. Elderly urban women tend to wear simple attire while the younger girls in cities try all kinds of fashions including jeans.

With the evolution of the Pakistani diaspora and the late Princess Diana and Jemimah Khan often wearing Pakistani designs, an entire fashion and textile industry emerged not only in Karachi and Lahore but also in London, Birmingham, and Manchester. The fashion magazines, television channels, and a number of Pakistani designers offering a wide mix of Pakistani traditional dress with a modern twist have further popularized Pakistani costumes. The fashion shows with models and television celebrities on the catwalks have certainly ensured the preservation of this tradition. Stores such as Khaadi in big cities offer a wide variety of Pakistani cotton dresses, shirts, trousers, waistcoats, shawls, coats, *chaadars,* and tunics, tailored to modern tastes yet strictly designed in indigenous styles. This patronage has instilled a renewed interest in the local products, textiles, and traditional patterns besides opening up an entire new spectrum of the fashion industry.

In the 1980s, for a time *dhoti-shalwar* (actually a *shalwar* but with more cloth added to make its upper part look baggier) became quite popular among Pakistani women, but the regular-size *shalwar* seems to have come back in recent years. The bottom ends of the *shalwar* are mostly decorated with matching embroidery or even with some silver jewelry to suit some happy family occasions. In the early years of Pakistan, the sari was a familiar choice in urban areas, but it has become rather less visible and confined to only very formal occasions. Still, it is not unusual to come across elderly women in Lahore and Karachi preferring saris over the *kamees-shalwar* combination. The hijab or a headscarf is a new arrival in Pakistan and might have come from Iran or the West; alternatively women either cover themselves with a full *chaadar* or in the rural and tribal regions may opt for full veil. The older form of veil has embroidered spaces for the eyes and is called a *burqa.* The more fashionable veil, usually in black, is in vogue among the traditional families across the subcontinent.[14]

Like most Pakistani men, women prefer the *shalwar* and may have several combinations for mix-and-match purposes. Despite the availability of ready-made clothes in stores and boutiques, many Pakistani women still prefer tailor-made clothes, which entails planning, shopping, and choosing the designs as well as the tailors. The Pakistani fashion industry has been growing steadily both within the country and among the diaspora in the Gulf, United Kingdom, and the United States. Before Bollywood became too preoccupied with scanty Western dresses for Indian actresses, it played an important role in popularizing newer fashions among South Asian women. Pakistani dramas watched across the region by millions have had enduring influences on choices and styles.

For a long time, South Asian women, especially Muslim women, have worn *gharara,* a loose garment, instead of a *shalwar* or sari. It is mostly made of silk or brocade with extensive handwork on it. Brides still wear it as a part of the wedding dress, and the preferred color is always red and golden embroidery added to it. The wedding combination is always red and gold, including dress, jewelry, and henna. Henna is meticulously added to the bride's hands and feet. Special make-up is applied and hair styling done either at home or at a salon. The groom may wear a suit, *kamees-shalwar,* and a pair of hand-made special shoes called *khussa. Khussas* are traditional footwear with a leather sole and intricate embroidered work in golden thread on their upper sections. Grooms may also don a long coat—*achkin*—made of expensive cloth. It is also called *sherwani* and like the *kurta* has a round, collarless neck with several buttons on the front.[15] It is more like a Mao jacket but of knee length, made of black serge for winter and perhaps white or creamy cotton for summer. The *sherwani* is always combined with a white *shalwar* or pyjamas and shiny black shoes. Shoes could be moccasins, *Kohati* sandals (leather sandals attributed to northern regions) or even brocaded slippers. On such occasions, the groom will certainly have a specially designed turban or a *karakul, astrakhan* cap. The latter is a cap made from the wool of a spring lamb, as usually worn by Jinnah, the founder of Pakistan.

Pakistani men, especially from rural, tribal, and traditional background, wear headgear varying from turbans and caps to loose *chaadars* or smaller scarves,

Family in formal dress at a wedding. Courtesy of the author.

depending on climate, customs, and religion. Chitralis and Hunza men may add a solitary feather to the front of their round woolen hats, which are mostly white or brown. During the Afghan resistance in the 1980s, these caps obtained a symbolic significance everywhere. The small skullcaps are worn by some tribal and urban dwellers who find them handy for prayers, as Pakistani Muslims—both men and women—cover their heads, especially during daily prayers. These skullcaps are mostly made of cotton and may have some interesting yet simple patterns embroidered on them. The tribal Pushtuns and almost all the rural Baloch wear massive turbans on their heads, which may have different color schemes and come in varying lengths. Like beards and moustaches, they are considered to be the traditional symbols of manliness. Some Afridi tribal Pushtuns living in and around the Khyber Pass prefer a round cap on a shaven head, although the beard remains a permanent feature. The Baloch usually wear huge, white turbans, whereas the Sindhis prefer an embroidered cap, generally in red with some small decorative mirrors shimmering in the sun.[16]

The waistcoat is another important item of Pakistani male attire, which has been in vogue on the Frontier and now is an important part of summer dress of the Pakistani middle class. These waistcoats vary in colors, material, and design according to the climate and occasion. Since the 1970s when the *shalwar* and *kamees* became the national dress for men, the waistcoat assumed an added significance, and politicians, poets, and artists began to retain a whole wardrobe of different colors and designs to match their choice of *shalwar* and *kamees*. In the Murree Hills, Kashmir, and Northern Areas with an arctic climate, big blankets and warmer shawls over sweaters and waistcoats protect the men from the harsh winter and cold breeze. In Hunza, middle-aged and affluent men traditionally wear a long woolen overcoat called *choogha,* which is always brown with floral patterns, sequined on the front and borders. Farmers, fishermen, and ordinary workers in lower Pakistan, like their women, can neither afford too many clothes nor have the luxury of choice. It is only on Eid festivals and wedding occasions that these people may find a chance to try on something new and a bit more fashionable. Gypsy men usually receive their clothes from charity, whereas gypsy women adorn their fewer possessions with an interesting mix of colors, patches, and some basic yet heavy jewelry. Their dress reveals a continuity of patterns and tastes through the centuries.

NOTES

1. Given the age-old familiarity with India and Indian commodities, as contrasted with the newness of Pakistan and Bangladesh, this cuisine is generally known as *Indian.* Its origins are mostly from the northern subcontinent with a heavy emphasis

on meat dishes, preferred by Muslims but usually avoided by practicing Hindus, who are typically vegetarian. For more than two centuries, curry dishes have been called *Indian* dishes, even though most of the restaurant owners in Europe happen to be Bangladeshis, Pakistanis, and Kashmiris. However, the wholesale suppliers are mostly Indian traders. In the same vein, trademark beer such as Kingfisher and Cobra are also Indian-owned. Madhur Jaffrey, the well-known writer of the Indian cookery books, is also an Indian by origin, and her books are quite familiar in British households.

2. *Balti* literally means a bucket, but it is a deeper pan for grilling and cooking. Now Balti stands for a whole variety of cooked dishes. In Britain and in South Asia, the restaurants advertise themselves as Balti or Tandoori varieties. *Tandoor* is a clay oven used for making naans and chapattis and is now part and parcel of South Asian cuisine. Its origins are again rural and ancient, yet is used widely today for roasting various meat varieties. A *karahi* is an oval-shaped metallic cooking dish where tender meat is cooked in fresh vegetables and various seasonings. The pot is used for cooking vegetables as well. *Karahi* is more native to the Frontier province.
Peshawari naans, in their British incarnation, may have coriander or basil mixed in the flour. The kabobs could be of minced meat or small cubes, all mixed in herbs and sauces, which are then grilled on an open fire. *Balti* and *karahi* dishes are made from fresh mutton, lamb, or chicken with a generous mixing of tomatoes and other fresh herbs. *Balti* and *karahi* are also the name given to two deeper metallic pans, and patrons like to eat from them with morsels of naan.

3. *Pulao* has Central Asian origins but is basically fried rice with spices, seasoning, and tender meat. Unlike simply boiled or pitched rice, *pulao* combines various ingredients and takes longer to prepare. It is a formal dish, and any feast will be incomplete without it. For vegetarians, the pulao could consist of peas, chickpeas, or beans. Usually, yogurt mixed with herbs, called *raita,* goes with *pulao* as yogurt is considered to be digestive with its moderating impact on spices.

Zarda means "yellow" or "orange," from the yellow of the saffron. The milk-based white rice pudding with added nuts such as almonds, pistachios, and raisins is called *kheer.*

4. *Nargissii* literally means Narcissus, and the word may have been derived from the appearance of the cut-in-half boiled egg within a meatball, which looks like an open eye.

5. The common name for bread is *roti*, but it could have various forms and names. The Peshawari naans are different from Lahori *kulchas,* which are rounder and a bit oily. Kulchas are a breakfast staple and with traditional spicy dishes such as curries made from trotters, boiled potatoes, and chickpeas make a large-scale Lahori breakfast. Hotels across the country offer both Lahori and Western breakfasts.

6. In Balochistan, the leg of lamb is roasted on skewers over an open fire and is called *sajji.* Now, many restaurants in cities offer this formal dish to their customers.

7. Pakistani Chinese are all multilingual and strictly based in cities.

8. For instance, on Eid festivals Pakistani Muslims prefer new, well-pressed, and, often, colorful clothes but during Muharram—the month of mourning—Shia Mus-

lims wear black shirts as a sign of grief. Christian men wear formal European clothes on special occasions such as Christmas and Easter, whereas Christian women wear saris or a combination of *shalwar* and *kamees*, with some even donning skirts in rare cases. All these clothes are tailored to suit the occasion and thus assume a formal status. The Christian priests wear robes and clerical garb like their Western counterparts. In rural areas, both men and women may prefer the traditional Pakistani clothes. The Anglo-Pakistanis—the descendants of the mixed liaisons dating from the British era—wear European clothes. They are a vanishing section of the Pakistani Christian community. Hindus and Sikhs usually wear *shalwar* and *kamees* with the Sikhs usually wearing turbans. Parsis prefer European clothes, although their priests try to adhere to traditional styles.

9. They are heavier over the top because of the various pleated turns and are tied around the waist through the knitted rope, locally known as *naara*. It is made of loose cotton strings, sometimes colored or patterned. Some women and men may use the ends of the strings for securing their keys.

10. They are gathered at the top, and the waistband *(naara)* creates several pleats.

11. Some Pakistani historians and archaeologists, who are enthused with the idea of Pakistan being a Muslim country with closer linkages with West Asia, trace the origins of *shalwar* from Central Asia, beginning in the Kushan dynasty of the first Christian century. The *shalwar* flourished in the 1970s and 1980s when Pakistanis made a conscious effort to nationalize their dress styles within an Islamic context. The shalwar was found all across the Ottoman, Safwide, and Mughal empires of the early modern period and even mountainous regions such as Kurdistan have continued to use it as a symbol of national identity. In Africa—both in the western and northern regions—the *shalwar* is worn with pyjama-style trousers and the tunic becomes longer than its *kamees* counterpart in Pakistan.

12. These are tight pyjamas, which look more like a formal type of leggings, and are a meter longer than the leg's length so as to make for a gathered look at the bottom.

13. It should not be confused with the upper loose garments that Muslim women wear.

14. The veil is justified in the name of religion and honor among the traditional groups. The Ahmadis, a sect following a late nineteenth-century publicist, have ordained stricter veiling for women. The veil's patterns identify an Ahmadi woman from others. Even in the diaspora, especially in England where the sect's leadership is based, Ahmadi women, irrespective of age and class, strictly wear this veil, which often makes them look more like Saudi women.

15. Pakistani leaders like to wear a *sherwani* on national occasions. It has a round grandfather's neck with an open front that can be buttoned up. Its smaller and sleeveless version is a waistcoat, called *waaskat*.

16. Other than *ajrak*, rural Sindh is known for a colorful bed sheet called *rilli*, which is an intricate but immensely artistic patchwork of various colors and patterns, always in squares. Sindh is known for its leather slippers with flowery patterns on them. Rural Pakistanis also make special efforts to decorate their camels, horses, and prized bulls with jingling bells, flowing tassels, ornamented headgear, and even

flowery sheets to cover their backs. The saddles reveal a unique combination of wool, cotton, and leather mixed with decorative glass and woodwork to match the traditions inherited from the ancient cultures.

SUGGESTED READINGS

The Desi Cookbook. www.desicookbook.com

Fashion Pakistan. www.fashionpakistan.co.uk

Husain, S. A. *Muslim Cooking of Pakistan.* Littlehampton, UK: Apex Books, 1983.

Siddiqui, Huma. *Jasmine in Her Hair.* Madison, WI: White Jasmine Press, 2003.

The Urdu Point. www.urdupoint.com/cooking/Pakistan/

Victoria & Albert Museum. *Colours of the Indus.* London: Victoria and Albert Museum, 2000.

Visage (Karachi). www.visage.pk.com

Zameen (London). www.zameen.com

6

Gender, Courtship, and Marriage

The best among you are those who treat women well.
—saying of Prophet Muhammad, (570–632)

The one who got married is repenting the same way as the one who did not.
—Urdu saying

As an overwhelmingly Muslim society, Pakistan might be presumed to be a land of rigid and rather sexist laws and customs where orthodoxy rules, women are oppressed, and there are honor killings and forced marriages. Most Pakistanis are not polygamous, yet the society is commonly viewed as patriarchal, where marriage might become an ultimate bondage with women—wife, daughter, or sister—all assuming a subservient role. The woman's role is seen as strictly domestic, behind the confines of boundary walls—*chaardiwari*—and totally invisible behind a veil or *purdah*. However, such views are rather simplifications of a complex phenomenon and fail to see Pakistan as a multifaceted and multilayered society. It may be true that unlike Western women, Pakistani women have lesser public roles, yet presumptions of the society being inherently oppressive and antiwomen are unfair. Excepting some cases of intolerance and bigotry, Pakistan is a land of pluralistic, traditional, and mostly egalitarian values where sacred and secular, and religious and profane exist side by side. Of course, like every other society there are strong pulls toward more puritanical views of customs and arts in Pakistan, yet the legacies inherited over centuries from a wide variety of cultural and regional sources remain to balance these. Usually, the outside preoccupation with gender relationships in Pakistan is focused on woman's subservient position at home and before law, and on practices such as honor killings and wife beating.[1] Islam, tribalism, feudalism, and a kind of elitism anchored on an abrasive modernity are caricatured as the linchpin of this sexist legacy. This chapter discusses the status of women, inter-gender relationships, courtship practices, and the significance of marriages.

Pakistani men tend to have a variety of attitudes about women. At one level, a woman is a mother and thus is to be respected, with a God-given authority. She deserves a level of affection and devotion. Like the earth, she is the source of all creations, and like Eve, embodies creativity and genius. Simultaneously, she is a wife and a companion, who combines both strength and vulnerability. Strength is derived from her creativity as well as from her unconditional love, whereas her vulnerability is to external threats, which may be linked to a fear of her being violated by some outside force. This could be traced back to the long history of invasions where once vanquished, men of the tribe would be either killed or simply enslaved, whereas women would be taken as concubines. As Pakistan is still a largely rural and tribal society, one cannot be totally negligent of such a fear-complex. Independence in 1947 caused significant human dislocations and their effects reverberate even today. The world's largest migration took place on the subcontinent with serious violations of human rights by Hindus, Muslims, and Sikhs when the British left India to its anarchic forces instead of monitoring and controlling the frenzied situation.[2] Barbarities were committed on a large scale, and thousands of women were either raped or kidnapped by the opposing

Kalasha women at a stream in front of the special dwelling where they live while menstruating. Courtesy of the author.

groups and never seen again. In several cases, young girls were mercilessly slaughtered. The creation of a Muslim state with almost no infrastructure amidst such gory circumstances often reverberates in the national consciousness, especially during the heightened Indo-Pakistani tensions.

ISLAM AND GENDER

According to some feminists—both Muslim and non-Muslim—Islam, like any other religion, is inherently sexist and women cannot enjoy equal rights as long as religion remains the main reference point.[3] However, Islamists believe that Islam gave significant rights to women long before any other society or government did. The right to seek divorce, share in property and consultation on several issues were some of the salient powers women gained under the Prophet. To these Islamists, sociocultural problems and gender inequalities in societies such as Pakistan can be overcome only if a pristine Islamic order is established in the collective interest. In other words, to them, Islam is not the problem, but rather a solution.[4] Another group believes that the Prophet certainly allocated significant rights to women, and women such as Khadija (Muhammad's first wife) and Ayesha (Muhammad's scholarly wife) are the role models for all, yet, over the successive centuries, male interpretation of the classical sources, feudalism, and clerical monopoly have created serious inequities.[5] Such reformists seek a new interface between early Islam and a modern regime of rights and citizens, which could empower women and thus offer tangible solutions to societal problems. Muslim scholars and activists such as Fatima Mernissi, Leila Ahmed, Shirin Ibadi, Riffat Hasan, Asma Barlas, and Asma Jahangir are, in fact, the architects of this reformism, also known as Muslim feminism.[6]

To them and many other male and female reformers across the Muslim world, the classical Islamic heritage comparatively offered wider empowerment to women, yet also highlighted intergender differentiation without turning into patriarchy. In such discourses, the Prophet's mother, Aminah,[7] emerges as the role model and his wife, Khadija, remains an ideal companion to be followed. His daughter, Fatima,[8] is again the role model both for women and men. The Prophet fell in love with a former divorcee, who was 15 years older and his employer. She also asked him to marry her—all radical things from contemporary or even current viewpoints. Men, especially in the early patriarchal societies, would usually prefer younger women and would avoid marrying older as well as financially independent women. Another of the wives of the Prophet, Ayesha, is seen as a specialist on Islam who narrated several prophetic traditions, and early Muslim men often sought her expertise on all kinds of civic and theological issues. Soon after the death of the

Prophet, she even led the believers in a war. Sukayna and Zainab, the grand-daughters of the Prophet and the daughters of Ali and Fatima, are deeply venerated by Muslims for their courage, patience, articulation, and interest in scholarship and arts. In the early Islamic era, there were female Sufis, writers, and architects all over the Muslim world, yet gradually male domination peripheralized women's role.

The emphasis on headgear (*hijab* and scarf) is a modern issue. In the early era of the seventh century, Muslim women did not wear the veil or practice total seclusion. Prophet Muhammad's wives did not wear a veil until later in life when they were advised to cover their heads and faces. This exhortation was specifically for these women. Both Muslim men and women were advised to dress modestly. Muslim women also began to wear the veil, a few centuries after Muhammad's death, which was basically a cultural norm and not a religious dictate. The wearing of a the veil by Muslim women in the diaspora is a personal choice, and many young European and North American Muslim women are trying to make a political statement of their religious and cultural identity with the veil.[9]

Islam does not prohibit polygamy or encourage it. The related Quranic verses made a second marriage contingent upon the agreement of the first wife, and more significantly, only if the husband could treat the wives equally. Thinking this impossible, many Muslims jurists and feminists have tended to believe that polygamy is not permissible. Moreover, most Muslims are monogamous. Today, Islam prohibits marriage without the assent of the bride and ensures her say through the presence of two witnesses during the wedding ceremony. Marriage is considered to be a noble institution because of the centrality of the family and also as the sole arena for sexual activity. Islam does not prohibit sexual pleasure between lawful partners but is against any form of extramarital activity. Purity, faithfulness, and honesty are deemed important virtues of a successful married life. Islam does not prohibit family planning, and even under emergencies allows abortion. Infanticide is abhorred, and preferring boys over girls and requiring unnecessary dowries are viewed negatively. Islamic instruction and practices delineate the relationship between the genders and guarantee certain inalienable rights for both the sexes, yet family and reproduction remain prioritized. Sex remains a joyous yet quite private affair within the parameters of a married life. In addition, classical Islamic teaching requires respect to fellow human beings including women and is deeply abhorrent of physical or even verbal torture.

MUSLIM WOMEN IN SOUTH ASIA

In South Asian history during the Muslim era, there are female mystics, queens, nabobs, writers, and artists, but with the invasions and political upheaval and the male monopoly over religious scholarship, Muslim women, like their counterparts elsewhere, were largely confined to homes and child bearing.[10] During the colonial era, despite some early liaisons between European men and some Muslim women, the Muslim introversion increased with more emphasis on traditional values, shunning modernist dictates.[11] After the dissolution of the remaining Mughal royal symbol in Delhi in 1858 by the British East India Company, Muslims were mostly singled out for staging the rebellion and received harsher and discretionary treatment from the British officials.

Amidst a great sense of loss and helplessness, the emerging Muslim socioideological movements vigorously advocated a back-to-roots strategy where revivalism was prioritized over reformism. The official indifference, accompanied by a missionary onslaught through schools, publishing, and other civic institutions such as hospitals and *zenana* (groups and activities run by missionary women and meant for Muslim and Hindu women) collectively exacerbated Muslim alienation. At this crucial stage, Syed Ahmed Khan (1817–1898) tried to orient Indian Muslims toward Western education and opened schools and publishing houses. Yet, even a liberal-minded reformer such as Khan generally advocated a strictly domestic role for women. Some of his colleagues, such as Deputy Nazeer Ahmed, wrote Urdu novels idealizing a home-based role for women while Akbar Allahabadi, a contemporary poet, simply ridiculed modernity and women not wearing the veil. Like the revivalists, these Urdu authors worried about the "corrosive" Western influences on traditional Muslim values, where a woman was viewed as a paragon of chastity and domesticity.

However, some Muslim cultural groups in Lahore, Amritsar, Gujranwala, Bombay, and Dhaka established pioneer schools for Muslim girls and here the efforts of organizations such as Anjuman-i-Himaayat-i-Islam and Anjuman-i-Islamiaya are noteworthy. In Bengal, Syed Abdul Latif advocated modern education both for men and women without neglecting the Islamic teachings. The gradual emergence of a new, urban, and ambitious Muslim middle class in Lahore, Bombay, Karachi, Madras, and Dhaka, and the increased politicization of the educated Indians in general facilitated the entry of some Muslim women into the public domain. The Mian families of Lahore and the Khojas of coastal India broke the taboos by sending their women to schools and by ensuring their higher education in the English-medium and missionary institutions. Quite significantly, they allowed them to drop the veil—*burqa*—worn by the contemporary urban Hindu and Muslim women. Given the respect and social stature of these families, there was no complaint from their communities, and educated Muslim lawyers, businessmen, and civil servants started marrying such outgoing, educated, and self-confident women.

Some Muslim notables such as Syed Ameer Ali, Abdullah Haroon, Muhammad Ali Jinnah, and Yusuf Ali even married non-Muslim women, and with the advent of Mohandas Gandhi and increased populist participation in politics, numerous Indian women began to participate in several public activities. Soon the Indian National Congress (INC) and the All-India Muslim League (AIML) would have women cadres, and the English and local press would often publish pictures of activists such as Begum Shah Din, Ruttie Jinnah, Fatima Jinnah, Begum Mahmoodabad, Viqarunnisa Noon, Jahan Ara Shahnawaz, and Shaista Ikramullah. Concurrently, some Muslim intellectuals such as Maulvi Mumtaz Ali began publishing Urdu magazines in India where women's issues were highlighted, allowing more space to ambitious middle-class families.[12] Fatima Jinnah, the sister of Muhammad Ali Jinnah, was a highly trained professional, who stood by her brother till his death in 1948.[13] She was an independent woman, who helped Muslim women gain education and actively participate in politics. Fatima Jinnah even sponsored some brilliant Muslim youths in their education and training abroad and thus is widely seen as a role model in Pakistan.[14] In 1964–1965 she took on the country's military dictator, General Ayub Khan, whose machinations resulted in his victory—otherwise she could have become the first-ever elected woman president of a Muslim nation. Known as *Maadar-i-Millat* (Mother of the Nation) she led an eventful and inspiring career.[15]

Begum Jahan Ara Shahnawaz was another such Muslim woman from an elite background whose family had been in the forefront of educational and political activities in the Punjab. Her father, Sir Mian Muhammad Shafi, was the founder of the Punjab Muslim League and encouraged his daughter to obtain higher education and come out of *purdah*. Like Shaista Ikramullah, Lady Abdullah Haroon, and Nawab Abida Sultan of Bhopal, Jahan Ara enjoyed lifelong political associations with Muhammad Ali Jinnah and Ranaa Liaquat Ali Khan. Based in Lahore, she and her daughter, Tazi, played a vanguard role in Muslim politics during the 1930s and 1940s, and both of them also wrote novels, traveled widely, and, after Partition, helped in the resettlement of refugees. Since the Round Table Conferences of 1931–1933 in London, she had been an ardent follower of Jinnah and even claimed to have prevailed upon him to change his mind on settling down in London.

She wrote of her visit to the Jinnahs in 1933 at their home in England: "I told him that he could not do it. Father was gone and there was no one but him to pilot the nation and he had to return to his country. He asked if I really thought so and I replied, not only did I think so but I had come to take him back home. The nation and the country needed him."[16] When in 1941 Jinnah asked all the Muslim members of the Viceroy's Defence Council to resign in a protest against the official unilateralism, she dithered and was expelled from the AIML. However, she claimed to have been persuaded by Sikandar Hayat Khan, the Unionist premier of the British Punjab, to continue as a representative of Muslim women on this council.[17] However, later on, she was allowed to rejoin the AIML. She claims to have seen Jinnah working on a French-style constitution for Pakistan, which somehow has never been found. She is the only one to have suggested that and observes that Liaquat Ali Khan also knew about it.[18] Jahan Ara Shahnawaz, accompanied by Hasan Ispahani, toured the United States to espouse the case for Pakistan and delivered lectures at several places. Deputed by Jinnah on this mission, she also met First Lady Eleanor Roosevelt and several American journalists, explaining Muslim politics to them. Her daughter, Tazi, also received encouragement from Jinnah for her creative writings and political activism.

On the other side of the spectrum, regional landholding families and tribal and rural societies continued with their age-old tradition of gender differentiation. Urban schools and colleges motivated more women to enter into higher education. However, even in the cities, the religious Muslim seminarians called for purdah and women's seclusion within the confines of the house, where education was meant to be simply Quranic knowledge and other home-based skills. Maulana Ashraf Ali Thanwi, a Muslim cleric of notable religious significance, wrote a voluminous book, *Bahishti Zewar* (Heavenly Ornament), which offered minute details on being an ideal woman by assuming a strictly home-based role. His prioritization of purdah and *chaardiwari* stipulated full-time attention to child rearing and helping the husband—something that has been a consensus point among all such clerics.[19] Many religious, tribal, and rural Muslims did not like the AIML and its demand for Pakistan during the 1940s simply because its leadership, to them, was Westernized and had an active cadre of educated *modern* women. The skepticism of a powerful yet morally lax West was a pervasive idiom among such objecting sectors, who held on to strong familial, tribal, and rural traditions by seeking religious legitimacy in them.

Thus, while on the one hand, the freedom movement empowered vast sections of the society, including women, it equally intensified the ideological polarization especially regarding the role and status of women. This divide remains evident even today, although over the last several decades, women's education has become widespread. Yet, it is coeducation, removal of the veil, and employment alongside men that continue to agitate many conservative sectors. Syed Mawdudi's book, *Purdah,* which appeared in the preindependence era, still has many followers who seek a reassertion of the home-based role for Muslim women. An eminent scholar and erudite political analyst, Mawdudi sought examples from Western society to forcefully argue that unchecked consumerism, extensive adornment of women's bodies, premarital sex, and nudity all had displaced the cherished moral values.[20] However, the nationalist struggle empowered women, especially in schools and colleges, and offered some respite to urban Muslim women from an enduring subordination.[21]

Independence mobilized large sections of society and educated women gained greater self-confidence as Muslim leaders such as Allama Muhammad Iqbal and M. A. Jinnah spearheaded the case of female education and equal opportunities. Iqbal's poetry and writings exhorted Muslim youths to seek dynamism and self-discovery by immersing themselves in a historical consciousness and by having a progressive outlook. Jinnah, in an address to the students at Aligarh Muslim University in 1944, spoke against women's exclusion. He observed: "It is a crime against humanity that our women are shut up within the four walls of the houses as prisoners. There is no sanction anywhere for the deplorable conditions in which our women have to live. You should take your women along with you as comrades in every sphere of life."[22] Earlier, in 1941, a Muslim Girls' Students Federation had been formed to muster support for a Muslim homeland, while in 1943, at the Karachi session of the AIML, woman delegates founded the Women's National Guard, whose motto was later adopted by the Pakistan Girl Guides. In the elections of 1945–1946 in British India, these organizations played a crucial part in seeking votes for the AIML while promoting the case for Pakistan. The high point in their movement came with the Muslim mass agitation against Khizr Hayat's Unionist cabinet in the Punjab in 1947, when Jahan Ara Shahnawaz and Salma Tassaduque Hussain led the civil disobedience campaign. It was during these demonstrations that a young Muslim schoolgirl waved the Pakistani flag on the steps of the Lahore's Assembly Hall.

OPPORTUNITIES AND CHALLENGES FOR WOMEN

With the formation of Pakistan, a number of organizations dedicated to the welfare of women came into being. The All-Pakistan Women's Association (APWA) was the most preeminent. It was formed at Karachi in 1949 as a voluntary body owing to the efforts of Ranaa Liaquat Ali Khan and was open to Pakistani women older than 16 years of age. Its goals have been the educational and social uplift of women, and it has opened several schools, colleges, and handicraft centers across the country, although in rural areas it has remained rather underrepresented. Amidst the criticism from the religious groups in 1955, APWA launched a campaign against the second marriage of Muhammad Ali Bogra, the contemporary prime minister, and intensified its efforts for further civil rights for women. It was largely because of this groundwork that the military regime of General Ayub Khan ratified the Family Law of 1961, which formally guaranteed proper procedures for marriage and divorce, besides making polygamy contingent upon the agreement of the first wife. It also established local arbitration courts to decide on family feuds and cases of divorce, barring men from completing divorce in a single day. It made the certification of marriage compulsory and considerably raised the marriage age both for boys and girls. However, as noted, the same regime ensured the defeat of an elected woman president, when through bureaucratic intrigues and feuds, Fatima Jinnah lost the elections.

During the 1970s, the elected regime of Zulfikar Ali Bhutto (d. 1979) ensured more political rights for women and established a high-power committee to proffer recommendations for the removal of sociolegal biases against women. The report by this committee (also called Yahya Bakhtiar Committee) was never made public, and soon General Zia-ul-Haq overthrew Bhutto in a coup in July 1977. Zia, partially to establish his own constituency outside the Army and mainly to appease clerics, introduced a number of discretionary laws in the name of Islamization, circumventing all those rights that the women as well as minorities had attained in the 1960s. Under these laws, the evidence of two women was declared equal to that of a man; the new punishment for adultery was death by stoning, and, concurrently, family planning was de-emphasized. In a crucial and insidious way, Zia's measures removed the difference between an adulterer and a rape victim, and several women were put in jail prompted by even a minor suspicion from a relative. Many land-based cases soon turned into cases of adultery, and Pakistan became a totally male-dominated society. Pushed against the wall, many urban women began to organize themselves into bodies such as Women's Action Forum (WAF), Shirkat Gah, Aurat, and Shelter and eventually mobilized to establish the Human Rights Commission of Pakistan (HRCP).[23]

The elected governments led by Benazir Bhutto and Nawaz Sharif (1988–1999) did not attempt to remove the oppressive laws of General Zia and instead tried to appease the conservative and clerical sections within the country. The HRCP and other non-governmental organizations (NGOs) have resolutely lobbied for the repeal of various political, electoral, social, and legal forms of discrimination against women.[24] General Pervez Musharraf's military government opened up the society largely because of pressure from within and also because of Western persuasion since September 11, 2001. There are more women in Pakistani assemblies, yet several discriminatory laws against them and minorities persist.

Suicides over dowry issues, honor killings, and forced marriages still take place in the rural regions, although a vigilant press and an alert civil society have maintained pressure against them. Investigative reporters and researchers, lawyers and human rights activists—both men and women—have been working in tandem for more equitable rights for women and other under-privileged people. Women are excelling in the universities and competing for jobs, yet Pakistan is still a transitional society where influence and afflu-ence operate largely in the interests of the privileged sectors, and women, minorities, and other disadvantaged groups remain disempowered.[25] Given the struggle in the recent past, there are certainly reasons to be hopeful for a better sociolegal status for Pakistani women, although it also depends on the level of political and economic stability in the country.

The high infant mortality rate initially affects girls, although their subse-quent survival rate and life expectancy remain slightly better. However, unem-ployment—both among the educated and uneducated—remains higher for women and there are serious discrepancies in salaries and job conditions as well. About 33 percent of Pakistani legislators are women, but they lack com-mon forums and strategies, and men make all the vital decisions. Early mar-riages have almost disappeared, but dowry deaths or honor killings, despite a growing public abhorrence, still occur. The inheritance laws and other legal rights, including the discretionary law of evidence or differentiation between rape and adultery, remain in place and the regimes, influenced by conserva-tive elements, prefer the status quo. However, there are more women teach-ers, doctors, nurses, and journalists, although the society still seeks sustenance from religion, where loyalty toward faith and family remain sacrosanct.

Drama, films, literature, and Urdu-language press all stress deference to such norms, while the English papers such as *Dawn, Daily Times, Newsline,* and *Frontier Post* often highlight the need for progressive reforms. The influ-ential and widely read magazines such as *Herald, Friday Times,* and *Newsline,* mostly started and penned by women, regularly expose sociolegal misdeeds in their investigative columns. The conservative press and especially the papers sympathetic to religiopolitical parties also publish reports on suicides, gang rapes, and other forms of brutalization of women, yet stop short of demand-ing modernist reforms. Instead, they emphasize the traditional life and malign modern living as a Western immorality. However, the West evokes envy as well as suspicion among Pakistanis at large, including women. Most of them would like to enjoy the latest fashions and Western education while still staying loyal to their own cultural values. Popular culture with its video music and email groups, and several NGOs feed into a forward-looking Paki-stani womanhood, short of radicalism either in the name of modernization or under the pretext of traditionalism. The fashion shows, music concerts, women role models, and a kind of celebrity culture, despite its specific class dimensions, remains ascendant in urban areas, whereas in rural and tribal regions, clerics and local leaders maintain a strong hold on communities.

Within the context of debate and reforms on human rights, the Islamists in Pakistan believe that going back to a purist religion will surely rectify all the maladies, whereas modernists and reformers want a progressive and enlightened synthesis where modernity does not have to be rejected because of its Western roots. Elimination of legal and social inequalities and greater participation in various fields of life are the objectives before the various reformers, women's groups, and other human rights NGOs. The nationalist struggles across the Muslim regions during the interwar period, and a global spotlight on Islam in the last two decades have definitely solidified these two divergent viewpoints. However, one sees a growing salience of Muslim feminism, which is resistant to clerical monopoly on power as well as to an unbridled drift in moral values and is sure-footed on the issues of gender-based discrimination. It is believed that a full democratization or universal empowerment of these societies accompanying holistic educational and economic uplift may gradually help postcolonial nations such as Pakistan obtain an egalitarian environment.

Pakistan's class structures and demographic varieties reflect as well as allow diversities impacting gender relationship. While rural and tribal women may have fewer or almost non-existent public roles, their urban counterparts are gradually making their presence felt. While Fatima Jinnah, Benazir Bhutto,[26] Asma Jahangir, Hina Jilani,[27] and several well-known women parliamentarians might have represented urban and somewhat privileged backgrounds, there are thousands of teachers, researchers, nurses, clerks, and telephone operators who are using their own achievements toward a greater women's participation across the board. The discriminatory laws introduced by General Zia-ul-Haq compromised human rights, especially those of women and minorities, and it will take many more efforts to dissolve these laws. During the 1990s, there were again worries that Pakistan might go the Taliban way with a growing accent on Islamic radicalism, sectarian violence and a clerical penchant for harsher laws, and these challenges to a more democratic and tolerant Pakistan are still there. In 2002, while General Musharraf deterred the mainstream political parties from fully participating in the elections, the religio-political parties cashing in on this political vacuum and a pervasive anti-Americanism gained exceptionally higher votes. The combined forum of religious parties (Muttahida Majlis-i-Ammal—United Action Forum [MMA]) was able to form provincial governments in the NWFP (North-West Frontier Province) and Balochistan and also began to introduce laws that reminded many observers of the Taliban. As long the army keeps the major political parties at bay from the mainstream national politics and Pakistan shies away from significant ameliorative measures including land reforms and civic rights,

there is always a danger of reactionary forces blocking universal empowerment. Pakistan's leaders are always under pressure to undertake ameliorative
measures to improve human rights records, yet authoritarian regimes have
only increased the chasm. For instance, the blasphemy laws—again a Ziaist
legacy—head the public agenda of debate, and so does the brutal custom of
honor killings.[28] Since 1979, three separate high-power national commis-
sions have been established to investigate a wider and multidisciplinary realm
of women's rights and predicament, and all of them have suggested several
significant systemic overhauls. It is the lack of will on the part of successive
governments that has not allowed these recommendations to be carried out,
except for piecemeal measures.

ROMANCE AND COURTSHIP

Invasions and turbulence from within have not stopped the romanticiza-
tion of women in Pakistan's folk and literary heritage. Pakistan's romantic and
folk literary traditions see virtue, beauty, and human excellence in woman,
and there is always a strong element of melancholy in meeting and seeking an
ideal partner. The beauty of a beloved—-both physical and in character—is
copiously praised, and steadfastness against social customs and societal pressures remain the hallmark of a woman's courage. Yet, while she is to be cov-
eted and courted, she is also to be protected.

Pakistanis have inherited several traditions in their history that, in their
own respective ways, elevate respect for women, neighbors, and the needy in
the community. Of course, because of economic stratification and some reactionary practices, one cannot overlook the cases of violence directed against
women, which are rooted in outdated customs such as dowry and disputatious
property issues. The ancient Indus Valley's sketches found on walls, ceramics,
and seals reveal the respect given to women. The artifacts from the Buddhist,
Jain, and Gandhara cultures, housed in the museums at Taxila, Peshawar, and
Lahore emphasize the numerous physical and spiritual attributes of womanhood. Elaborate jewelry shows the centrality of aesthetics in intergender relationships. The Hindu female deities, despite embodying contrasting powers
of fertility and destruction or wealth and desolation, allocate a larger-than-life
role for women. Woman's sensuality becomes the cornerstone of Hindu classics such as *Kama Sutra,* while Sita's kidnapping causes the great campaign by
Ram Chandar, the hero god of *Ramayana.*

The advent of Islam and the emergence of the Indo-Islamic culture provide
the powerful backdrop to all the literary, artistic, and cultural dimensions permeating intergender relationships. Persian mostly dominates the highbrow
literature of this one-thousand-year-long era, but its Turkish, Arabic, Hindi,

and Urdu representations are equally diverse and creative. The poets such as Masud Salman Lahori, Abdul Qadir Baidal, Abdur Rahim Khankhanan, Nazeeri Nishapuri, Mirza Ghalib, and Muhammad Iqbal are some of those luminaries whose Persian verses reveal an unprecedented collection of romantic lyrics—*ghazals*—epics, poems, eulogies, and quartets.

Prose writers such as Al-Beruni, Abul Fazl, Abdul Qadir Badayuni, Gulbadan Begum, Jahan Ara Begum, Dara Shikoh, Zebunnissa, and Shah Wali Allah broadened the intellectual discourse, although it was left to the poets to dwell on romantic themes, where a woman is celebrated not simply as a paragon of physical beauty but mainly for her creativity and personality. The Urdu poets such as Wali Deccani, Mir Taqi Mir, Mir Dard, Mir Sauda, Mirza Ghalib, Daagh Dehlavi, Muhmmad Iqbal, Josh Malihabadi, Faiz Ahmed Faiz, Ahmed Faraz, Nadeen Qasimi, Mustafa Zaidi, Parveen Shakir, and scores of others have built on these traditions over the last three centuries. Like Jumna Das in Hindi, Urdu master writers such as Ghalib, Iqbal, and Faiz have gone beyond the familiar themes in ascertaining human psyche and intergender relationships. A few examples may suffice to suggest that the literary and intellectual ethos allocated more esteem to women than did traditional societies as a whole.

Ghalib is known for his wit, and his romance would never shirk even from blaspheming some of people's convictions, especially among Muslims. A witness of the destruction of Delhi and the displacement of the Mughal Empire, Ghalib still would not allow otherworldliness to overtake his penchant for romance. In one of his verses, he asserts that he knew the reality of the world hereafter yet would hold on to the creed since it gave him a good feeling. On another occasion, he counted his lifetime possessions as only the portraits and letters of beautiful women *(tasweer-i-buttan aur haseenoon kay khutoot)*. Ghalib's beloved is smart and quick-witted like him and poses a formidable challenge to the lover. One of Ghalib's contemporary poets wrote a beautiful Urdu verse, which, in translation, would mean that the beloved is eternally with the poet when no one else is around. Metaphysically, the poet was acknowledging the ever-presence of a beloved, to whom he remained faithful, yet Ghalib was so impressed by this verse that he figuratively offered his entire Persian and Urdu collection in exchange for just this single couplet. In another verse, Ghalib ruminates on being in love with beautiful women *(buttan)* all his life, and for the next world he would have nothing to show to the Almighty. To a rebel poet, the steadfastness in one's own conviction supersedes every other human activity, as he suggests burying a devout Brahmin in the Holy Kaaba just because the Brahmin has been unflinching in his commitment.

Muhammad Iqbal wrote of Muslim consciousness and the great heroes and heroines of Islam, yet reverted to romance whenever he found an opportunity. Even his moving poems written about deserted Muslim monuments such as the Cordova Mosque or Sicily turn into romantic rhapsodies with the lover crying over separation and long-lost love.

Faiz's poetry is a reiteration of class conflict and struggle against oppression, and here a working woman becomes a heroine, because the poet does not have the time for romantic love. Faiz courts the indifferent community like a lover beseeching a beauty whose powers and creativity remain bound because of societal inhibitions.

Josh Malihabadi, Mustafa Zaidi, Mahmud Sherani, and Ahmed Faraz use romantic symbolism to evoke human sensibilities, and the unattainability of a woman becomes a formidable challenge for a bereaved lover. These poets, in many cases, even do not shirk from naming their lovers, whose separation they bemoan, yet it keeps instigating their agitated humanity and creativity.

Literary women prominently figure in Pakistan's highbrow literature with their presence not merely as objectified beloveds but as empowered lovers, concerned humans, and politicized individuals, who feel the ordinary pangs and pains of life. Parveen Shakir's poetry is more romantic and focuses on sensory love. while Kishwar Naheed and Fahmida Riaz go beyond the subtleties of romance. To them, women's empowerment, protest against oppression, and secularist ethos are more important. Even in the historical novels by Naseem Hijazi and Rais Jafari or fiction by Altaf Fatima, Hajra Masroor, and Qudsia Bano, the Pakistani woman refuses to be a mute sufferer; she becomes an active partner and motivator. The television plays by Haseena Moeen and Surrayya Bijjyia focus on educated urban women establishing their own autonomous space within the society and interpersonal relations. Even the plays by Noorul Huda Shah and Asghar Nadeem Saiyid, focusing on rural women or gypsy girls, refuse to portray them as vulnerable victims of an oppressive manhood. Quratulain Hyder, perhaps the most preeminent Urdu fiction writer of the twentieth century, has always combined crosscultural traditions, where her characters never surrender their individuality and are elevated above the usual ornamentation and objectification.[29] The English writings by Tazi, Bapsi Sidhwa, Kamila Shamsie, Mohsin Hamid, and several other Pakistanis, despite a clear class and urban bias, include stories of independent women deromanticizing subordination and invincible manhood.

Other than Urdu and English writings, it is the folk literature and culture of Pakistan that may offer further insight into these dual aspects in a woman's persona—a romantic heroine and a valorous individual. In the folktales such as *Heer-Ranjha,* Heer is not the heroine because of her beauty but because of her courage to withstand taboos. In *Sassi-Punnon,* Sassi traverses across the barren and forbidding deserts of Sindh and Balochistan to seek out her Punnon (also known as Punnan), a Baloch nomad, who has moved on. Both immortalize love despite all the human and natural impediments. In the oft-quoted romance of *Mirza-Sahiban,* popular across the Indus regions, Sahiban falls in love with Mirza, a Turk from Takht Hazara, and is not willing to conform to tribal pressures. In *Sohni-Mianwaal,* Mianwaal sits on the other side of the bank, while a courageous Sohni from the family of potters swims across the Chenab to meet her lover. Eventually, this ordinary woman of Punjab drowns because of jealousy of another woman but emerges as the ultimate heroine. Other similar romances such as *Leyla-Majnoon* and *Shirin-Farhad* in the regional and folk tales reveal empowered and fearless women, who are faithful to their lovers and are able to withstand all kinds of pressures from their own families, clans, and class. The story of Madhu Lal Hussein is a love affair between a Muslim Sufi and a Hindu disciple and is eternalized in lucid Punjabi verses. An annual fair, *Mela-i-Charaghan* (the festival of lights), is held at their shrine in Lahore where thousands of people congregate to pay their homage.

Especially in rural and tribal areas of Pakistan, in traditional society unmarried men and women are not allowed to meet. However, romances have occurred and occasionally ended on tragic notes. The poetry, music, and songs all reflect the sorrows, pangs, challenges, and threats to this kind of courtship, which may suffer because of jealousy or sexual segregation. The most popular songs and traditional verses are those where lovers use eloquent words and melancholy vibes to reach out to a beloved, whose beauty and courage are surmised through piercing words and enchanting similes. The Beloved, for a Sufi lover, is always God with Muhammad as an intercessor, while for others it is plain mundane love that has to be consummated through marriage. Thus, courtship is the medium to the ultimate and entails hardships as well as joyous union *(milaap* or *wissaall).* Lover's messages are mostly in sign language across the rooftops during hot summer days or could be short phrases and verses thrown at the vantage points or exchanged through some confidants. For villagers, the courtship may happen while the young women go out to the village wells to fetch water or visit some shrine on Thursday.

In urban towns, students may meet at school or college. Now, the Internet and cellular phones are immensely popular ways to communicate privately. Poetry, movie dialogues, and clips from dramas are used by couples to impress each other, and thus, without a direct physical contact, courtship continues through words, gestures and secret escapades, which may have their own risks and disasters. Whereas the rural and tribal sectors frown on any free mixing of opposite sexes, in urban colleges and universities younger couples find ways to meet, although not every love affair ends in marriage. The considerations of family, class, religion, and even of caste play their role in establishing or even vetoing partnerships. Television dramas, films, and fiction, and an ever-growing industry of popular songs focus on man-woman relationship and all the accompanying romantic nuances, yet marital liaisons occur only through families and other such societal facilitators.

MARRIAGE: A MORAL AND SOCIAL NECESSITY

Marriage is not only a religious duty, it is a social obligation besides being the main medium for sexual relationship and procreative activities. Marriages are largely arranged through families, friends, or by a growing sector of matchmakers. In villages, either the elderly relatives or women from barber families seek out possible partners for young people while sounding out families on possible suitors. The prestige, property, and the character of the individual and his family always precede such investigations, which are mostly undertaken on behalf of the would-be groom. Education and jobs are major considerations as the immediate family plans on expanding its economic and physical reach. In urban areas, the personal selection of a mate, often a love match, is further facilitated through friends and cousins. Young people meet at college or at someone's wedding. Their courtship starts with meaningful gestures and secret meetings or messages on mobile phones and online until the in-betweens venture in. The children from elite families have more chances of meeting at parties or even while studying abroad.

Many middle-class and upper-class marriages, despite a veneer of being arranged, are increasingly personal choices. For such individualistic Pakistanis, ethnicity is not an important factor, although religion, education, and profession remain major considerations and they marry someone of the same class. Pakistani men, studying or working in the West and Japan, have been marrying foreign women.[30] Traditional families, however, insist on a marriage within the same clan and locality and would usually frown upon marriages of personal choice to a foreigner. Women eloping with their lovers by obtaining a civil marriage certificate from the court are mostly excommunicated by their immediate families or may, in some cases, be murdered, especially if they ever return. Men involved in such cases may also be killed by the members of the rival tribe seeking revenge or, in certain cases, by their own relatives. The government has been under pressure to ban such killings since they have been occurring in rural regions and the NGOs and media have been publishing harrowing stories of such gory events.

Marriage is to be preceded by an engagement *(mangni)* where rings, clothes, and sweets are exchanged and a feast with music is given by the groom's family. An elaborate program for the wedding, including traditional folk and Bollywood music, display of dowry, feasts, henna ceremonies and, most of all, registration of marriage *(nikah)* take place over an extended period of time. The *nikah* is led by the local imam of the mosque and is recorded in the register in the presence of several witnesses on both sides. Under Islamic teachings, seeking the bride's willingness to marriage is compulsory before such a ceremony can be entered in the register; prayers and distribution of sweets follow. For the *nikah* ceremony, the groom is taken to the bride's home along with his family and friends, where they are hospitably received and some amusing rituals are played out on the groom and his friends. The groom comes back again with a procession *(baraat)* and at this time the bride finally departs with him. It is a happy occasion, although parents may feel a sense of loss over their daughter leaving for a new home. The parents may also have an equal sense of satisfaction for being able to get their daughter married. Finding an appropriate groom may be a difficult proposition, but marriage means that the parents have fulfilled their religious and social obligations.

After her arrival in the new home, a specially decorated room *(aroosi)* awaits the bride, and local women venture in with presents to see her. She is the center of attention for a few days as festivities with music and special dinners continue until life goes back to normal. Couples in the cities may get married in expensive hotels or in marriage halls and may even go on honeymoons within the country. Christian, Sikh, Parsi, and Hindu marriages take places within the churches and temples, but the cultural rituals are very similar with traditional songs, colorful dresses, and elaborate jewelry to be seen and feasting and music going on for days until the new couple is finally settled. The bride's wedding dress is made of bright red silk with golden embroidery depicting traditional Mughal patterns. The groom may don a long tunic, embroidered shoes, and a turban. Urban grooms—both Muslim and non-Muslim—may

Bride and groom at henna ceremony. Courtesy of the author.

Newlyweds with family and friends. Courtesy of the author.

prefer Western suits. Marriages not only bring two families together; they are also meant to repair relations with annoyed kin. That is why gifts and presents are generously exchanged and the dowry *(jahaiz)* is proudly put on display in the courtyard. Traditionally, the bride's family is expected to offer an elaborate dowry and the groom's family may offer accommodation to the new couple.

Divorces are rare in Pakistan, which does not mean that every marriage is totally successful as it is often children and peer pressure that may keep families together. However, divorces certainly take place, although Islam considers it to be the last option and would urge for reconciliation. A divorce occurs over an extended period of three months so that the couple may still have the opportunity to resolve their differences.

Notes

1. A woman or a man accused of eloping or an extramarital affair will be stigmatized by the society at large and will certainly become a serious problem for the immediate family. Either they have to be married and sent off to some other locality or, in some cases, they might be quietly murdered by the nearest kin so as to "cleanse" the family's honor. Such killings, although illegal, are known as honor killings, in which mostly women and occasionally men are secretly murdered by the close relatives to avoid social stigmatization. Civic groups have been collecting figures on such deaths—also known as *karo kari*—which usually happen in the tribal-based rural localities.

In some rural landowning families of Sindh, women may never get suitors or their parents might have been unwilling to marry them into other clans out of a pervasive fear that their lands might go to others. This happens in those families where there are no male heirs and the parents are reluctant to bequeath their property to women. Such families, so as to meet the moral obligations, hold mock marriages of their daughters with the Quran that include all kinds of marital rituals. They believe that not only they have completed the marital obligations but have also ensured land staying within the family. Many Pakistanis did not know about such mock marriages until British television documentaries during the early 1990s made them aware of it. Other than educated Pakistanis, several ordinary people were shocked to know of these strange and rather cruel practices. However, while honor killings happen across the country quite secretly, like in neighboring India and elsewhere, the marriages with the Quran are not so frequent and both are certainly anathematic to most Pakistanis.

2. One only reads and hears of these three communities being the sufferers as well as perpetrators, and it is only in recent times with more diversification of historical scholarship that academics have begun to focus on Punjabi Christians as well, since they also underwent division across the new borders. However, most of the Punjabi Christians have been concentrated in Pakistani Punjab with a very small portion on the Indian side. The works by several writers and studies by scholars such as Suvir Kaul, Urvashi Buttalia, and Gyan Pandey have focused on the human dimensions of these dramatic events. See Muhammad Umar Memon, ed., *An Epic Unwritten: The Penguin Book of Partition Stories* (Delhi: Penguin, 1998); Alok Bhalla, ed., *Stories about the Partition of India* (Delhi, Indus, 1994); Jason Francisco, "In the Heat of the Fratricide: The Literature of India's Partition Burning Freshly," *Annual of Urdu Studies*, 2, 1996; Khalid Hasan, trans., *Kingdom's End and Other Stories* (London: Verso, 1987); Suvir Kaul, ed., *The Partitions of Memory: The Afterlife of the Division of India* (Delhi: Permanent Black, 2001); Urvashi Butalia, *The Other State of Silence: Voices from the Partition of India* (London: Hurst, 2000); and Gyanendra Pandey, *Remembering Partition: Nationalism and History in India* (Cambridge: Cambridge University Press, 2001).

3. There are several references to this, although many writers would avoid being defined as Eurocentric. Some Muslim writers such as Salman Rushdie (*The Satanic Verses,* New York: Picador, 1988), Tasleema Nasreen (*Lajja,* Calcutta: Vami, 2001), and Monica Ali (*Brick Lane,* London: Doubleday, 2003) have raised similar issues. In more recent years, a rather more blunt critique has appeared in *The Trouble with Islam,* (Toronto: Vintage, 2005) written by Irshad Manji, a North American–based writer. In this impressionistic work, she finds serious problem of sexism and anti-women sentiments within the teaching and practices of Islam. In general, Muslims ignored her critique, although some in the Western media found in her a "progressive Muslim," flagging an overdue revolt.

Such idealization not only views Islam as a monolith, it inherently perceives it as a stalemated oppression. For instance, *Newsweek* gave its verdict on Muslim societies being antiwomen: "In some Muslim societies women are systematically mutilated, in others merely humiliated. Last week Britain Crown Prosecution Service announced it had identified 117 cases of female deaths and disappearance over the last 10 years that may have been honor killings: executions of girls and women by men in the family who feel they've brought shame on them." Christopher Dickey and Carla Power, "Rocking the Casbah," *Newsweek,* 20 December 2004. http://www.msnbc. msn.com/id/6700425/site/newsweek/. Here, Britain's pluralistic communities are monolithicized as totally *Muslim,* which is incorrect. In addition, female circumcision has nothing to do with Islam and rather predates it. For a detailed response by a Muslim author, see Habib Siddiqui, "The Making of Manji: Her Master's Voice," http://world.mediamonitors.net/content/view/full/12165/.

4. The Muslim organizations such as the Muslim Brotherhood in the Arab world, Jama'at-i-Islami in South Asia, Taliban in Afghanistan, and Hizbul Tahrir elsewhere have regularly emphasized a strictly home-based role for women. Many of these organizations have strong women's cadres that also subscribe to similar views. Some Western converts to Islam, such as Maryam Jameelah (an American living in Pakistan) and Yvonne Ridley (a British journalist) also seek separate gender roles.

5. Khadija's success as an independent businesswoman in a tribal and male-dominated society and her love for the Prophet eventually leading her to propose to him despite her being senior to him by 15 years reveal a woman of strong and steadfast determination. She was also Muhammad's employer and was impressed by his honesty and diligence, and quite significantly she became the first-ever Muslim soon after the start of his espousal of Islam. Thus, her multiple roles are seen as inspirational for all Muslim men and women. Muslim feminists have emphasized her pioneering and enterprising qualities and see in her an early symbol of intergender equality.

6. A native of Iran, Shirin Ibadi is the first Muslim woman Nobel Laureate, whose own legal, political, and academic pursuits have helped women in her country. While receiving her prize in 2003, Ibadi highlighted the feasibility of human empowerment through a synthesis between Islamic values and contemporary discourse on human rights. She is certainly a role model for millions of women in West Asia.
A Pakistani lawyer by profession, Asma Jahangir is the founding president of Pakistan's Human Rights Commission, a private-sector watchdog group known for its espousal of and training in human rights across the country. In addition, she has established shelters for battered women in Pakistan and Afghanistan. Based in Lahore and helped by nationwide groups of lawyers and activists, Jahangir has been a fervent supporter of democracy and has also worked as the UN Rapporteur on human rights on Afghanistan.

Fatima Mernissi and Leila Ahmed are pioneers of Muslim feminism, which has been further strengthened by Muslim academics such as Riffat Hasan, Asma Barlas, Asghar Ali Engineer, and many other writers, often defining themselves as "Progressive Muslims." See Fatima Mernissi, *Women and Islam: An Historical and Theological Inquiry,* trans. Mary Jo Lakeland (Oxford: Blackwell, 1992); Leila Ahmed, *Women and Gender in Islam* (New Haven, CT: Yale University Press, 1992); and Omid Safi, ed., *Progressive Muslims on Justice, Gender, and Pluralism* (Oxford: Oneworld, 2003).

7. Aminah's devotion to her son despite an early widowhood and her exemplary upbringing of the Prophet make her a role model for Muslim mothers and wives.

8. Fatima was Muhammad's daughter with Khadija—his first wife and close companion. Muhammad was survived only by Fatima as all her siblings died during the Prophet's lifetime. The Prophet was close to her and confided in her. He arranged her marriage to Ali, a great scholar and Muhammad's own cousin, known for his courage as well as devotion to the Prophet. Fatima gave birth to Hasan and Hussein, who were also very close to their grandfather. Fatima's simple marriage ceremony, her devotion to her family, and her generous disposition to her sons and daughters earned her an unprecedented esteem among all Muslims. Thus, Muslims continue to respect and revere Aminah, Khadija, Fatima, and Ayesha not simply because they made up the Prophet's immediate household but largely due to their own respective attributes as exemplary human beings, affectionate parents, loving partners, and scholars in their own right. Ayesha, Muhammad's youngest wife, has been the most quoted authority on classical Islamic knowledge over the last 14 centuries. The Prophet died in her arms and she is viewed to be the authentic source of most of his sayings *(hadith)* and deeds *(sunna)*.

9. In the United Kingdom, the second generation women of South Asian background in some cases have adopted the wearing of a scarf, while in the lands of their ancestors the scarf remains unfamiliar, as women would mostly wear a *chaadar* or a simple wrap-around *(dupatta)*.

10. Queens such as Razia Sultana, Chand Bibi, Noor Jahan, and Mumtaz Mahal proved to be successful administrators and military commanders in their own rights. Gulbadan Begum, Jahan Ara Begum, and Zebunnissa were known for their literary and scholarly pursuits, whereas Muslim Begums of the same Khan family ruled the princely state of Bhopal from the early nineteenth century until 1948. See Shahryar M. Khan, *The Begums of Bhopal: A Dynasty of Women Rulers in Raj India* (London: I. B. Tauris, 2000); Siobhan Lambert-Hurley, "Contesting Seclusion: The Political Emergence of Muslim Women in Bhopal, 1901–1930," Ph.D. dissertation (University of London, 1998); and Abida Sultan, *Memoirs of a Rebel Princess* (Karachi: Oxford University Press, 2004). Princess Abida Sultan (1913–2002) was herself the last Begum, an heir to the throne of Bhopal, but in 1947 she opted for Pakistan and left central India for Karachi. The first book listed here is, in fact, authored by her son, who later on retired as Pakistan's Secretary for Foreign Affairs.

11. See William Dalrymple, *White Mughals* (London: Flamingo, 2002), a best seller devoted to this subject.

12. For more on this, see Shaista S. Ikramullah, *From Purdah to Parliament* (Karachi: Oxford University Press, 1998) (reissued); and Dushka H. Saiyid, *Muslim Women of the British Punjab: From Seclusion to Politics* (Basingstoke: Macmillan, 1998).

13. Fatima Jinnah, *My Brother* (Karachi: Academy, 1987). (This is a rather short monograph, since she could not complete the biography.)

14. See Khalid Hasan, ed., *Memories of Jinnah* (Karachi: Royal, 1990). This volume is based on the diary of Mr. K. H. Khurshid, a former secretary of the Jinnahs, who was sent to London's Lincoln's Inn for his bar-at-law by Fatima Jinnah.

15. For more on Fatima Jinnah, see Rizwan Malik and Samina Awan, *Women Emancipation in South Asia: A Case Study of Fatima Jinnah* (Lahore: University of Punjab, 2003); and Agha Hussain Hamdani, *Fatima Jinnah: Hayyat awr Kidmaat* (Islamabad: National Institute, 2003) (reissued).

16. Jahan Ara Shahnawaz, *Father and Daughter: A Political Biography* (Karachi: Oxford University Press, 2002) (reissued), p. 141.

17. Ibid., p. 163.

18. Ibid., pp. 229–30.

19. Barbara D. Metcalf, *Perfecting Women: Maulana Ashraf Ali Thanwi's Bihishti Zewar: A Partial Translation with Commentary* (Berkeley: University of California Press, 1990).

20. Syed Abul Ala Mawdudi, *Purdah* (Lahore: Islamic Publications, 1972) (reissued).

21. Ayesha Jalal, "The Convenience of Subservience: Women and the State of Pakistan," in *Women, Islam and the State,* ed. Deniz Kandiyoti (London: Zed Books, 1991).

22. Quoted in Khawar Mumtaz and Farida Shaheed, *Women of Pakistan: Two Steps Forward. One Step Back?* (London: Zed Books, 1987), p. 7. Also see Sarfaraz Hussain Mirza, *Muslim Women's Role in the Pakistan Movement* (Lahore: Research Society, 1969).

23. For details on all kinds of efforts including the recommendation of the statutory commission of 1987, see Iftikhar H. Malik, *State and Civil Society in Pakistan: Politics of Authority, Ideology and Ethnicity* (Oxford: St. Antony's Series, 1997), pp. 146–67.

24. For more on this, see Iftikhar H. Malik, *Islam, Nationalism and the West: Issues of Identity in Pakistan* (Oxford: St. Antony's Series, 1999). There are several NGOs across Pakistan, operated by a variety of groups and communities. The Edhi Foundation, the Agha Khan Rural Support Programme, The Orangi Pilot Project, Shaukat Khanum Memorial Cancer Hospital, Foundation Schools, and All-Pakistan Bishops Conferences are some of the noteworthy organizations.

25. I have discussed these issues in a report, which mainly focuses on non-Muslim minorities. See Iftikhar H. Malik, *Religious Minorities in Pakistan* (London: Minority Rights Group, 2002).

26. Author of *Daughter of the East* (London: Hamish Hamilton, 1988), Bhutto is the daughter of a former president of Pakistan, Z. A. Bhutto. After her education at Harvard and Oxford, she returned to Pakistan to fight for democracy and was twice elected prime minister. In October 1988, she became the first-ever woman ruler of a Muslim country, although her government was twice dismissed in 1989 and then in 1996 on corruption and nepotism charges. Convicted by a court in corruption cases, she has been living in exile in Dubai and London but her political party—Pakistan People's Party—remains the largest political organization in the country. However, charges of corruption and nepotism have continued to haunt her, making headlines even in her self-imposed exile since 1997, deterring her from returning to Pakistan. Her husband, Asif Zardari, remained in jail for eight years on similar charges and was released in December 2004. See Jeremy Carver, "The Hunt for Looted State Assets: The case of Benazir Bhutto," in Transparency International, *Global Corruption Report 2004* (London: Pluto, 2004), pp. 102–4.

27. They both are trained barristers and human rights activists. Asma Jahangir has fought court cases for battered women and persecuted individuals, besides pioneering

the Human Rights Commission of Pakistan. Despite various threats to her life, she has fought on civic fronts and is a role model for millions of Pakistanis. Hina Jilani is her close relative and a fellow activist in Lahore; aligned with several other activists, she has founded several women's organizations, including Women's Action Forum (WAF) and Shelter. They have resisted authoritarianism and discriminatory laws and thus have been shadowed by the intelligence agencies as well as by intolerant clerics.

28. It is not unusual to come across daily news and commentaries on innocent victims of honor killing, also known as *karo kari*. The Pakistan Senate, the Parliament's upper house, was presented in 2004 with the figures of *karo kari* victims by the regime, much to the chagrin of all. According to this report, 4,000 individuals were killed from 1998 to December 2003, out of whom 2,200 were women and the rest were men. These individuals had been blamed by their relatives or clans for elopement and marriages outside the immediate families. As explained, their own close relatives quietly eliminate them. The government promised to introduce a new law to declare this practice illegal, although not enough progress has been made on that front. The figures also gave details of the ratio of incidence in the Punjab, followed by Sindh, Frontier, and Balochistan. Courts had several cases pending before them while quite a few criminals had been already convicted. For details, see *Dawn*, 10 July 2004 (www.dawn.com). In 2004, about 1,000 cases of honor killing were documented in Pakistan by the Human Rights Commission of Pakistan (HRCP). See HRCP, *State of Human Rights in 2004* (Lahore: HRCP, 2005).

29. She migrated to Pakistan in the early years but subsequently left for India in despair.

30. Usually religion and nationality assume rather contentious positions. Men may convert their non-Muslim partners to Islam even though, in most cases, they end up staying in the adopted countries. Marriages between Muslim men and women from "the People of the Book" (Jews and Christians) are allowed, whereas Muslim women, under the strict Islamic interpretations, are not allowed to marry non-Muslim men. But there have been such marriages at places like India or in the West, though in exceptional cases. Marriages between Pakistani men and Indian women, especially during the times of inter-state tensions, can prove problematic when it comes to acquiring nationality.

SUGGESTED READINGS

Ikramullah, Shaista S. *From Purdah to Parliament*. Karachi: Oxford University Press, 1998.

Mernissa, Fatima. *Women and Islam: An Historical and Theological Inquiry*, translated by Mary Jo Lakeland, Oxford: Blackwell, 1992.

Mumtaz, Khawar, and Farida Shaheed. *Women of Pakistan: Two Steps Forward. One Step Back?* London: Zed, 1987.

Saiyid, Dushka H. *Muslim Women of the British Punjab: From Seclusion to Politics*. Basingstoke: Macmillan, 1998.

Sultan, Abida. *Memoirs of a Rebel Princess*. Karachi: Oxford University Press, 2004.

7

Festivals and Leisure Activities

Pakistan has a number of festivals and holidays to celebrate religious, historical, and social occasions during the year. National holidays and some festivals
have fixed dates falling within the Gregorian calendar, whereas others follow its lunar counterpart or the ancient Indian Bikramajit (also Vikramajit)
calendar. Muslim festivals follow the lunar cycle, whereas folk and traditional festivals are according to the agricultural cycle. The festivals, fairs, and
sports mean holidays from work and they are also opportunities for socializing and relaxing. Such holidays and collective activities disburse economic
and human resources across the board and thus help many local economies
besides encouraging tourism within the country. Holidays and festivals are
eagerly awaited, especially by children.

Sports are an integral part of Pakistani leisure culture. Cricket, squash,
and hockey are a major national preoccupation. These sports allow Pakistan
to strengthen its nationhood and afford global recognition. The Indo-Pakistani cricket matches, since their inception in 1952, have always been heated,
although in recent years the spectators on both sides tend to show more
warmth and reciprocity. Pakistan also has its own share of traditional sports
such as wrestling and other forms of local physical pursuits that combine Indus
Valley traditions with extra-regional influences. Sports are mostly played on
the weekends and during the holidays so as to draw more of an audience.
Picnicking, open air theaters, and concerts, traveling to summer resorts, and
attending literary evenings are some of the other leisure pursuits.

NATIONAL DAYS

National days in Pakistan honor cultural and political heroes. For instance,
Sir Muhammad Iqbal (1873–1938), the famous poet-philosopher, born in

Sialkot and buried in Lahore, is considered the national poet of Pakistan. His widely quoted works are in Urdu, English, and Persian, and his ideas of political redefinition of the Indian Muslims as a separate nation unto themselves made him one of the important founders of Pakistan. Sir Iqbal's portraits are found in offices and galleries across the country and quotations from his writing and poetry are recited in laudatory speeches to inspire the nation. His birthday is celebrated as a national holiday on April 21.[1] On November 11, the anniversary of his death, selections from the Quran are recited at gatherings and families visit his grave in Lahore's historic district. Senior government officials lay wreaths on his resting place.

In the same vein, the birthday as well as the death anniversary of Pakistan's founder, Muhammad Ali Jinnah (1876–1948), also known as the Quaid-i-Azam (great leader), are national holidays falling on December 25 and September 11, respectively.[2] His mausoleum in Karachi is always thronged by visitors and on the holidays becomes a focal point for several special parades and bouquet-laying official ceremonies. Jinnah's mausoleum is guarded by a smart contingent of Pakistani troops who, periodically, rehearse their choreographed movements. On his anniversaries as well as on the country's independence day, seminars, prayers and rallies are organized to commemorate his contributions, newspapers print special supplements, and leaders issue laudatory and commemorative messages. The British partitioned the subcontinent into the new states of India and Pakistan on August 14, 1947, and this day is the main national holiday with parades and other gala activities being held across the country.

In the same vein, March 23 is another national holiday, as it was on this day in 1940 that the Muslim representatives from across the subcontinent met in Lahore to form a consensus on sovereign statehood. The rally took place at Minto Park, renamed Iqbal Park, where there is now a memorial tower, designed by a Turkish artist and built a few decades ago. This day is also called Yom-i-Jamhurhiyya (the Republic Day), as most of the country's constitutions have been traditionally promulgated on this day. However, military regimes have usually shied away from the political and democratic symbolism of this day and have instead focused more on the Independence Day. Pakistan's army celebrates September 6 as National Defence Day, while the Pakistan Air Force has it own commemorations the next day.[3] Because of the army's unilateral role in Pakistani politics and economy, these days have assumed more significance and Pakistan's missiles and other advanced weapons are displayed with great pride.[4] The inhabitants of the Himalayan state of Jammu and Azad Kashmir celebrate October 27 as their national day to commemorate the inception of their struggle for liberation in 1947 from the former princely Maharajah.[5] They also celebrate Pakistan's independence day and other national holidays.

The religious festivals reflect the Muslim majority in the Pakistani population. Muharram, the first month of the lunar year, is devoted to the remembrance of Imam Hussain and his family, who were martyred in Karbala in A.D. 680. Hussain had come from Medina to challenge the rule of the Umayyad caliph, Yazid, and, in the process, was killed. He was killed by the Euphrates River on the 10th of Muharram, also known as the Day of Ashura.[6] He is buried in Kufa and Pakistani Muslims visit his shrine. All Muslims, especially Shias, remember the sacrifice and pain of Hussain's venture by wearing black clothes and walking in mourning processions. The Prophet Muhammad's birthday falls on the 12th of Rabbi-ul-Awwal, the third month of the lunar/ Hijri calendar, and it is a gala day.[7] It begins with prayers in the mosques and special Quranic recitations on radio and television. Many Muslims celebrate this festival, also called Eid Milad-un-Nabbi, by walking in processions and singing hymns.[8] The roads and bazaars are tastefully decorated and special feasts are organized at the Sufi shrines. The singing of mystical poetry, known as *na'at* and *qawalli*, is the main feature of the day's activities and distribution of cooked food, water, and other items among the needy takes precedence over other routine work.

The month of fasting or Ramadan is the ninth month of Hijri calendar. Adult Muslims are expected to fast from dawn to dusk every day. The sighting of the moon for Ramadan is a happy occasion, and all through the month itself, more people pray in the mosques and listen to the recitation of the Quran, especially during the nightly prayers. This is considered to be a month of purification, and people do not drink even a sip of water or eat any morsel of food all day until nightfall—a trial, especially during summer months. The end of Ramadan is again dependent upon moon sighting, which augurs the happy festival of Eid-ul-Fitr. This Eid begins with special midmorning prayers in the mosques, and then feasting continues for the next three days. Muslim adults are expected to offer charity—*fitrana*—to the poor before they pray in the mosque. Children put on new clothes and relatives visit one another and grievances are put aside.

Like Christians and Jews, Muslims consider Abraham to be one of their important prophets, and a holiday in his honor falls 70 days after the Eid-ul-Fitr. This festival occurs a day after the completion of Hajj—the annual Muslim pilgrimage to the Holy Land in Saudi Arabia—and thus is of dual significance. Affluent Muslim families are expected to slaughter animals and distribute the meat among the relatives and the needy and to ensure that the tradition of Abraham, who was ready to sacrifice his son to please God, is fully followed. The morning of this occasion—Eid-ul-Azha or the Eid of Sacrifice—begins with special prayers in the big mosques. The priests remind everyone of the prophetic traditions and exhort for generosity and kindness. They also sermonize on Hajj, and the Prophet Muhammad's own last pilgrimage where he had made a historic speech denouncing racism and violence while emphasizing a transregional bond among the believers *(ummah)*. For the next three days, there are feasts as Muslims all over the world prepare for the end of the Hijri year in the next 20 days.

In addition to Ashura (the 10th of Muharram) and Eids, Pakistani Muslims periodically visit Sufi shrines that have their own annual prescribed celebratory days, called *urs*. Here, specially cooked *pulao*—rice with meat and spices—and sweet rice or *zarda* are distributed while the *na'at* and *qawalli* sessions go on until very late at night. Some strict and literalist Muslims are not in favor of such festivities and downplay the role of Sufis as intermediaries between God and the people. The leading Sufis are buried in Lahore, Multan, Golra, Pak Pattan, Uchh, Sehwan Sharif, Kaka Sahib, Bhit Shah, and Taunsa, yet there are shrines and monasteries *(dargahs)* all over the country whose blue and green domes shimmer in the tropical sun. The descendants of these Sufis maintain these shrines, and the disciples and their families send in their offerings from all over. The shrines offer places to stay for visitors and have a continued tradition of free food *(langar)*. Some of these shrines, such as those of Gunj Baksh in Lahore, of Golra Sharif and Bari Imam near Islamabad, of Shahbaz Qalandar and Sachal Sarmast in Sehwan Sharif, of Shah Latif in Bhit Shah, and of Bahaud Din Zakariya in Multan draw incomes from such offerings in addition to the wealth from the properties bequeathed to these

Sufi shrine of Shahbaz Qalandar. Courtesy of the author.

tombs by the past Muslim monarchs. But, in almost every village and town across Pakistan, shrines of local Sufis and spiritual mentors *(pirs)* attract a steady stream of visitors and offerings. The men maintaining these shrines and graveyards around them are called *dervishes, saieens,* or *malangs,* and the local people greatly respect them and look after their mundane needs.[9]

Pakistani Christians celebrate Christmas and Easter by going to the churches and visiting graveyards of their relatives. Hindus have religious festivals such as Diwali, Holi, and Dusehra, which are also holidays, and the Sikhs have their holy days celebrating the important events from the lives of their Gurus.[10] The visits to Nankana Sahib and Panja Sahib—the two holy Gurdawaras—are special occasions for Sikhs.[11] Parsis or Zoroastrians are a small and affluent community mostly confined to Karachi and celebrate their religious festivals, especially remembering the Prophet Zoroaster and the beginning of the old ceremonial Persian year. They are known for their charity.[12]

Baisakhi is one of the oldest surviving festivals from the ancient Indus Valley culture and is shared by Hindus, Christians, Sikhs, and Muslims as it falls during the harvest season. This festival, like Diwali, is a happy occasion and is characterized by fun and rural fairs. Holi is another colorful and happy occasion when Hindus make special feasts, have musical performances, and throw colored powders on one another to show good feelings.

Basant is a happy festival of special significance that falls on the first day of spring, and kite flying in the Old City of Lahore has transformed it into a gala tourist attraction. This festival certainly predates the advent of Islam in South Asia, but over the successive centuries, Punjabis have celebrated it as a major occasion. Following a lull soon after Partition it resurged. It takes place in the older parts of Lahore and has revived some of the historic landmarks there. Weeks before the kite-flying contests, professionals prepare kites and strings of various hues and sizes. They ensure the razor-like sharpness of the string *(doar)* to allow their kite to cut off other kites. During the contest, locally known as *paicha,* spectators become impassioned and then run after the fallen kite and rip it apart. Thus, it becomes a boisterous occasion with the shouting and exercise overwhelming everyone. Some old-time Lahorites take great pleasure in taking their guests to their ancestral houses in the old city, where elaborate food is prepared with the focus on traditional dishes. Women wear their best and most colorful attire. With thousands of colorful kites on the skyline, the rooftops come alive with parties and a mosaic of colors. Basant has attracted major domestic, regional, and foreign tourism, and its symbolism in reviving an age-old Punjabi identity at all levels is quite significant.[13] Basant also often coincides with the cricket season in South Asia

Dhani bulls on parade in the Salt Range. Courtesy of the author.

and the Gulf, with the Indian spectators often coming over to Lahore to enjoy the matches as well the Basant fiesta.

Rural fairs take place either in the proximity of the Sufi shrines or are held in the open spaces. Rural Pakistan is shown at its best with a permeating influence of ancient Indus Valley traditions. The rural fair is a time of rest and recreation for villagers with a respite from the tough life cycle. Here, traditional sports such as *kabbadi*,[14] wrestling, horse races, *chowgan*,[15] and camel races are held. Farmers, who are rewarded on such occasions by the government for rearing healthy cattle, parade their prized bulls and other animals, accompanied by drum beats. Some farmers may bring quails, partridges, and roosters for fights and contests. The boisterous competitions amidst some betting go on till late in the evening.

The telling of stories and jokes occurs in the evening when the water pipe *(huqqa)* and endless supply of tea add to the relaxed ambience. Small tea stalls and sweet shops are set up next to the animal pens. Traditional sweet pudding mixed with raisins and almonds *(halwah)* is the main rural dessert and remains the specialty of all such feasts. Barbers, who for countless generations have shared the ancestral and professional tradition of preparing *halwah* and other festival cuisine, display their special cooking skills out in the open.

The camel race is a favorite pastime in the desert regions, but there is always the fear that some camels may go astray, taking their riders into the crowds. Camels are also made to compete to lift the maximum loads. The race horses are well-trained professionals who run in a straight line at a full speed with the rider holding a shiny spear for tent pegging. Bouts of wrestling, running races, and boxing matches are other events at such fairs. Astrologers, traditional mendicants *(hakims)*, snake charmers, jugglers, men with monkeys, and impersonators *(behroopias)* entertain everyone.

The central and provincial governments also encourage special festivals such as Jashn-i-Khyber to promote the Pushtun component of Pakistan and Jashn-i-Murree to celebrate Pakistan's melting-pot hill resort, where people from all over the country annually throng to avoid the scorching heat of the plains and deserts. Jashn-i-Kohsaran celebrates Pakistan's pride in having the world's highest mountains peaks, such as K-2, Rakaposhi, Tirich Mir, and Nanga Parbat. They tower over some of the largest glaciers in the world, which are constantly feeding the mighty Indus. The Shandur Pass in the Karakorams lies at the altitude of 12,000 feet and is known to be the birth-place of polo. Each year during the brief summer season, the grassy mountainous terrain comes alive with the numerous horsemen, their supporters and general fans streaming in from across the valleys to see the annual contest between the teams.[16]

The tribal Pakistanis also celebrate religious and national festivals and have similar cattle shows. The tribal fairs on the Frontier are exceptionally unique as here men carry all kinds of guns and wear turbans of various sizes and colors that—along with their accents—identify their clans. At these fairs, unlike in the Punjab and Sindh, one finds a greater use of snuff—both brown and green—although the youths would not consume it in front of the elders. The fairs at the Sufi shrines here share rituals and offerings like their counterparts in Balochistan, Punjab, and Sindh. The poetry sessions, joke telling, accounts of travels into the interiors of Afghanistan and Pakistan, and stories of hunts across the mountains rejuvenate the communal atmosphere at such fairs.

The shrines of well-known Sufis are quite acculturative as people from various ethnic backgrounds mingle together, expecting minimum comfort and sharing similar rituals and experiences. It is not unusual to come across Afghans or Iranian Baloch at the Sufi festivals in Pakistan. The visitors go back satisfied after having accomplished their mission and carry alms and charms with them to share with the relatives back home. The visitors from distant lands use donkeys, mules, and camels for transportation while the poor amongst them simply walk for days, but are looked after by the rural communities all along their routes. These informal networks of hospitality and generosity fall within the cultural and religious milieu where travelers are viewed as God-sent guests who have to be tended to. A humane and generous folk culture supersedes all other considerations and guarantees a safe chain of mosques, shrines, and hamlets all interlocked in a rather curious network. Even the jugglers, snake charmers, monkey men, and *hakims* (traditional physicians) find shelter and food at the local mosques or in someone's guest room.

Sufi festival with dervishes preparing for dhammal on the drums. Courtesy of the author.

LEISURE AND PLEASURE

Leisure is certainly part and parcel of every human society, although it is essentially contingent on factors such as economy and national security. While modern-day travel, holidays, and gala celebrations may require wealth and resourcefulness, the traditional and less-privileged Pakistani communities find ways to entertain themselves. The religious and national holidays afford Pakistanis time to relink with families, and marriages and even funerals have their social and cathartic impact. In addition, the traditional breaks within the agricultural cycle allow time to enjoy some rural fairs and festivities. For instance, even during harvest season, inviting other farmers to share the work usually turns into a festivity with drums and flutes played by village minstrels, who egg on youths to use their sickles more rapidly. Similarly, because the time for ploughing and sowing is short, peasants help one another. On such occasions, elaborate food—several meat dishes accompanied by the essential—*halwah*—is prepared to invigorate the bodies and spirits, while village minstrels play on their drums and flutes. Farmers find time in the evenings or during the fairs to talk about their crops, fields, and cattle, and share information. The *huqqa* certainly becomes a major bonding tool as the farmers sit in the open during the summer evenings or bundle up inside some room during winter.

The rainy season—Monsoons—is fun for everyone in the village as the rivers, streams, and water reservoirs fill up and swimming competitions are held. The Monsoons may also wreak havoc through floods and by flattening the mud houses owned by these farmers. Yet this remains the greenest and brightest time of the year. Dams at Tarbela, Mangla, Rawal, and Warsak fill up, with the country expecting fewer power breaks and better harvests in the irrigated areas downstream. The Indus River with all its four other counterparts—the Jhelum, Chenab, Ravi, and Sutlej—fumes with splashing currents while several other tributaries, such as the Kabul, Kurram, and Soan turn into big expanses. The Chenab, flowing through the middle of the Indus Basin, comes alive with gushing water and fresh soil brought down from the Himalayas and Kashmir Hills. Mangoes and other tropical fruits and vegetables fill the grocery markets. Most of the fairs take place during this time, and the traditional Indus Valley sweets made by local bakers attract everyone. Competitions are held at these fairs when barter trade, tea sessions, and traditional sports such as hounds running after hares add flavor to the village life.

SPORTS: OLD AND NEW

People in cities and small towns organize cricket matches or play football and hockey. Pakistanis enjoy playing and discussing cricket and many of them have their favorite teams and players. The Indo-Pakistani cricket matches are the most engaging and emotionally taxing games of their type as both the nations sit glued to their television sets. Even in faraway villages, tribal hamlets, or Afghan refugee camps, children are seen playing cricket or watch running commentary on the screen. However, the rural children usually play with marbles or have games such as chowgan, which is the origin of modern-day polo. Cricket, quite similar to baseball, evolved in England several centuries back, although it gradually became an elitist pastime over the village commons on a summer afternoon.[17] Soon, it engaged the empire builders in the subtropical regions all the way from Africa to New Zealand, although it was not able to make inroads into North America. The twentieth century was the time of expansion and popularity for cricket across the British Empire, often remembered as its golden past.[18]

In South Asia, the colonial officials and local educated Indians also organized teams to play test matches extended over several days. Indian players mostly came from princely families or urban elite groups. After independence, India and Pakistan developed their own cricket teams, and they were admitted into the world's governing body, now known as the International Cricket Committee (ICC). The West Indies had the first foreign team to visit Pakistan in 1948. In its first overseas tour in 1949, the Pakistani cricket team, captained by Mian Saeed, defeated Sri Lanka, but the major turning point occurred in 1952, when the India-Pakistan match series was inaugurated. On their first-ever visit to the rival neighbor, a comparatively new team spectacularly defeated India at Lucknow, and national celebrations were jubilant.

This was the beginning of the era of the well-known trio of cricketers, Omar Kureishi, Jamshed Marker, and Abdul Hafeez Kardar.

In 1954, Pakistan proved to be the only country to win a test match in England, because of Fazal Mahmud's bowling and Wazir Mohammed's batting at the Oval. Kardar, Mahmud, and Mohammed took Pakistani cricket to a new height, adding to the country's pride and establishing a celebrity culture.[19] Cricket was no more a mere national pride, it was a passion, and players such as Mushtaque, Hanif, and Intikhab soon ensured the continuity of a golden era.[20] After a brief lull in the 1960s and early 1970s, with the infusion of new blood with the arrival of players such as Zaheer Abbas, Asif Iqbal, Javed Miandad, Imran Khan, and Abdul Qadir, Pakistani cricket experienced a revival at a time when India also prided itself on the advent of Sunil Gavskar, Kapil Dev, and Ravi Shastri. The fans on both sides eagerly waited for the India-Pakistan encounters at a time when one-day series were growing in popularity because of their quick results and exuberant action within a limited time, unlike the extended test matches. Simultaneously, given the presence of a South Asian diaspora in the Gulf States, soon Sharjah began to attract matches outside the subcontinent.[21]

The appointment of Imran Khan as the captain in 1982 ushered greater coherence and coordination among Pakistani cricketers and the game took a new turn.[22] In 1986, with his sixer at the decisive India-Pakistan match at Sharjah, Javed Miandad made it into cricket's history books, ensuring Pakistan's dramatic victory over India, and his was called "the shot of the century" by the television commentators. Imran Khan was greatly helped by two new talented bowlers, Wasim Akram and Waqar Younis, whose fast speed and maneuvers, along with the spin bowling by Mushtaq Ahmed, ensured more wickets for Pakistan until in the World Cup Series in 1992, when Pakistan emerged as the champion. Pakistani cricketers such as Saeed Anwar, Salim Malik, Inzimamul Haq, and Shahid Afridi have significant scores to their credit, but after the retirement of Imran Khan, Wasim Akram, and Waqar Younis, the team needs persistent batsmen and fast bowlers. Shoaib Akhtar may have been the fastest bowler in the world, but the team seeks spinners and batsmen brimming with self-confidence and staying power.

The contributions by non-Muslim Pakistani cricketers such as Yousaf Youhana and Danesh Kaneria are universally recognized in the country. Constant and lively television coverage, the Indo-Pakistani competition, and the Internet commentaries all have ensured the popularity of cricket, even though it actually began as an English pastime and only symbolized at that time an imperial pursuit. Pakistanis play cricket in inner cities, parks, and rural compounds, and in the winding alleys of tribal settlements, and any visitor to the land is aware of the nation's preoccupation with cricket.[23] The influence of the game has been so pervasive that the children of the Afghan refugees born in Pakistan also developed a fondness for the game and even the Taliban had to relent during their brief tenure in Afghanistan. Pakistani youths discuss cricket in their social get-togethers and debate over the careers of famous cricketers, especially when their team is not performing well. A loss to India delivers a serious blow to the nation's mood, and column after column in dozens of English and scores of Urdu newspapers keep on analyzing the performance and pitfalls of the individual batsmen and bowlers. On such occasions, rumors of match fixing are also routinely aired, more out of grudge as the nation invests a great amount of its hopes in the team.

Other than cricket, field hockey and squash have been the major sports where Pakistanis have won championships, and, like cricket, these sports have also witnessed their ups and downs. The proverbial Khans[24] such as Jahangir and Jan Sher—all from the same family—with their unique achievements in squash, and Samiullah—"the flying horse"—in hockey[25] took these games to their new heights, although in recent years it has been difficult to maintain those standards. But it is cricket that excels all other games and sports in the country. There are some women cricketers in the country, but it is mainly in table tennis and field hockey that Pakistan has its major women's teams. During the 1980s, under the strict Islamist regime of General Zia-ul-Haq, sports among women experienced a serious decline as women were under pressure to assume traditional roles. Wearing shorts or swimsuits was abhorred, and the country's entire focus turned toward cricket.

Despite the salience of modern games and sports, Pakistanis, for the most part, have persisted in their traditional heritage of leisure activities. One such game, wrestling, involves traditional families of *pehlawaans,* mostly from central Punjab, whereas *kabbadi* remains popular across rural Punjab. Wrestling, as in Iran, requires regular practice sessions *(kasrat)* and special arenas, trainers, and rituals all characterizing this game, where other than body building, the knowledge of a variety of tactics is certainly vital.[26] *Kabbadi* is played by five to six players on each side who stand in a semi-circle with a line drawn in the middle dividing the two teams. Each player goes over to the other side and while repeating a word such as *kabbadi,* challenges the opposite side to tackle him. If he loses the breath and is unable to make it to the dividing line, his team loses the point to the rivals. In other words, keeping the breath and being able to touch the line after a tackle are the objectives, which certainly require some amount of stamina and physical prowess. More than one rival cannot tackle the player at a time, although he is free to challenge the semi-circle manned by the rival team. This game is usually played on summer afternoons and at the village fairs. Often, two localities of the same town may have two rival teams, and matches could easily end up in emotional outbursts, but the local leaders, volunteers, and police officials try to maintain order between the noisy and feuding supporters.

Schools, police, and defense forces are all encouraged to have regular *kabbadi* teams, and the government sponsors regional and national championships. Another form of *kabbadi* involves a player who runs fast ahead of two players from the rival team and is supposed to make it back to the starting point after a complete circle and also without being felled by the chasing players. This form does not involve any verbal exercise but rather depends more on running and tactics to outdo two rivals fully determined to bring one down. These games have local sponsors, but cricket, squash, and hockey have international sponsors, mostly the cigarette companies, who have been concentrating on the developing world since their decline in the West. The rural games also involve cockfights and similar contests between quails, partridges, and dogs. Usually considered to be cruel by serious-minded people, these contests nevertheless take place illicitly, causing quite a bit of gambling and betting.

The rural children improvise with some old and new games and pastimes, which may involve hide-and-seek, marbles, catching birds, or swimming in the local pond. Rural girls, after helping their parents in the fields and visiting the local mosque to gain basic Islamic instruction, might engage themselves with dolls or embroidery. Their urban counterparts may have computers, mobile phones, and opportunities to try some dance movements, depending upon the reaction from their elders. Indian films and Pakistani dramas naturally pull them toward the world of fashions and beautification of hands by creating floral patterns from henna. The urban youths have computer games and school teams of hockey and cricket, and they might arrange occasional matches with friends in the neighborhoods. They may also venture into a growing number of gymnasiums, and some of them, especially from the affluent families, might afford swimming, horse riding, and motorcycling.

Pakistanis like picnicking in the evenings during the summer months, as it gets very hot and humid in the Indus Valley. The parks fill up with families and vendors. The well-to-do go to Murree, Swat, Ziarat, Abbotabad, Northern Areas, and other cooler resorts. Parties and feasting on family and religious occasions offer excuses to try on newer fashions and gather to talk. Live or recorded music accompanies such occasions. In urban areas men and women may not be totally segregated from each other and even may be dancing together at some parties, although the society generally frowns upon the free mixing of sexes. Most of the leisure activities remain communal and often under the watchful eyes of peers and elders.

Many affluent Pakistani families go abroad on holidays. Britain, the United States, the Gulf, and Southeast Asia are the main destinations for prosperous

Pakistanis who may combine trade with tourism. Dubai, in recent years, has emerged as a major shopping and sporting spot for South Asians, especially in view of travel difficulties between India and Pakistan. In addition, the Gulf Emirates account for a considerable South Asian diaspora—both skilled and unskilled—who organize cricketing and charity events besides holding special fashion shows. Most of the informal trade and travel in South Asia, worth several billion dollars, passes through Dubai, and the local educated Pakistanis make special arrangements on national and religious holidays. They hold literary functions such as poetry recitals *(musha'airas)* and art shows, making Dubai and Sharjah the extended centers of their leisure and creative pastimes.[27] Pilgrimage or Hajj to the Holy Places in Saudi Arabia and visits to shrines in Iraq remain the major desires of religious Pakistanis, who save money for years to buy their passage and stay at these places. Young people work to ensure the sponsorship of their elders to the Holy Places at least once in their lifetime and consider it as an important step in their atonement. People help others in the same locality and also donate money for the upkeep of shrines and mosques. The diaspora Pakistanis also assist these institutions and their attached seminaries, while more and more educated professionals help national organizations. Despite serious restrictions on Muslim charities after the events of September 11, 2001, at the behest of the United States and some other governments, Pakistanis are able to operate several reputable organizations in the diaspora. They enthusiastically support the commendable work by charities in Pakistan, including the Edhi Foundation, which runs several free hospitals, shelter houses, ambulances, and orphanages.

Depending upon class and taste, Pakistanis enjoy a variety of other activities including concerts, *qawallis*, and art exhibits at private and national galleries. Pakistanis like watching Indian films. They listen to Bollywood music, although the religious and traditional among them would prefer their own plays and *qawalli* music. The middle class and urban Pakistanis enjoy listening to their favorite Urdu *ghazal* singers or folk musicians and also heatedly discuss political and religious issues.[28] The *qawalli* sessions held at private residences or at Sufi shrines especially on Thursday evenings have their own spiritual and culinary attraction. Pakistani women enjoy shopping, often on their own or accompanied by servants and drivers, as their men are mostly not interested in shopping. However, there are always young men in these markets and bazaars looking appreciatively at well-dressed girls. The ice cream parlors, *paan* shops, and fast food restaurants stay open until late with groups of young men and women arriving in their cars or on motorbikes. During the summer months, in the evenings and late at night on the weekends, many areas in big cities come alive.

Pakistan can certainly afford more sporting events and literary and cultural festivals, as there are not enough activities especially for younger people and women. However, given the growing population, economic bottlenecks, and ideological contentions, such pastimes can be understood also in the context that for most of the ordinary Pakistanis just making ends meet remains the main concern. Here, both the government and the affluent sections of the society would have to affirm a more charitable attitude, away from the familiar mundane chorus of other national priorities.

NOTES

1. There are hundreds of books on this prominent Muslim thinker of the twentieth century, focusing on his poetry, politics, philosophy, and personality. His efforts were devoted to enthusing Muslims by inculcating a greater self-awareness *(khuddi)* and dynamism, which he considered an important prerequisite for a Muslim renaissance *(Nishat-i-Saaniya)*. Iqbal believed in reconstructing Islamic thoughts and practices, away from clerical and monarchical authoritarianism. See Muhammad Iqbal, *The Reconstruction of Religious Thought in Islam* (Lahore: Ashraf, 1999) (reprint). Iqbal's Ph.D. dissertation was devoted to the study of metaphysical developments in Persia and was published in 1934. His poetry collections—both in Urdu and Persian—are widely read by Pakistanis, Iranians, and Central Asians. Interest in Iqbal has reemerged in recent years in the former Soviet republics and likewise among other Muslim communities, given the challenges from a powerful modernity.

2. For more on him, see Stanley Wolpert, *Jinnah of Pakistan* (Berkeley: University of California Press, 1984).

3. The sixth of September has a specific significance as on this day in 1965, Indian troops crossed the international borders to attack Pakistan. Pakistanis fought a five-times bigger and more resourceful enemy rather valiantly and this 17-day war over Kashmir ended in a stalemate. A smaller Pakistan air force also won the heart of the nation and thus the seventh of September is devoted to its remembrance.

4. For the military's role, see Hasan Askari-Rizvi, *The Military and Politics in Pakistan, 1947–1997* (Lahore: Sang-e-Meel, 2000); and Stephen P. Cohen, *The Idea of Pakistan* (Washington, DC: Brookings Institution, 2004).

5. For more details, see Alastair Lamb, *Kashmir: A Disputed Legacy, 1846–1990* (Hertingfordbury: Roxford, 1991).

6. For information on Shia Islam, see Yam Richard, *Shi'ite Islam,* trans. Antonia Nevill (Oxford: Blackwell, 1995).

7. The Hijri calendar traces its origins from the Prophet Muhammad's migration from his native Makkah to Medina in A.D. 622. He eventually died and was buried in Medina. "Hijra" means migration, and the Hijri calendar is based on lunar movement and is thus shorter than its Gregorian counterpart by 10 days. Therefore, Muslim festivals such as Eids or Ramadan occur at different times and seasons.

8. The Prophet's centrality in the Islamic ethos and beliefs remains supreme and Muslims consider it their duty to defend his personality. For more on him, see Karen Armstrong, *Muhammad: A Western Attempt to Understand Islam* (London: Gollancz, 1992).

9. Many of these ascetics look like Sadhus and hippies with long, unwashed hair, and layers of beads around their necks. Like Buddha they also carry begging bowls and often dance at the shrines until they enter some kind of trance *(haal)*. The purists criticize such practices and rituals; ascetics remind them of non-Islamic influences and fatalist attitudes.

10. It is also called a festival of lights when scores of earthen oil lamps *(diyas)* are lit signaling hope and happiness. Dusehra is meant to celebrate the recovery of Sita by Ram after he had defeated Rawan.

11. Guru Nanak was born in Nankana Sahib into a peasant family. The town lies about 30 miles outside Lahore. Punja Sahib is situated by the Grand Trunk Road and is adjacent to the historic towns of Taxila and Wah. Located by a hillside, a stream flows through the temple, which is sacred to Sikhs. It is believed that a rock was falling off the hill yet was stopped by a Sikh Guru with his bare hand. A rock in the temple carries the print of the hand with five fingers. That is why it is called *Punja*—the palm with five fingers.

12. The trained ministers conduct the ceremonies and festivals in the temples. The ministers also look after the funerary place, called *Maabad Khana* or the Tower of Silence.

13. For an interesting study of Basant, see Richard McGill Murphy, "Performing Partition in Lahore," in *The Partitions of Memory: The Afterlife of the Division of India,* ed. Suvir Kaul (Delhi: Permanent Black, 2001).

14. Two teams divided by a line, which is the demarcation point for them, play this game. One player goes to the other side and is to be tackled by an opponent while trying to get back to the line within a specified time. The players wear loin cloths and are usually young males of the rival clans or villages fighting it out in sport.

15. This is again an old Southern and Central Asian game, which is akin to polo and is played by horse riders. It is, however, different from *Buzkashi*, the famous Afghan game in which a slaughtered goat replaces the ball.

16. For an eyewitness account, see Michael Palin, *Himalaya* (London: Weidenfeld, 2004), pp. 36–40. This volume is based on a BBC Television series.

17. Cricket has its own supporters and defenders from all kinds of class and ethnic backgrounds. The well-known West Indian thinker, C.L.R. James, was a great cricket fan. See his *Beyond a Boundary* (London: Serpent's Tail, 2000) (reprint).

18. David Frith, *The Golden Age of Cricket, 1890–1914* (Guildford: Lutterworth, 1978).

19. For details, see A.H. Kardar, *Test Status on Trial* (Karachi: National Publications, 1955).

20. For details, see Omar Noman, *Pride and Passion: An Exhilarating Half Century of Cricket in Pakistan* (Karachi: Oxford University Press, 1999).

21. These matches developed their own festival-like atmosphere and ensured the participation of celebrities from Bollywood and Lollywood. For more on Pakistani cricket see Q. Ahmed, *Pakistan Book of Cricket, 1991* (Karachi: Cricketprint, 1992).

22. See, Imran Khan, *All Round View* (London: Mandarin, 1988); and I. Tenant, *Imran Khan* (London: Gollancz, 1995).

23. Geoffrey Moorhouse, *To The Frontier* (London: Hodder, 1984). This intrepid English travel writer, while crisscrossing the country during the early 1980s, found himself playing cricket with the local players near the train station in Quetta.

24. See Dicky Rutnagur, *A History of Squash in Pakistan* (Karachi: Oxford University Press, 1997).

25. Sydney Friskin, *Going for Gold: Pakistan at Hockey* (Karachi: Oxford University Press, 1997.

26. These wrestlers have their own diet and masseurs and regularly visit the Sufi shrines. They patronize the traditional horse-drawn *tonga* for their movements and have huge followings in the older cities.

27. South Asians have significantly uplifted the cultural and economic life in the Gulf States. Other than running businesses and trade, South Asians are represented in the local English media. News and views on South Asia make banner headlines and take visible space in the English-language press.

28. *Ghazal* is a romantic form of poetry where each verse embodies a different theme and is sung in a semiclassical style. The genre originated in Arabic poetry and came into Urdu via Persian.

SUGGESTED READINGS

Khan, Imran. *All Round View.* London: Mandarin, 1988.

Noman, Omar. *Pride and Passion: An Exhilarating Half Century of Cricket in Pakistan.* Karachi: Oxford University Press, 1999.

Palin, Michael. *Himalaya.* London: Weidenfeld, 2004.

Rutnagur, Dicky. *A History of Squash in Pakistan.* Karachi: Oxford University Press, 1997.

8

Performing Arts and Film

To Europe leave the dance of serpent limb:
The prophet's power is born of spirit's dance,
That breeds the craving flesh, the sweating palm,
This breeds the race of pilgrim and of prince.

—Muhammad Iqbal[1]

Pakistani art represents transregional and crosscultural influences. The powerful realities of Pakistan including its ancient and modern heritage and its location as an Asian crossroads, and a pluralistic ethos collectively are reflected as well in its arts and crafts. The performing arts can be grouped into classical, folk, and popular varieties. Classical performing arts include dances, such as Khattak, Bhangra, Jhoomer, and Ludi, and musical genres such as *qawalli*, *ghazal*, and ballads. These folk traditions are performed on special occasions and have been inherited from an ancient past. The popular culture consists of popular songs, films, dramas, and even Westernized dances. These arts are recreational.

Music

Before Pakistani ancestors started drawings sketches on the cave walls or on the boulders in prehistoric times, they had already developed communications through spoken languages aided by signs and specific body movements. Like the birds and animals, sharing the same kingdom, these early human communities used their leisure time and creativity to make music. Early ballads and epics were performed individually or in a chorus. They ensured bonding and a shared heritage for generations to come. These songs were about battles, defeats, loves, deaths, and favorite animals and were symbolic tributes to powerful forces of nature all around. Artifacts from the Indus Valley include the well-known Indus seals, which include depictions of deities happily dancing and others who may appear angry and intent upon revenge. Dances were meant to pacify the enraged divine ego so as to solicit rain and a bountiful harvest. Pestilence, famine, and invasions were other scourges that had to be warded off through communal entreaties. Thus, during the subsequent Hindu, Jain, Buddhist, Greek, and Muslim phases, collective activities, both for pleasure as well as for sacred purposes, recurred. The devotional hymns *(Bhajans)* and circular dance movement *(Bhangra)* date from the ancient era, as do the various classical Indian songs, called *Ragas,* which are sung at specific times of the day or night and require years of practice—*riaz*—to acquire a command over their styles, tunes, and contents.[2] They combined sacred and secular dimensions of the ancient Hindu, Jain, and Buddhist periods and are not mere praises of deities but, allegorically, like Persian and Urdu romantic poems *(ghazals)*, celebrate human physique, virtues, and pathos.

In Pakistan there were classical dancers who were adept in Kathak and such other specialized varieties of dance traditions. They were born into families *(gharanas)* that had practiced this art form for centuries. After Pakistan's independence, Prime Minister H. S. Suhrawardy during the late 1950s invited Ghanshyam and his wife to open up a dance and music academy in Karachi. By the 1960s, there were a few such dance schools still operational, but in the 1980s they were closed down. The regime and its affiliate elite narrowly defined traditional Indian dances as Hindu culture and imposed all kinds of restrictions. Many leading classical dancers like Naheed Siddiqui went into exile. A few, such as Seema Kermani, stayed.

Intentionally ignoring the Indus Valley origins of these traditions, General Zia-ul-Haq's Islamization suffocated art forms including music, dances, and the theater, and the laws especially oppressed women. Like Women's Action Forum (WAF) and such other organizations, the women classicists established their Tehrik-i-Niswan (women's movement) in 1980 to confront these formidable challenges to the arts. In its conference in Karachi in 1981, the Tehrik determined to fight these official restrictions and societal strictures. It has worked to preserve classical dance, theater, and music via lectures, seminars, and video material. It appears that in the new century there might be more prospects for such creative activities.[3] But, again it depends upon the Indo-Pakistani relationship and also if Pakistan reverts to its original charter of maturing into a tolerant and democratic society.

CLASSICAL AND QAWALLI TRADITIONS

Pakistanis have varying attitudes toward poetry and music, based on their religious views. Most of them would have no problem with poetry, especially if it is of devotional kind, although they, by temperament, relish romantic witticisms. However, music, despite its popularity amongst a vast section of society, is still a taboo among the extreme religious sections. They would prefer only oral renditions with no musical accompaniment.

Pakistani religious festivities and ceremonies, on occasions, include singing and performing. Poems praising Allah *(hamad)* and the Prophet *(na'at)* are sung without any instrumental accompaniment or dancing, although the processions on religious days involve wider communal participation. The Prophet's birthday, the twelfth of the third month in the lunar calendar, includes processions of people singing. During the first month *(Muharram)*, the martyrdom of Imam Hussein, the Prophet's grandson, is commemorated not only by singing moving elegies but also by rhythmic chest beating as black-clad men and women take to the streets to weep and mourn. Even the memory of Hussein's personal horse *(Zuljinnah)* is evoked by parading specially decorated horses, reminding the mourners of the great tragedy that befell the Prophet's household. The chest-beating Shias may also use chains and small knives to bleed themselves. In the mosques, clerics and special singers recount the stories of Hussein's turbulent experience. The Saraiki language usually becomes the lingua franca on such occasions because of its poignant eloquence.

The classical South Asian dances and accompanying lyrics, despite their roots in the pre-Islamic era, developed over the subsequent centuries, especially during the Muslim era (A.D. 712–1857) when arts and literature flourished within a larger context of Indo-Islamic culture. Persian, and likewise Arabic and Turkish, not only connected India with a larger world of Islam to the West, North, and East; it equally offered an entire heritage of various arts that have been inherited by the contemporary states in the regions. Despite a greater emphasis on political and cultural separatism, these common antecedents still remain visible. For instance, *qawalli* is a collective semiclassical form of music in which Persian words mingle with Urdu or Hindi or borrow heavily from other widely used regional languages. The instruments and tunes reflect synthesis and thus become an authentic South Asian medley. *Qawalli* flourished under the Delhi Sultans when Muslim Sufis established their monasteries across South Asia and offered an egalitarian fellowship to people of different creeds and castes. The eleventh-century poetry, mainly in Persian, celebrates human dignity and spiritual rootedness with God through Light—*Noor*—where a saint *(pir)* is the mentor *(murshid)*, whose disciples *(murids)* follow him to seek intercession with the Creator. The saint not only creates an equitable sense of community, he or she also ensures the realization of their earthly and spiritual needs.

Data Gunj Bakhsh, buried in Lahore, Moeenud Din Chishti at Ajmer, Nizamud Din in Delhi, Bahaud Din Zakariya in Multan, and several other well-known spiritual personalities all across the subcontinent were linked with other Sufi orders in West Asia and China.[4] Ali Hajveri, known as Data Gunj Bakhsh, was one of the earliest Sufis to reach the Indus Valley, and besides his propagation of Islam, he left two classical volumes of research in Arabic. Famous as the leading spiritual mentor of Lahore even after more than eight centuries, his shrine is thronged by thousands every day and his annual *urs* during the summer attracts millions more to Lahore, which is itself known as *Data Ki Nagari* (Data's City). The shrines of Gunj Bakhsh, Mian Mir, Bhit Shah, Shahbaz Qalandar, Farid Gunj Shakar, Shah Chan Chiragh. and Bari Imam have *qawallis* taking place most of the time, although Thursday turns into a special occasion when large numbers of Pakistanis visit with their offerings. It is here that one thinks of Amir Khusrow of Delhi who, in fact, pioneered many of these lyrics and their renditions.

Khusrow, a disciple of Nizamud Din Auliya, and buried next to him in Delhi, was the synthesizer of several lingual and musical traditions. A saint and poet in his own right, Khusrow invented the harmonium, the quintessential Indian musical instrument and an essential part of the *qawalli* music. While benefiting from the old *ragas*, the poet-Sufi-musician Khusrow promoted *qawalli* songs and music and equally pioneered several classical Indian lyrics. Khusrow remains the major influence in South Asia even after almost a thousand years, and the application of technology and a bit of Western tunes have further consolidated his preeminence not only as a Sufi master but also as a pioneer-artist.

A harmonium, a few smaller Indian drums *(tablas)* and a *sitar* (literally, three strings) are the main instruments used in the *qawalli* chorus. The number of the *qawalls* could vary from 4 to 10 and even more, although the lead *qawall* is always seated in the middle and, besides conducting the entire rendition, sings most of the verses. His lyrics are repeated by other *qawalls*, whose rhythmic handclaps accompany the tunes at the right intervals. The singers at Buddhist, Hindu, Jain, and Sikh temples have also adopted these *qawalli* tunes. They can be seen performing early in the morning on the numerous Indian cable and satellite networks.

All across South Asia there are these traditional families—*gharanas*—performing classical music including *ragas* and *qawallis* or even simply instrumental music. The universal popularization of *qawalli* in Asia and in the West results from the great professional skills and personal devotion of people such as the late Nusrat Fateh Ali Khan, the late Ustaad Wilayat Khan, and Salamat Ali Khan. Nusrat Fateh Ali Khan, before his death in London in 1997, had already put *qawalli* and Pakistan both on the world map. His Persian, Urdu, Sindhi, and Punjabi lyrics, which enthralled all types of audience, brought a unique pluralism to this neoclassical form of music. He would always begin his session with a devotional praise for Allah, followed by his homage to the Prophet and all the saints, before moving on to subsequent Sufi literature.

In the 1990s, Peter Gabriel, the British rock star, helped Nusrat in mixing Western tunes with the classical *qawalli* pieces, where tablas, sitar, and a rhythmic handclapping would usually accompany Nusrat's chorus of six singers. Nusrat's own renditions within a synthesized and captivating Sufi tradition made their mark on Pakistani and Western audiences who could relate with this powerful effort at a time when media mostly harped on "a clash of cultures." Some of his solo songs, performed as *ghazals* or mixed with the faster Western beats, have equally proven popular. At this juncture, Nusrat combined Punjabi Sufi literature with its Persian, Sindhi, and Urdu counterparts, and his multidisciplinary immersion and melodious presentations turned *qawalli* into the mainstream music. In the early 1990s, Nusrat's concerts, both in Pakistan and abroad, used to be sell-outs, and it appeared that this master artist had turned this classical heritage into a respectable popular genre with East reaching West. Nusrat donated most of his money for charitable causes in South Asia and lived a rather austere life.[5]

Nusrat Fateh Ali Khan's versatile music was not merely confined to the popularization of Sufi music or *qawalli*; it equally universalized *ghazal* and other popular songs through a semiclassical medium. Thus, his intermixing of old and new, Eastern and Western themes and styles turned him into a familiar household name everywhere. For instance, his "Mustt, Mustt" is an old lyrical song, which the Muslim ascetics *(dervishes, malangs,* and *fakirs)* sing at the shrines until their whirling moments become ecstatic, or a state of *haal* descends upon them.[6] The purists may ridicule trance brought about by *qawalli* and by dancing dervishes, yet many young people also join in the repetitive beats of "Yaa Ali, Yaa Ali," or "Lal Qalandar." To the literalists, such actions are a travesty or merely a result of hashish, but for many it is a purific state where all kinds of divides come to an end and the body loses control to a transcending soul. *Mustt* is an Urdu word for an ecstatic elephant, which might have been otherwise quite gentle but becomes enraged.

In the same vein, "Hey Jamalo" is a famous Sindhi lyric, which *murids* and *malangs* sing at the shrines of Lal Shahbaz Qalandar in Sehwan Sharif, and herein the Sufi is literally addressed seeking his personal help and guidance. Every *qawall* has tried this mystical song but Nusrat's rendition remains the best. The Urdu poem, "Afreen, Afreen," written by Javed Akhtar, the well-known Indian Urdu poet, or Nusrat's remix of Qabil Ajmeri's "Sitaro Tum to So Jao" are two good examples of his diverse art, although the total number of his renditions may go into the hundreds. Even in the diaspora, other than Pakistani Muslims, Indian Punjabis, Gujaratis, and other lovers of mystical music enjoy this ode to Shahbaz Qalandar, who is referred to as Jamalo—the beautiful and magnificent. The best duo performance of this Sindhi folk-*qawalli* song was undertaken by Allan Faqir and Muhammad Ali Shehki, performed during the 1980s. Faqir, with his beard, colorful turban and an archetypal Sindhi costume, and Shehki in his Western clothes, offered mixed Sindhi and Urdu lyrics besides performing variants of two separate dance forms. Yet the synchronization proved quite effective.

Several other groups across Pakistan perform *qawallis* at shrines or at private parties and are also seen on television and in the diaspora. Ghulam Farid Sabri, Abida Parveen, Matkay Wallay, and several other *gharanas* have contributed greatly to the popularization of *qawalli* at a critical time when an onslaught by overpowering pop culture and movie music from Bollywood and Lollywood threatened its existence.

Ghazal may occasionally induce slow dancing while *qawalli* could, in some cases, lead to an ecstatic mood—*haal*. The performance by the Sufis during a *qawalli* session is a slow rhythmic dance, which eventually leads a few to a trance, until the living *pir* offers his consolation. These dances can be witnessed only at the shrines during the annual festivities—*urs*. The most famous dance performed across Pakistan at the Sufi shrines is called *dhamaal;* however, its origins are from Sindh and lower Punjab. It occurs during the annual *urs* and occasionally on Thursday evenings at Sehwan Sharif, where the famous Sufi-poet, Lal Shahbaz Qalandar, is buried. Almost every popular and semiclassical Pakistani artist has tried *dhamaal,* but melody queen Noor Jahan with her beats of "Ho Laal Meri Pat Rakhiyo" remains unsurpassed. She also attempted *dhamaal* tunes in her other songs, devoted to other Sufis, such as "Pak Pattan Tey aan Khalothi," "Bari, Bari, Imam Bari," "Mustt Qalandar Lal," "Ali, Ali, dam Ali, Ali," and "Jhoolay Lal, Jhoolay Lal," which were basically Sufi hits adopted for movies and performed by well-known actresses.

Across Pakistan, Thursday evening being reserved for Sufi offerings, one occasionally comes across dances by Sufis and dervishes at the shrines of Shah Abdul Latif of Bhit Shah in Sindh and also at the shrine of Bari Shah Latif near Islamabad. These dervishes—austere-looking wandering ascetics—who come to these shrines usually have long hair and wear green frocks, with several beads around the neck and bangles on their wrists. They may carry some instruments or even the traditional begging bowl—possibly symbolic of Buddha—and are greatly respected by the rural people. Men as well as women attribute all sorts of superhuman powers to these *pirs*, Sufis, and dervishes. Some of them may smoke hashish and are called *malangs,* but their attachment with any specific Sufi shrine ensures shelter and food as well as several disciples *(chela'as).* Even otherwise secular people may tolerate these *malangs* because, by temperament, most of the Pakistanis are not literalists and follow synthesized versions of Islam.

GHAZAL

Ghazal is a special form of poetry, which came into India from West Asia and combines love, pathos, yearning, and grief in a single couplet. A typical *ghazal*, using symbols and metaphors, would comprise several rhyming couplets. Singing a *ghazal* requires proper training as well as a mellow temperament, because a faster tempo for a *ghazal* is almost impossible. *Ghazal* is not dance music, as both the artist and listeners have to offer full attention to the sound and music, although some *ghazals* may be used in the movies as background to platonic love scenes.

The poets hold recitals—*musha'airas*—to read their poems and *ghazals* before appreciative audiences.[7] Special poetry recitals have been unique to South Asia and now to Pakistan. Here the poets gather to read out or sing their poems before a diverse audience who ponder over their expressions, imagery, metaphors, and similes while showering the poets with praise. With the decline of Urdu in post-1947 India, Pakistan has become the center of such poetry recitals. Quite a few women participate in such recitals.

Composing *ghazal* verses remains the most challenging achievement for any poet. Each couplet has to have a different meaning—*khayyal*—but rhyme and rhythms have to remain the same all through the poem. Words may matter, but it is the ideas and their expression through similes and metaphors that make this genre the most challenging. The restriction of one couplet requires mastery with ideas and words, and not every poet can achieve it; thus a tutor is often needed.

Famous Pakistani *ghazal* singers have included Malka Pukhraj, Mehdi Hassan, Iqbal Bano, Naseem Begum, Noor Jahan, S. B. John, and Tahira Sayyid. Malka Pukhraj, like other neoclassicists, grew in a household of preeminent Urdu poets and professional artists, and her renditions focused on a Mughal style. Proper hand movements and facial gestures synchronizing with the flow and ebb in the verse itself melt into the accompanying music of tablas, sitar, and harmonium. Her "Abhi To Mein Jawan Hoon" has achieved a global fame among the fans of Urdu *ghazal*. Tahira Sayyid, the daughter of Malka Pukhraj and a lawyer by training, has sung *ghazals* by Mir, Ghalib, Iqbal, Daagh, and Faiz, and in the early 1980s was selected for the cover of *National Geographic*. Attired in a traditional Mughal costume and jewelry while holding a majestic sitar and seated on a *diwan*, she reminded music lovers of the by-gone era of the Great Mughals. Iqbal Bano, Fareeda Khanum, Nahid Akhtar, and Ghulam Ali have, other noted *ghazal* singers (*gulooka'ars*), have sung for movies and also at select concerts.

Ghulam Ali, like Shaukat Ali, has tried both Urdu and Punjabi *ghazals* and songs, whereas Mehdi Hasan has simply focused on Urdu poetry. Amanat Ali

Khan and Salamat Ali Khan, scions of a noted Lahore *gharana*, represented Pakistan across the world in the specialized areas of classical and semiclassical music. Asad Amanat Ali Khan carries on their tradition. Like the *qawalls*, such artists have family traditions going back to the Mughals and even to the times of the Delhi Sultans. Noor Jahan has been a unique artist, who, to a great extent, embodied several realms in her persona and skills. She started singing in the pre-1947 era for the Bombay film industry (Bollywood) and then shifted to Lahore with her director husband, Shaukat Hussain Rizvi. She demonstrated her acting skills in some of the earliest movies, besides producing a few, but persisted with her singing. Her songs have varied from semiclassical to popular and from *qawalli* to folk, both in Urdu and Punjabi. There are several of her *ghazal* collections and some of the renditions are superb.

FOLK TRADITIONS

Given the predominantly rural composition and traditional disposition, Pakistani society enjoys its vernacular mediums, music, and jokes. Sindhi, Saraiki, Punjabi, Hindko, Pothowari, Pushto, Balochi, Shina, Brohi, and Kashmiri are some of the oldest expressions of the words, although they somehow, get defined as regional or vernacular languages. Compared with Urdu, their role as the repositories of oral and folk traditions is unparalleled and the intermixing of sacred with profane within these popular expressions is amazing. During marriage ceremonies and local concerts, amplifiers may blast the latest popular dance music from the Bollywood and Lollywood films, yet it is their folk counterpart in Punjabi or Sindhi that really enthralls the participants. In Pakistan, there are rural singers and musicians in every locality and hamlet, yet many of them have not been able to make it to the commercial markets as their skills and outputs are quite localized and undocumented. However, since the 1960s, there has been a steady effort to record various realms of folk culture, and such forms of music are being eagerly preserved. The establishment of the Institute of Folk Heritage in Islamabad has, among several others of its achievements, introduced Pakistanis to their rich and largely undocumented folk heritage. The songs, narratives, jokes, musical instruments, regional crafts, sports, and costumes all have been recorded for researchers and posterity, allowing not only a greater recognition but also ensuring their preservation. The annual Folk Festival *(Lok Mela)* in Islamabad brings in craftsmen, folk artists, and tourists from all over the country and ensures wider participation in various activities, including specialized workshops, so as to diffuse these long-held skills. The documentation of the traditional and folk music, with its strong Sufi and regional romantic components, has been preserved on cassettes and CDs, while the Internet is making it easily accessible to a global audience.[8]

Pakistan's regions have produced well-known names who have immortalized folk and semiclassical music, and they include the late Pathanay Khan, Khameeso Khan, the late Allan Faqir, Reshmaan, Abida Parveen, Ataullah Issakhelvi, and Ghulam Ali. These artists have tried *ghazals, bhajans,* and *kafis* besides the familiar terrain of *qawalli*.[9] They have mostly used Sindhi, Saraiki, and Punjabi for their music or have simply focused on instrumental music. For instance, Khameeso Khan and Allan Faqir, while always dressed in Sindhi attire, played instrumental music, whereas Pathanay Khan sang old Punjabi and Saraiki songs and kafis. In his concerts, Pathanay Khan, a native of southwestern Punjab, would either play harmonium or drums and would perform as the lead singer. People enjoyed his rendition of Baba Farid, Bulleh Shah, Waris Shah, and such other classicists. He would repeat each verse several times using varying chords and tunes, and the attentive audience would sit simply bewitched by his mastery and skills.

Reshmaan, a gypsy woman, appeared on the Pakistani music scene in the 1960s and with her husky voice and gypsy lifestyle captured the urban hearts. The themes of her songs are mostly Indus Valley romances with Sufi lyrics. She also sang ascetic poems by Manzoor Jhalla and other well-known contemporary Punjabi poets besides trying her own traditional gypsy folk lyrics.[10] Abida Parveen, a native of upper Sindh, is known for her *qawallis, kafis,* and *dohras,* which like those of Pathanay Khan, mix Sindhi with Saraiki and Punjabi. She has tried some modern Urdu *ghazals,* but her forte is semiclassical music and folk poetry.[11] Issakhelwi is not from a professional singing family background, but his folk renditions focusing on love, separation, and envy, all sung in the Mianwali accent of Punjabi and Saraiki, made him quite popular across the country. He sounded direct and different, and even non-Punjabis admired him, although his main following has come from Punjab and the Punjabi diaspora. The other folk artists known for their immersion in the Punjabi and Sindhi folk music and ballads, include Iqbal Baho, Surraya Khanum, Mussarat Nazeer, Alam Lohar, Asad Amanat Ali Khan, Mai Bhagi, Tufail Niazi, Zahida Parveen, Hamid Bela, and Jumman Khan.[12]

POPULAR MUSIC

Before the information technology revolution and the advent of satellite television and channels totally devoted to popular music, *ghazal* singers and folk musicians were devoutly watched on Pakistani television and their cassettes were always in a great demand, played in homes and by truck drivers. But the arrival of new urban groups on the music scene with the latest technologies and young audiences across the continents have largely marginalized the erstwhile monopoly of the folk musicians. Pakistani popular music, until recent times, has largely depended on the movie industry, as a typical feature film would have six to seven songs for dance purposes and also to assimilate several other themes within an otherwise longer story. Songs, thus, provided income and outlet to the poets, musicians, and dancers besides being played on the radio stations. The rise of the popular songs in Urdu and Punjabi—followed by Sindhi and Pushto—resulted from the independence of the country, establishment of radio stations, and the growth of a movie industry in Lahore (Lollywood).

The marginalization of Urdu in India and its consolidation in Pakistan as the national language, especially in the western part, created more opportunities for musicians, singers, and songwriters in the latter. Punjabi music persisted with its pre-1947 traditions but became more popular with the evolution of more Punjabi films, especially since the 1970s. With the separation of East Pakistan, Punjabis now made up the largest ethnic group, and their major share in the national economy, civil service, armed forces, and the economy, as well as the very location of Lahore in the province all ensured a large market for Punjabi music. The greater recognition of folk culture and respect for regional languages also ensured the popularization of Punjabi music. It experienced its heyday during the 1990s, when a number of pop groups from mostly affluent urban families began to adopt Punjabi as the main language of their creations. The English-speaking young men and women were soon singing Punjabi folks lyrics while sporting Punjabi clothes or plain *shalwar-kamees* combination and choosing rural locales for their video material. This ascendance of pop, and especially of Punjabi folk plus pop music, is nationwide and has occurred at a time when Urdu films and music have been experiencing a decline, largely because of more resourceful Hindi music and films from across the borders and their increased availability. The mushrooming of Bollywood-related satellite channels has also weakened the Urdu film industry and music in Pakistan, although its Punjabi counterpart has proved resilient.

The discotheque music of the 1970s provided a fillip to Urdu popular music, when the Nazia and Zohaib Hasan duo burst on the cultural scene in a significant way. This sister-brother team, brought up in London, sang popular Urdu songs to disco tunes. The sales of their cassettes were immense and a fan culture dedicated to their lifestyles sprang up. The duo held concerts and played on TV, and a major breakthrough came with generous offers from Bombay. The idolization of these anglicized Pakistani youths across South Asia sent all kinds of vibes. It became evident that the South Asian music could be modernized and adopted by all types of people and did not have to be the monopoly of certain families and *gharanas*.[13] It also meant huge wealth and fan clubs—both these features attracting many younger groups to attempt this new form of the Western-traditional popular domain. However, because of the official strictures under General Zia-ul-Haq, the new, young pop groups had to wait for another decade to make their entry. The information technology revolution, satellite and cable televisions beaming from abroad, and an increased demand for Pakistani music in the diaspora led to the outburst of videos and CDs. Several groups and individual artists now received important promotion through their concerts in the West and also benefited from the television coverage across South Asia. It might be difficult to enumerate all the Pakistani bands, which have urban roots, and comprise ambitious, well-educated, and equally wealthy family backgrounds. While there are individuals and bands still catering to the traditional and folk tastes, these popular bands have, in some cases, become the role models and celebrities for many Pakistani youths.[14] Their music is not symptomatic of revolt but rather reasserts Pakistani identity by focusing on its historic, cultural, and scenic aspects.

The first significant and enduring band to emerge in the late-1980s in Pakistan was called Vital Signs, led by Junaid Jamshed, whose patriotic songs such as "Dil, Dil Pakistan" have remained prominent on the charts. Soon after the death of the General Zia in 1988, the group played to the huge crowds across Pakistan, promising a new era of cultural revival, although some conservative groups were critical. Pakistanis welcomed these handsome, confident, and well-dressed musicians as a new chapter in their history, and like the Beatles, the members of Vital Signs soon became celebrities. While Noor Jahan, Mahdi Hasan, Nusrat Fateh Ali Khan, Abida Parveen, and Salma Agha remained mostly attached to the film industry and catered to specific audiences, Vital Signs was reaching across the regional and class barriers by holding concerts. Their concerts attracted a large number of young women, and the release of their singles and cassettes would turn into a major cultural trend in the country. By this time, video music and satellite televisions had arrived to give the band a more global audience; it split and in 1999, Junaid Jamshed went solo and gradually began to immerse himself into more Sufi lyrics.

By that time, another band, Junnoon, had emerged on the popular scene with its roots in Karachi. Their mixing of Sufi and semi-rock traditions gained these young singers a significant audience across Pakistan. Unlike the bilingual diversity in Urdu and Punjabi of the Vital Signs, Junoon initially focused only on Urdu songs and adopted several of Allama Iqbal's songs, which enthused their fans. Led by Ali Azmat, the band soon began to sing Punjabi Sufi music and produced a hit song, "Bullayah Ki Jana Mein Kaun," composed by the Punjabi classicist, Bulleh Shah. This was one of the earliest Pakistani bands that sang for Bollywood films such as *Papa* in 2003 and produced a track titled "Garaj Baras." Rahat Fateh Ali Khan, the nephew of Ustad Nusrat Fateh Ali Khan, also contributed to this track with his song, "Manu Ki Lagan."

Another contemporary of these two bands, featuring similar music, has been Strings, a Karachi-based group that emerged from a local college. The band, named after the strings of a guitar and led by Bilal Maqsood, plays mostly mellow and slow songs, so its hits include "Sar Kiya Yeh Pahar" and "Du'ur Say Koi Ayay." They joined mainstream pop with their official song for the Pakistani cricket team during the 2003 World Cup, which was titled: "Hai Koi Hum Jaisa…" Their songs have become immensely popular and one of their tracks, "Dhaani Chunnaria," won the B4U's "India Top Ten."

Since the late 1990s, Jawad Ahmad, a solo singer from Lahore, has been singing popular songs by mixing Sufi and Bhangra tunes. His entry into the pop world took place through his hit song, "Saiyann Ni Mein Teri Aaan," composed with a woman model in Lahore's National College of Arts. She is a Pakistani "girl next door," who is quite confident in her movements while wearing Sindhi clothes. Ahmad's more recent hit has been again a folk song, "Uchian Majajan Walley…," which offers a traditional context to a romance.

One of the well-known Pakistani singers, Abrarul Haq, has become synonymous with his hit songs like "Asan Tey Janna Billo Dai Ghar" and "Nutch Punjaban Nutch," the latter causing some outcry among feminists and conservatives. He subsequently changed it to "Nutch Majjajan Nutch" so as not to stigmatize Punjabi women.

While mostly urban men have dominated this youthful popular visual music, women have also made their presence felt in the audience and as models and singers in their own right. One such urban singer has been Hadiqa Kiyani, whose Punjabi hit songs, "Boohay Barian" and "Dopatta Mera Malmal Da," attained legendry popularity in South Asia. Shazia Manzoor's song, "Ghar Ajaa Sonia" has provided the title as well as theme to a Bollywood feature blockbuster.

A few other well-known Pakistani solo male pop singers include Shahzad Roy, Rahim Shah, Ali Haider, Ali Zafar, Fakhar, Haroon, and Ahmed Jahanzeb. Roy's popular Urdu songs have included "Tera Kangna," "Teri Soorat," and Iqbal's poem, "Yaa Rubb," and he remains popular among all age groups. Ali Haider has maintained a steady following although he has not made it to the big charts. Ali Zafar, a graduate of NCA, has become well-known with his semi-rock focusing on rural themes and sung in Punjabi. His "Hooqa Paani" was a hit during 2004. Ahmed Jahanzeb appeared on the music scene in 2002 with his song, "Ek Baar Kahoo" from his album, *Laila Majnoon*. Sport-

Pushtun with his rubab instrument and prized rugs. Courtesy of the author.

ing long hair and singing Sufi music in a melodious voice, he was an idol among young fans. Rahim Shah, from Balochistan, has brought in Pushtun musical tunes into his Urdu songs, especially "Teri Pail Bajay Chun Chun," which reveals rhythmic energy within the background of raw natural scenery. Fakhar and Haroon were a duo until recently, and their "Jadu Kay Chiragh" became a hit in 2000–2001, yet they decided to go their own separate ways. Fakhar has been comparatively more successful than Haroon, although they both have yet to attain their full creativity and following. This brief resume shows the diversification of Pakistani music and the recent input by younger urban singers, who have added new techniques, themes, and energies into it at a time when the film industry remains weak because of strong and rather unilateral influence from across the borders.

DANCES: THE FOLK STYLE

Pakistan is rich in folk music and dances, which have regional, agrarian, and romantic roots. They are often performed with the accompaniment of harmonium and tablas, played by rural bards who are folk institutions unto themselves. Sometimes, known as Bhats or Mirathis, they are the oral repositories of local genealogies and folk tales. To the throbs of big drums *(dhoal)*, they sing love songs from the past epics and romances and also perform Sufi quartets and special short poems called *dohras* (duets) and *mahiyyias* (romantic epics). The emphasis on such occasions is not just on merrymaking but to reignite nostalgia for a romantic past and celebration of youth as well as its rural rawness. Popular folk dances that accompany such songs may involve young as well as old and are called *ludi* and *bhangra*. *Ludi* and *bhangra* are communal dances mostly popular in Punjab, where farmers in their colorful attire dance to the rhythmic sounds emanating from the big drums, handclaps, and flutes, locally known as *shahnai*. The flute is also locally known as *baansari* because it is made of a hollow bamboo with several round openings to refine variegated sounds. *Ludi* is always danced in a circle both by men and women, whirling around the musicians. Handclaps and ecstatic shouts accompany the folk songs. *Ludi* builds up gradually, and specialists dressed in traditional costumes gradually add up speed and momentum into their circular movements. *Bhangra* is faster and could have anywhere from just two dancers to several and, like *ludi*, involves circles and hand claps by turbaned and colorfully clad youths.

These folk dances, like the folk and Sufi poetry, have been adopted for screen, and the younger artists imbued in Western traditions have been successfully experimenting with them to ensure their longevity. *Bhangra*, in particular, has seen a great revival and transethnic energy in Britain where Punjabis, both Indian and Pakistani, have transformed it into a mainstream form of recreation in the clubs and pubs, and at private parties.

The tribal Pushtun on the Frontier, especially the Khattaks, have a special traditional dance, called Khattak dance, which is akin to a faster form of *Ludi*. Here young men with traditional haircuts *(patta)* and attired in usually white *shalwar-kamees* combination and shiny red waistcoats dance in a circle while holding swords. The fast body movements synchronize with the flashy movement of the metallic swords, together creating a uniquely absorbing scene. The Khattak dances have, to a great extent, symbolized the cultural vitality of Pushtun folk traditions where manhood, martial spirit, and physical alacrity all come into play with a powerful and resounding music emanating from instruments such as *dhoal*, flute, and *rubaab*.

FILMS

After the evolution of Hollywood in the era of still and silent movies, India also began to build cinemas and theaters. Bombay, Lahore, Calcutta, and Delhi were the earliest places to experiment with cinematography. Bombay and Lahore took the lead where a mixture of Hindi and Urdu—called Hindustani—emerged as the lingua franca for this most important medium of popular culture. In 1913 India produced its first silent movie, called *Harishchandra*, although no woman agreed to perform in it. However, in Lahore it was because of the efforts of Abdur Rasheed Kardar that the first silent film, *The Daughter of Today*, was produced there in 1924, followed by *Mysterious Eagle* and *Husn Ka Daku*. But faced with competition from a more resourceful competitor, Kardar's *The Loves of a Mughal Prince*, focusing on the romance of Anarkali and Prince Saleem, proved a flop. However, he never lost hope and produced a string of movies on all kinds of topics, mostly using Hollywood as the model. In 1931, Bombay's *Alam Ara* came out as the first talkie, while Lahore in 1933 produced its first sound film, *Heer Ranjha*, based on the famous Punjab's romance. Noted Urdu playwrights such as Imtiaz Ali Taj and Agha Hashar were soon writing scripts for these films, while Noor Jahan began her career as an actress in 1942 with the film, *Khandaan*.[15]

After Partition, Pakistan's first movie, *Terri Yaad* (1948) did not prove a success. However, Lahore soon saw the emergence of three studios, and the arrival of Noor Jahan and Shaukat Hussain Rizvi rehabilitated faltering confidence. Noor Jahan's singing and acting in films like *Dopatta* (1952), and the completion of Hollywood's *Bhowani Junction* (1955) kept Lahore on the film scene. The major break came during the 1970s when actresses such as Sabeeha, Nayyar Sultana, Mussarat Nazeer, and Shameem Ara were joined by Rani, Zeba, Shabnam, Firdaus, Nishu, and Mumtaz, and actors such as Muhammad Ali, Waheed Murad, Nadeem, Munawar Zareef and Shahid burst on to the scene. Films such as *Anjuman, Umrao Jan Adaa* and *Aieena* proved to be box office hits. Because of a ban on the Indian movies, Pakistani films flourished for a decade until the 1980s, when popular television plays and restrictions by General Zia-ul-Haq almost strangled the industry. The introduction of videos and of Dubai as the new supply center for Indian films lessened the confidence that the movie moguls of Lahore had earlier acquired. During the 1990s, Lollywood further suffered because of the easily available and more resourceful Indian movies, which were now being watched on the cable networks.

Unlike popular music, Pakistan's film industry is not experiencing any quick recovery, and hundreds of cinemas across the country have been lying unused, or were converted into shopping plazas. Some people, sharing their skepticism of Lollywood, even suggested formally opening up the market to the Indian movies, which could mean more revenues and jobs in Pakistan. While Lollywood has been mostly focusing on Punjabi films, some Urdu feature films like *Moosa Khan* and *Yeh Dil Aap Ka Huwa* have proven valuable efforts in recent years. The latter received wider acclaim in the Gulf States and Britain and proved that individuals such as Jawed Sheikh and actors like Shaan, Resham, Zara Sheikh, Meera, and Sameena Peerzada can certainly make a difference through quality art. On average, Lollywood has been producing between 40 and 60 films per year, most of them being Punjabi, and a few in Urdu and Pushto. For instance, in 2004, Pakistan produced only one

Urdu film, *Salakhain,* which grossed a hefty sum, but most viewers watched Indian films in their homes, and cinemas remained rather underused. There were 11 film studios during the 1970s and now only one is left in Lahore.

Many Pakistanis do not see the situation as hopeless, however, and quote several unique features of the brief career of the Pakistani film industry. They mention *Chan Way* (1952) as a pioneer film, which was directed by a woman, Noor Jahan, and also mention *Aieena* (1977), which ran for four years, also referring to movies such as *Zarqa* (1969), devoted to the Palestinian struggle, and *Dosti* (1971), which focused on immigrants in Britain. According to such booster views, Pakistan is the tenth largest film producing country; Noor Jahan recorded 3,000 songs during a professional career of 60 years; Nasir Adeeb, a scriptwriter, produced 400 scripts; while Punjabi actor, Sultan Rahi, beat the world record by appearing in key roles in 535 films within a 40-year career.[16]

THEATER AND PUBLIC ENTERTAINMENT

The stage plays in Pakistan are either classical Urdu pieces or could be adoptions from Western languages. The Shakespearian plays are often presented under the auspices of the National Council of Arts, which promotes high-brow arts across the country through its provincial branches. Often, the British Council has offered its premises for staging such plays. Lahore and Karachi are the main centers of this form of visual arts, and especially in Lahore, the Rafi Peer Theatre group has been quite active even during the rough 1980s. Films and cable television have certainly impacted the plays, and the youths seem to be more interested in music and the Internet than watching semiclassical plays. Concurrently, elderly groups are more attuned to religious activities and to them, stage plays are simply Western traditions meant for a particular class. Like the classical Indian music and films, theater is not very popular in the country. In some urban schools and colleges there are drama clubs where Western and Urdu plays by writers like Hashar, Taj, and others might be performed. Television programs also retain some comedies where actors such as Moeen Akhtar, Anwar Maqsud, Zeba Shahnaz, and Omar Sharif have been quite popular. During the 1990s, stage shows where jokes, songs, and comedy acts were combined were enjoyed by people of all ages. These sessions and the television comedy serials such as *Jazeera, Fifty-Fifty, Sona Chaandi,* and *Chhoti Si Duniya* earned a significant reputation because of their raw humor.

It appears that with urbanization and newer modes of leisure and pleasure being easily accessible, the age-old tradition of the impersonator *(beroopia)* is withering away. This local clown would dress in all kinds of shocking costumes, make the audience laugh, and earn a modest living. His famous acts would involve dressing like a murderer holding a knife with blood gushing from his face. His performance rested on an element of awe and drama by scaring ordinary people through sudden and frightening actions. The rural bard may still play the role of a local jester at marriage ceremonies and may try to amuse guests with Punjabi jokes, which are usually bawdy and sexist, but the wordsmithery and appropriate gestures guarantee laughter.

In Pakistan, traditional mendicants *(hakims)* and roving gypsy healers *(sanyasis)* come to town and select a central point in the market to sell their herbal medicines. Each of their medicines, according to their verbose commentary, will cure several diseases and can be defined as a panacea. Their Pushto-Punjabi mixture of expression with an element of bluntness regarding sexual matters certainly make all the men milling around these *babas* blush. Fully attired as tribal Pushtuns, they elaborate on several kinds of sexual diseases until all the men are persuaded to buy their potions, which will supposedly transform them into lions and cheetahs. A typical *hakim baba* has a hennaed beard, a loose turban, and a waistcoat with a chain watch showing from one of the pockets and would always carry a bag full of potions. Often, he has a life-size painting of lions and cheetahs jumping over boulders, symbolizing the prowess that his potent medicines provide. This huge colorful portrait on cloth is hung behind the *baba* on a wall at a vantage place to make its mark on impressionable youths. These *babas* sell their herbal mixes to eager audiences. Then they take a swipe of snuff from a mirrored box before disappearing into dusty horizons.

In Pakistan, there are still a few circuses left, especially if one visits the village fairs or festivals at the shrines. People like to see lions and tigers up close and pay money to get into the enclosures, while jokers keep them busy with their tricks. These circuses mostly feature transvestites *(heejras)*, who for generations have been performing to rural audiences.[17] There might be a few songs, acrobatics, jokes, and shows involving monkeys and bears. Snake charmers, monkey men, and jugglers with bears and goats are still seen across the rural settlements, although they strictly avoid cities where the police and the mischievous children may pose problems for them. They usually have a gypsy background and move with the seasons.

NOTES

1. Muhammad Iqbal, "Dancing," in *Poems from Iqbal,* trans. Victor Kiernan (Karachi: Oxford University Press, 1999), p. 192.

2. There are several names for them such as *kathak, thumri,* and so on. Famous classical musicians such as Tan Sen have obtained proverbial fame based on their compositions and renditions. Tan Sen was a great musician during the time of Emperor Akbar in the sixteenth century. He followed Amir Khusrow's tradition besides making his own mark in innovative ways. All kinds of stories, including the superhuman power of his music to cause rain, are still popular across the subcontinent.

3. "Culture as Politics: An Interview with Seema Kermani," *The Times of India,* 10 December 2004.

4. This fourteenth-century Moroccan traveler to the Middle East, India, Sri Lanka, and China has left copious records of the element of transregionality among these Sufis. See Tim Smith-Mackintosh, ed., *The Travels of Ibn Battutah* (London: Picador, 2003).

5. He arranged the music for films like *Dead Man Walking* and *The Bandit Queen.*

6. "Mustt (Lost in His Work)" in Womad Production for RealWorld, CD 0777 7862212 3.

7. These poetry recitals take place in North America, Europe, and the Gulf whenever Urdu and Punjabi poets come together. In Pakistan, the tradition is quite alive with the patronage from television and an alert literary community, but in the diaspora, it may soon face several challenges when the first-generation native speakers pass away.

8. For instance, the *kafis* of the Punjabi classicists such as Baba Farid, Bulleh Shah, Sultan Bahu, Waris Shah, Mian Muhammad, Qadir Yaar, and several others have been preserved by the Islamabad-based Shalimar Recording Company and are available from the official shops of the Institute of Folk Heritage.

9. A *ghazal* is a romantic, often melancholy poem with each verse containing an independent subject. A solo artist in a semiclassical style usually sings it. *Kafi* is a four-verse Punjabi poem with powerful Sufi and populist undertones. *Bhajans* are sung in the praise of Hindu deities either in the temples or at home.

10. Reshmaan has been equally popular in India, where Bollywood made a whole feature film on her in the early 1970s.

11. Like Reshmaan, she is popular in all of South Asia and in the diaspora, where her concerts have been quite well subscribed. They both have accompanying musicians and singers who, like *qawalls*, have their own specializations.

12. *Kalaam Wa Kafiaan*, a two-volume selection of traditional and mystical music, Rawalpindi, n.d.

13. After an arranged marriage that turned sordid, Nazia Hasan, now again living abroad, fell ill and died an early and tragic death in the early 1990s. Her brother also went into oblivion.

14. Adnan Sami, a Pakistani singer known for his husky voice and *ghazals*, moved to India for personal and professional reasons. Similarly, Salma Agha, a well-known singer-actor of the 1980s, known for her ease with semiclassical traditions, decided to move to London following her marriage.

15. For a more detailed historical and illustrated study, see Mushtaq Gazdar, *Pakistan Cinema, 1947–1997* (Karachi: Oxford University Press, 1998).

16. See Ummer Siddique's write-up in http://pakistani_films.tripod.com.where_do_we_go_from _here-m. Accessed on 7 January 2005.

17. The *heejras* of old Delhi took a budding British author to India, where his journey led to several masterpieces. See William Dalrymple, *City of Djinns: A Year in Delhi* (London: Penguin, 1998). The author followed with more bestsellers like *White Mughals* (London: Flamingo, 2003).

9

Social Customs and Lifestyles

You are free; you are free to go to your temples, you are free to go to your mosques or to any other places of worship in this State of Pakistan. You may belong to any religion or caste or creed –that has nothing to do with the business of the State.... We are starting with this fundamental principle that we are all citizens and equal citizens of one State.... Now I think we should keep that in front of us as our ideal and you will find that in course of time Hindus would cease to be Hindus and Muslims would cease to be Muslims, not in the religious sense, because that is the personal faith of each individual, but in the political sense as citizens of the State.

—Quaid-i-Azam M. A. Jinnah's address to
Pakistan's First Constituent Assembly, 11 August 1947

Pakistani culture has its diverse sources, numerous manifestations, and regional variations, and embodies various class-based dimensions. It is part of an overarching Islamic civilization rooted in the historical Perso-Indic traditions. The ancient Indus Valley civilization is the fountainhead of this Indo-Islamic culture, which is derived from a number of successive Hindu, Jain, Buddhist, Zoroastrian, Greek, Persian, Arab, and Turkic contributions. At times, it becomes rather difficult to differentiate its West Asian characteristics from their Indian counterparts, although the culture equally reflects the forces of continuity and change. Pakistani culture, as exhibited through numerous social customs, attitudes, lifestyles, and creative arts, may be overwhelmingly Muslim, but in its more mundane domains it shares several traits and mores with neighbors in the east as well as to the west.

About five million Pakistani Christians and a similar number of Hindus may share religious beliefs and customs with their co-religionists elsewhere, yet they also represent a visible Pakistani imprint. Muslim and non-Muslim Pakistanis share numerous similarities in clothes, languages, food, and lifestyles. This is not to deny that, like any other such pluralistic society, Pakistani cultural and artistic traditions are diverse and the push toward majoritarianism certainly causes tensions and even dismay across the various divides. Pakistanis, in general, are religious people, and the efforts for a collective sense of national identity exist across all the communities in the country. Pakistan's pronounced emphasis on its Muslim credentials, although originally not aimed at marginalizing non-Muslims, also engenders concerns as the textbooks and various symbols and national practices have to be monitored carefully.

Thus, while the apparent prerogatives of a unitary form of nationalism may pull the country toward a greater Muslimhood, pluralism proffers its own requirements and modalities, necessitating a delicate balancing act. While Muslims are not a single monolithic community thinking and acting alike, in the same vein, Christians, Hindus, and other religious communities also exhibit similarities as well as denominational and other variations. Thus, whereas Pakistani culture, to a large extent, may purposefully symbolize the dominant Islamic ethos, its pluralistic aspects equally need to be taken into account, which is certainly a gargantuan task.

Pakistan's customs reflect a vast plethora of forces of modernity and tradition, although the divide may not be always so explicit. The feudal, rural, and tribal realities of Pakistan are not merely confined to some forlorn areas; ethno-regional loyalties may persist even in the urban localities based on strong clan-based bonds and operating through common hierarchies, shared memories, and dialects. For instance, Balochistan may account for 43 percent of Pakistan's territory, but population-wise it has only six to seven million inhabitants, mainly divided into two larger ethnic groups—Baloch and Pushtun. There are more Baloch in just one locality of Lyari in the megapolis of Karachi than in the entire province of Balochistan. The Zikris, for a long period, have been confined to the Makran (Kech) district of Balochistan with their spiritual center in Turbat, yet because of recent migrations, now demographically Karachi accounts for their largest concentration.[1] In the same vein, the Frontier may hold an aggregate Pushtun majority in the settled and tribal regions, yet Karachi and not Peshawar is now the largest Pushtun city.[2] These migrations, especially over the last four decades, have transformed the demographic contours across the country and have also had on impact on customs and cultural norms in a radical manner.[3]

For instance, Pushtun or Baloch women may not venture out of their homes in their native areas, but once in cities such as Karachi and Islamabad they have more opportunities at their disposal, and their venturing out, in most cases, would not be frowned upon by their men. However, when these families visit villages and ancestral lands, women again tend to wear the veil *(purdah)* and retire into the family quarters *(zenankhana)*. Some of these newly urbanized women are actively pursuing an education, although some may not be able to pursue jobs and especially so after their marriage. However, these newly settled Pushtuns and Baloch in cities are gradually becoming more receptive toward women's education and are being affected by stronger forces of modernity and acculturation.[4] In the same manner, women from the Syed[5] and such other *ashraaf* (genteel or upper caste) families routinely resume their traditional roles once they return to their homes and homeland. However, in most cases, such visits are quite short and happen infrequently. The younger groups certainly are more urbanized and, to them, the rural or tribal life may be only a short exotic adventure, as they would certainly not like to surrender their sedentary lifestyles forever. Rural and tribal men, while on visits home over the Eid festivals or to attend marriages and funerals, may also replace their Western trousers with a tunic and *shalwar*, and may become more visible in the local rituals, yet also hasten back to their urban pursuits.

The feudal traditions in Pakistan have stronger presence, especially in Sindh and Southern Punjab where they have endured in all the local matters. Here the emphasis is on prestige and honor for major landlords *(waderas, sardars)* and strict seclusion for their women and greater emphasis on arranged marriages within the extended family *(biradari)*. However, such feudal nomenclatures also feature an element of benevolence while dealing with the peasants or village professionals, who are grouped together as lower castes. The feudal landowner assumes the role of a local patriarch besides operating as an intermediary between the peasants and the government. He will arbitrate in the local feuds while treating his farm workers *(haris)* and peasants as his children, although certainly not equal to his own. Some of these landlords retain huge landholdings of thousands of acres of arable land and pastures, which may also include dozens of villages. Landholding ensures the local primacy of these notables, besides securing them seats on the elected assemblies.

The political parties, also dominated by such land-holding elites, seek the loyalty of these influential persons, and in reward for their support in forming governments, the latter are offered several incentives. Such politics of patronage, aided by the status-quo bureaucracy, have never allowed substantive land reforms in the country. Instead, the feudal elements have been further strengthened through their acquisition of urban property and by bringing

their relatives into the country's defense and civil structures. In a predominantly agrarian country with an already meager tax base, most of these agricul-
turalist classes are absolved from tax payments. In many instances, successive
regimes have offered them soft loans besides providing them subsidized seeds,
fertilizers, and machinery.[6] Thus, instead of developing a more equitable,
progressive, and egalitarian system, Pakistani planners have often preserved
the feudal system and have even colluded with the rent-seeking element at the
expense of national civic prerogatives.

The feudal model of political economy is so well entrenched that even
the urban politicians, senior military officials, and businessmen often end
up seeking a similar lifestyle for themselves with a retinue of servants and
unlimited local power. Several Pakistani generals and retired officials from the
armed forces receive generous land grants both in the rural and urban areas,
and their socioeconomic patterns are not different from their feudal counterparts. Almost every major city in Pakistan has "defense colonies," meant as
modern residential areas reserved for senior military officials, and they surely
account for the most expensive and choicest real estate endowed with all the
latest amenities.[7] These vast settlements featuring palatial houses and leafy
boulevards, like such other military-run businesses and corporations, represent a Pakistan that is starkly removed from the slums and poverty-stricken
hamlets.[8] Since most of these allottees, now making a new neo-feudal class,
are from Punjab, the local resentment in Balochistan and Sindh against them
often turns volatile. In cities, however, the defense housing schemes remain
the most cherished and secure property and, other than some middle-class
critics and think tanks airing their resentment in the media and poignant
reports, no major movement exists as such to seek out a more egalitarian
alternative for the rural and urban poor.

This class of nouveaux riches or land-based entrepreneurs is not ritualisti-
cally feudal, because they lack the traditional wherewithal that a local chieftain might have from his hold on the area extending over several generations.
The traditional chieftains, often known as *sardars, waderas, chaudharis,* or
tumandars, have a curious relationship with the local and national adminis-
trations that vacillates between mutual accommodation and sheer extortion.[9]
Often, they may demand more money and facilities from the government
in return for ensuring peace and support; while on other occasions, they
may even sponsor some miscreants to embarrass the local administration.
Pakistani regimes have often used troops to quell disturbances in the rural
Sindh and tribal Balochistan so as to reassert their authority at times when
the local chieftains were sponsoring insurgencies or harboring outlaws from
other towns.[10]

In Balochistan, a typical tribal chieftain or *sardar* will be the head over several clans, and his ancestral genealogy, excessive landholding, and crucial linkages with the official machinery will earn him preeminence in the local hierarchies.[11] On the Frontier, where landholdings are small, the local khan will inherit the tribe's or clan's headship on the basis of his own stature and also because of a commitment to preserve the collective honor *(izzat)*. The tribal regions, largely outside Pakistan's legal system, pursue their own customary laws through the assembly of elders *(jirga)* and allocate more unilateral powers to these khans. The notable khans are offered stipends by the government, and even the local development of schools, power lines, and telephone connections and such are conducted by seeking the good offices of these intermediaries. Their role, despite a smaller land base, allows them a very important status, largely because the rugged terrain on the sensitive Pak-Afghan borders would otherwise demand more radical measures involving troops and police, which the governments since the British era have tried to avoid. The local sociolegal autonomy and the incentives to make more money through illegal trade across the borders not only consolidates the tribal system, like its feudal counterpart in southern Pakistan, it equally makes successive governments dependent upon these intermediaries.

Consequently, the ordinary people on all sides suffer as the local power elite mostly siphon off the benefits. The local khan may occasionally work in tandem with the local cleric *(mullah)*, and thus while dealing with the external forces, tribal honor and religion may get enmeshed together. While some Pakistanis may romanticize the tribal system for its promptness in deciding on communal matters and also for providing security to the community, many believe that tribal people cannot be left to the whims of a few intermediaries or outmoded hierarchies while rest of the world moves on.[12]

Smaller towns, irrigated regions of central Punjab, and big cities across the nation have influential families, but here the associations are based on professional commonalties and marital networks. Often, the ethnic or clannish solidarity may come in handy during elections and for other such contests, but these loyalties are more obvious in far-flung rural and tribal cases. Pakistan's ethnic affinities have, in general, become more fluid because of migrations, evolution of newer generations, and professional and class-based alliances over and above ethnicity and localism. But ethnic solidarity has not become redundant; instead, in some cases such as the Urdu-speaking descendants of migrants from India *(Muhajireen)* in Karachi, it has been further solidified among the local-born second generation.[13] However, despite the ethnoregional diversities, sectarian divisions, and class-based chasms, Pakistani customs governing one's entire life retain an unmistakable semblance of similarity. They all have a strong religious context but certainly feature a cultural vitality permeating through a tradition of hospitality within the ethos of a shared camaraderie.

Pakistani customs are uniquely reflected in areas such as marriages, funerals, dress styles, food habits, literature, leisure activities, sports, and attitudes toward the rest of the world. Rituals and customs regarding childbirth—certainly with a preference for boys in many families—religious instruction through the home, mosque, or church and temple, and an emphasis on education from parents, older siblings, and tutors. certainly diffuse similar attitudes and practices across the board.[14] Marriage remains the major bond—after religion perhaps—and all the way from engagement to consummation a plethora of ceremonies and customs based on celebration and hospitality underwrite this age-old institution. In villages and tribal regions, such ceremonies may last longer, but in cities there is more emphasis on functionality, although neglecting relatives and friends from such activities is unthinkable. Thus, rituals and rites help weld the family, clan, and caste networks together while mobility and professionalism may weaken them.

In the religious customs, both the *ulama* (religious scholars) and *pirs* (spiritual mentors) assume a central role by virtue of being considered the custodians of sacred traditions. Each family may have their own spiritual guides and shrines to give periodic offerings and in return, these will operate as guardians and aids through turmoil and triumph. The *pirs* would lead special prayers or distribute charms, which offer solace to their disciples *(murids)*, seeking intercession on imperatives such as having a job, a son, or a good fiancée for one's son. The *pirs* may even specialize in removing the evil spirits who might have been causing fits in a younger, unmarried maiden, or could disburse some spiritual panacea for infertility.

The *pirs*, like Hindu astrologers *(jotshis)*, might draw zodiac diagrams so as to foretell the fortune of the attentive *murids*. In the same way, professional fortune-tellers, without assuming any spiritual authority, claim to foretell the future using palmistry that they have learned from their forbearers. They would use signs, stars, palmistry books, and even especially trained parrots to forecast for their clientele. Such astrologers *(najumis)* usually are found in the older and commercial parts of the inner cities and strictly avoid urban educated groups. Most of their customers, such as the visitors to the Sufi shrines, would be women, who find these fortune tellers *(aamils)* reliable and may have their own favorite. A typical *aamil* will sit by the roadside with a brooding and often balding parrot and several cards turned upside down in front of him or her. The parrot, on receiving a special signal, picks up a card from the pile, which will then lead to more intimate revelations. For a pittance, the astrologer will offer an overview of a mixed future besides cautioning on do's and don'ts. This is a tradition dating from the classical Hindu era, and one can spend days visiting these *najumis* to seek out their professional acumen. Lahore's Circular Road and Peshawar's Qissa Khawani Bazaar thrive with these astrologists and their visitors.

These old sections also have a number of traditional physicians *(hakims)*, who offer herbal medicines to their patients. These *hakims* have usually inherited the classical Greek and Indian skills and prescriptions from their ancestors, followed by apprenticeship with some seasoned professional. Their shops or wayside stores have rows of earthen ewers filled with herbs of various hues and scents, and the potions are guaranteed to be effective boosters, especially for those men who might be otherwise worried about their sexual prowess. Some of these *hakims* enjoy a wider acclaim guaranteeing them a busy practice. They start by feeling the pulse while the patient is narrating his/her predicament. The *hakim* busies himself in jotting down the prescription in his unique writing style. The well-established practitioners have several assistants working in smaller alcoves who provide medicines on the basis of the scribbled notes forwarded by the *hakim*. Rawlapindi's Bohr Bazaar or similar specialist localities known as *mohallah-i-hakeeman* or *bazaar-i-hakeeman* are found in all the bigger and older cities.

These settled *hakims* are a separate category from the trained allopathic physicians and homeopaths, and still different from the roving *hakim babas* who visit villages and tribal hamlets carrying satchels full of potions. Most of the latter *hakims* are Pushtuns and sell their panaceas using a unique blend of several languages and dialects. Their eloquent oratory on sexual diseases and

Fortuneteller sitting on a cot, Swat. Courtesy of the author.

the potency of their special potions often causes laughter among the blushing youths.

Pakistan still has a thriving tradition of traveling vendors and hawkers who visit towns to sell their goods, books, and groceries. At the old and narrow bridges over the rivers and at the bus stations, vendors come to sell their medicines *(manjans)*. These medicines of varying categories are usually powdery elements meant to treat chronic toothache, upset stomach, arthritis, or weak eyesight. Some of the vendors carry tablets meant to kill rats in the house. The unique singsongs by these vendors are quite amusing, and they always succeed in selling some within a few seconds even if the bus may begin to move. Young men throng bus and train stations to sell boiled eggs, dried fruits, potato chips, spicy beans, cakes, water, newspapers, and soft drinks as their livelihood depends upon vending. Women, children, and rural people are the main customers for such hawkers, who are customarily proficient in their persuasion.

The older cities and smaller towns have their own tea stalls or even private areas for socializing in the evenings. On the Frontier, the local khan usually has his nightly session in a specific section of his well-fortified house that is locally known as *Hujjra*. Here snuff *(naswaar)*, green tea *(qahwa)*, tea, and a smoking pipe *(huqqa)* are offered to the local men who come to discuss a variety of issues. On a starry night during summer months, neighbors and friends sit on cots, while in winter everybody retires inside where carpets, blankets, and pillows keep the temperature quite warm. This is an informal way to relax, gossip, and spread information. In Sindh and lower Punjab, an evening session takes place at someone's open compound or in a hall, often called *bhathak*. In cities, food places and ice cream parlors or even private parties may offer a place for socializing for like-minded families and friends.

The most important entertainers for rural people are local bards and barbers, who engage in menial works besides cooking, cleaning, and singing. The barbers often operate as matchmakers and messengers, moving between families and localities, and they thus assume a vivid sense of self-importance. The impersonator *(behroopia)* is gradually disappearing from the South Asian rural scene where television and other urban influences have marginalized such local entertainers. However, transvestites *(heejras)* still move about between villages and in the inner cities where families lavishly support them during religious and other festivities. *Heejras* carry harmoniums and also tie bells around their ankles *(paaill)* so as to create rhythmic sounds while they dance to a medley of folk and popular tunes. They can get away with jokes and often strike sexy poses to solicit more money and offerings from the male and female audience. They can visit women's quarters in the rural areas of Punjab and Sindh, but in the tribal regions it is not so easy. In general, people allocate special attributes to these transvestites and likewise do not like to hurt the ascetics *(faqirs* and *malangs),* who are viewed as holy men in the service of some saints.

Modern contours of Pakistani customs include clusters of urban institutions, western-style education, greater mobility, competitive professionalism, and an overall move toward middle-class lifestyles. While Hindus may be underprivileged in rural areas in Sindh, their educated and professional counterparts may have more leverage and rights in cities, although localism based on rural or tribal hierarchies may also guarantee some kind of patriarchal protection. Accordingly, powerful and resourceful men continue to hold predominant social positions in exchange for ensuring protection for women and minorities. The tribal Pushtuns, Baloch tribals, rural Sindhis, Zikris, rural Kashmiris, and Pothowaris may feel safer in cities with more economic and educational opportunities, yet their relatives back home still prefer more traditional ties and local customs, although some might desire to own brick houses with all the latest amenities.

It is in the cities where modernity is not only bringing people of different professional and ethnic backgrounds together, but equally spawning a rigorous quest for identity, often banking on exclusivist religious interpretations. However, the urban elite and some feudal families may send their children to highbrow English-language institutions such as grammar schools or Lahore's Aitchison College, whereas a huge public sector education system absorbs a vast majority of people. The poorer among them will end up at religious schools—*madrassas*—and the poorest will either beg, or simply be inducted into an informal economic sector that depends on child labor. Several from amongst them may never be able to make it to adolescence, succumbing to child diseases or drugs. Although mortality rates have been coming down steadily, poverty remains a harrowing reality.

COMMUNITY

Social attitudes and customs show an element of conservative stability in a society where the official machinery may be corrupt yet community supports and protects its own vulnerable members through various private mechanisms. Without having any official social security system in place, individuals look after their parents, siblings, and even grandparents. That is why, for a long time, many parents in societies such as Pakistan have preferred boys to girls. Boys help fathers as breadwinners and look after their parents and other close dependents during illness and old age. Elder boys assume major responsibilities toward the family as one generation bequeaths these shared values to the next. Pakistanis in the diaspora also help their parents and close relatives back home in various ways, and marriages within the extended family just become an added mechanism to further consolidate these traditions and kinship. Islam further underlines the moral responsibility toward parents, relatives, neighbors, and underprivileged people. Many beggars and other such vulnerable people are seen on the streets and by the mosques, shrines, and bus stations seeking charity from others. Alms giving, a widely shared custom, is justified in the name of common goodness, spiritual elevation, and divine blessings. Ordinary people always help elderly people, saints, and even disabled individuals living on charity at the shrines. In rural areas, travelers are allowed to spend the night in the local mosque where worshippers may bring them food. The peasants usually apportion a share from their harvest for mosques, shrines, and people performing menial jobs.

Pakistanis, in general, may not be highly literate as a nation, but there is deep respect for educated people, poets, and religious scholars. Issues such as political instability, economic disparities, unemployment, and known cases of corruption and coercion dishearten the people at large and they continuously pray and yearn for strong leadership. Pakistanis are vulnerable to what they read in the textbooks about their history and relations with neighbors such as India and are also deeply moved by Western and Israeli policies toward other Muslim communities. A nationwide politicization often is reflected in the media, rallies, and special prayers in the mosques, besides a massive amount of literature in Urdu and other local languages.

Pakistanis may have sectarian tensions that occasionally turn violent, yet there are still close-knit families and neighborhoods. Despite numerous social and gender-based hierarchies, the citizens are mostly steered by wider public morality and folk wisdom. Tribal societies are certainly very localized. Many young men have gone to the Gulf or are working in cities such as Karachi, but they remain in touch with their native lands and customs. Towns and cities have all types of groups following different attitudes and lifestyles varying from immensely conservative to totally liberal pursuits.[15] Certainly, the society has been transitioning from rural to urban and from overwhelmingly agrarian moorings to more industrial and commercial focuses.

NOTES

1. This is based on my extensive fieldwork in Balochistan and Karachi during 2003. Interviews with the local members of several communities including the Zikris, visits to Koh-i-Murad outside Turbat, and a study of relevant literature revealed that while demographic changes have been motivated by economic factors, they have also engendered new ethnic configurations. This community got the name because of *zikr,* or constant recitation of Allah's names and attributes.

2. Peshawar has certainly been the crossroads of various ethnocultural groups, although until recently the inner city was largely inhabited by the Hindko-speakers,

who are non-Pushtun, yet are bilingual. After 1947, with the departure of the Hindus and Sikhs, such business families were further strengthened. However, the steady arrival of largely rural and tribal Pushtuns into Peshawar and likewise into Kohat has changed the local demography. Since 1979, the arrival of the Afghan refugees, and the emergence of Peshawar as the center of the Afghan resistance, led to a greater influx of newcomers into the city. Now, the city has a visible Pushtun majority, although it remains quite pluralistic.

3. For an interesting perspective, see Feroz Ahmed, *Ethnicity and Politics in Pakistan* (Karachi: Oxford University Press, 1998).

4. City life allows more autonomy and the chance for a public role to these women. They may attend school, go out shopping, and manage the family life, which may even involve driving.

5. Literally, "leader" in Arabic but in Pakistan, Syeds are the descendants of the Prophet and thus deserving of more respect from amongst the "commoners."

6. The Pakistani state structures suffer from a serious malaise because of corruption and nepotism. Many of Pakistan's landlords, businessmen, and officials are known defaulters, who have been reluctant to return public loans. These loans, as frequently discussed in the media, amount to several billion rupees but are often written off by the obliging regimes in Islamabad.

7. Pakistan's huge military defense establishment receives preferential treatment and is the most decisive pressure group when it comes to domestic policies, budgetary allocations, and foreign policy matters. In fact, the army has ruled the country for most of its existence. It controls its nuclear program and its intelligence agencies run their own political programs. The armed forces have often been helped by the United States and other Western powers because of their own global imperatives. These domestic and external forces have decimated Pakistan's political and constitutional prerogatives while the country continues to suffer from economic disparity. Ayesha Jalal, *The State of Martial Rule in Pakistan: The Origins of Pakistan's Political Economy of Defence* (Cambridge: Cambridge University Press, 1990).

8. These officials are simultaneously allotted several plots besides houses through concessionary schemes and, in addition, are given freehold lands on the borders and in the interiors of Sindh, much to the ire of the local people. The disturbances at places like Okara in central Punjab during 2003–2004, in rural Sindh during the 1980s and 1990s, and also in Gwadar and elsewhere in Balochistan were due to the advance of these "outsiders," who in many cases happened to be from Punjab. Over the last several decades, many Pakistani intellectuals have been highlighting these serious dichotomies while demanding a complete and unfettered democratization of Pakistan with the military going back to the barracks, but such initiatives have been mostly vetoed by the commanders, who have steadily received support from the outside.

9. Certainly, there are exceptions but the feudal traditions are discriminatory, sexist, and oppressive. For a closer view of such a scion, see Tehmina Durrani, *My Feudal Lord* (London: Corgi, 1995). Even educated women such as Benazir Bhutto proudly detail their landholdings. See Benazir Bhutto, *Daughter of the East* (London: Hamish Hamilton, 1988). The feudal legacy is discussed in Iftikhar H. Malik, *State and Civil Society in Pakistan* (Oxford: St. Antony's Series, 1997), pp. 81–93.

10. During 2004–2005, the Bugti tribal area of Balochistan was restive, as the chieftains wanted Islamabad to pay more in royalties on natural gas to them. About 60 percent of Pakistan's natural gas comes from Sui, an area within the Bugti tribal region. See http://www.bbc.co.uk/2/south_asia/4167299.stm.

11. For a useful although less critical study, see Paul Titus, ed., *Marginality and Modernity: Ethnicity and Change in Post-colonial Balochistan* (Karachi: Oxford University Press, 1996).

12. Imran Khan, the former cricketer and a politician, has often eulogized the tribal customs and the *jirga* system, which has certainly shocked some of his urban supporters. See Imran Khan, *Warrior Race: A Journey through the Tribal Land of Pathans* (London: Chatto and Windus, 1993). This volume and works by M. Amin, I. Husain, and Michael Palin have breathtaking pictures of villages, glaciers, mountain peaks, rivers, and tribal people on the Frontier. See Mohamed Amin, *Journey Through Pakistan* (London: Bodley Head, 1982); Irfan Husain, *Pakistan* (London: Stacey, 1997); and Michael Palin, *Himalaya* (London: Weidenfeld, 2004). One of the earliest works to focus on the scenic and historic features of Pakistan was by two British women, who had been living in the country and thought that it was largely unknown to the outside world. The Asian Study Group in Islamabad published their work. See Hilary Adamson and Isobel Shaw, *A Traveller's Guide to Pakistan* (Islamabad: Asian Study Group, 1981). The work has since undergone several more printings. Isobel Shaw, who has been writing and living in Pakistan, has contributed a few more works on the country. See Isobel Shaw, *Pakistan Handbook* (London, John Murray, 1989).

13. Sociologists often identify such urban loyalties as a new form of tribalism, which may add to segmentation and fragmentation.

14. Peers would include parents, elder siblings, and specially hired tutors. In addition, the role of media, schools, worship places, and other public institutions in transferring all types of attitudes remains quite significant.
Muslim boys—not the Muslim girls or non-Muslim boys—undergo circumcision, which is certainly a major event of socioreligious significance. In cities, initiation may happen at birth, while in rural and tribal regions it is arranged in early childhood followed by celebrations and gift exchanges. Christian, Parsi, Hindu, and Sikh children have their religious initiation through baptism or similar rituals at the worship houses but this would not involve circumcision.

15. For an interesting novel depicting the noveaux riches, see Mohsin Hamid, *Moth Smoke* (London: Granta, 2000).

SUGGESTED READINGS

Amin, Mohamed. *Journey Through Pakistan.* London: Bodley Head, 1982.

Hamid, Mohsin. *Moth Smoke.* London: Granta, 2000.

Husain, Irfan. *Pakistan.* London: Stacey, 1997.

Khan, Imran. *Warrior Race: A Journey through the Tribal Land of Pathans.* London: Chatto and Windus, 1993.

Mannheim, Ivan. *Pakistan Handbook.* Bath: Footprints, 1999.

Glossary

Aaamil Fortuneteller

Achkin Formal overcoat with a round neck and buttoned front

Ahimsa Nonviolence (advocated by Mahatma Gandhi)

Ajrak Patterned Sindhi wraparound, mostly of cotton

Akhara Arena

Alim Muslim religious scholar

Anjuman Cultural or literary association

Ashnaan Morning bath by Hindus

Ashraaf Genteel or upper castes

Azaan Call for Muslim prayer

Baansari Flute made of bamboo

Baba Elderly gentleman

Bain Elegy

Baraat Marriage procession

Basti Settlement

Bashalini Headgear worn by Kalasha women in Chitral

Bawali Staired Hindu well

Beera Form of snuff

Behroopia Impersonator

Bhajan Hindu devotional song

Bhand Rural minstrel/jester

Bhangra   Fast Punjabi dance

Bhasha   Language

Bhat   Rural bard

Biradari   Kinship, extended family

Biryani   Rice dish with spices and meat

Burfi   Sweet made of milk, sugar, and flour

Burqa   Traditional veil and caftan covering the entire body of a woman

Chaat   Savory salad made of fruit, vegetables, and chickpeas

Chador/Chaadar   Loose wraparound for women

Chapatti   Unleavened baked bread

Chardiwari/Chaardiwari   Within the four walls of the home

Charpoy   Cot

Chashma   Spring

Chattri   Umbrella or canopy

Chaudhari   Punjabi notable

Choogha   Woolen overcoat worn by men in Northern Areas

Chooridar   Tight pyjamas

Chowgan   Form of polo

Daastan nawisi   Fiction writing

Dal/Daal   Dish made from beans or split peas

Dargah   Sufi shrine

Dervish   Ascetic

Dhamaal   Devotional dance at Sufi shrines

Dhoal   Big drum

Dhoti   Loincloth

Diwan   Urdu poetry collection

Doaha   Punjabi duet

Doar   String for kite flying

Dupatta   Loose wraparound for head and shoulders

Eid   Joyous Muslim festival

Fiqh/Fiqah   Jurisprudence

Firni   Sweet cream dish made of ground rice and milk

Fitna   Feud, dissension

Fitrana   Charity before Eid

Gajraila   Carrot pudding

Gharana   Family of traditional musicians

Ghararra   Traditional loose pleated skirt worn by women in place of loose trousers *(shalwar)*

Ghazal   Romantic poem

Ghee   Clarified butter

Gulookaar   Singer

Haal   Ecstatic mood or trance

Hadith   Saying/tradition of the Prophet Muhammad.

Hajj   Annual pilgrimage to the Hejaz, Saudi Arabia

Hakim   Traditional physician

Haleem   Dish made with several kinds of meat, beans, and herbs cooked at low temperature

Hallal   Muslim way of slaughtering animals

Halwa/Halwah   Traditional sweet pudding

Hamad   Devotional hymn to Allah (God)

Hari   Landless farm worker in Sindh

Haveli   Traditional house

Heejra   Transvestite

Hujjra   Khan's (Pakistani notable) guest house

Huqooqul Allah   Duties unto God

Huqooqul Ibaad   Duties unto humanity

Huqqa   Water pipe for smoking tobacco

Imam   Islamic religious leader

Insaan-i-Kamil   Perfect human being

Izzat   Honor

Jahaiz   Dowry

Jali   Lit: net. Perforated stone slab, metallic piece, or wood plank

Jihad   Holy struggle

Jirga   Assembly of elders

Jotshi   Astrologist

Julaibi   Thick, sweet dish made with butter that looks like spaghetti

Kabbadi Traditional sport, similar to wrestling

Kabob Grilled or cooked meat dish

Kafi/Ka'afi Short Punjabi or Sindhi mystical poem

Kamees/Kamis Long shirt

Karo-Kari Honor killing

Kasrat Wrestling practice

Khareef Summer crops

Kheer Sweet rice cooked in milk

Khichri Kedgeree, which is a sweet dish that contains rice, milk, and sugar

Khussa Embroidered shoe

Kofta Spicy meat or vegetable ball, with herbs and cooked in curry

Kulcha Baked bread, especially for breakfast

Kurta Shirt or tunic

Langar Free food distributed at a shrine

Lassi Churned buttermilk

Ludi Group dance popular in rural Punjab

Lungi Formal and patterned loin cloth

Madrassa Islamic religious school

Majlis Cultural association or Shia sermon

Malang Ascetic

Mandar Hindu temple

Mangni Engagement

Manjan Potion for toothache

Mantra Hindu prayer

Mari Multi-storied traditional residence, mostly owned by richer Hindus in pre-1947 Northwestern Punjab

Marsiyya Elegy

Maulvi/Mullah Muslim religious leader

Mela Fair

Mihrab Niche in the mosque for imam to lead congregational prayers

Mimar Mason

Mistri Local mason

Mithai Traditional South Asian sweet

Mohallah Urban place

Muhajir Muslim migrant

Muhajireen Pl. of *Muhajir*

Mujahid One who undertakes *Jihad* (holy war)

Mujahideen Pl. of *Mujahid*

Mullah Less scholarly cleric

Murid Disciple of a Sufi (mystic) or *pir*

Murshid Spiritual mentor

Musha'aira Recitals by several poets

Naan Leavened baked bread

Na'at Devotional poem praising the Prophet Muhammad

Najumi Astrologist, a fortuneteller

Nanbai Traditional baker

Naswaar Snuff

Nikah Marriage ceremony

Noor Light (usually referring to the Prophet Muhammad)

Paan Beetle leaf

Paicha Kite-flying contest

Pakora Spicy deep-fried vegetable appetizer

Paratha Round bread cooked in clarified butter

Pehlawaan Wrestler

Pir Sufi saint

Puja Hindu worship

Pulao Spicy cooked rice

Purdah Veil, also seclusion

Qahwa Green tea

Qaseeda Eulogy

Qawalli Devotional music

Rabih Winter crops

Raga Classical melody

Raj British rule of India

Raita Yogurt mixed with coriander and parsley

Riaz   Music practice

Rilli   Colorful, patched Sindhi sheet

Roti   Plain unleavened bread, cooked on a hot plate

Rubayyat   Quartets

Sadhu   Hindu ascetic

Sajjada Nishin   Muslim dynastic Sufi order

Samosa   Pasty with spicy ground meat or vegetables inside

Sanyasi   Roving healer

Sardar   Baloch chieftain

Shahnai   Flute

Shalwar/Shalwaar   Loose trousers

Sharia/Shariat   Islamic law; jurisprudence

Shia/shi'ite   Follower of Caliph Ali, a doctrinal Muslim sect

Silsilah   Sufi order

Sohbat   Shared rice dish in Bannu area of the Frontier

Suf   Wool

Sufi   Islamic mystic

Sunnah   Prophet Muhammad's practices/examples

Sunni   Lit. a follower of the Prophetic traditions, a majority doctrinal sect

Tablas   Small Indian drums

Tabligh   Propagation of Islamic knowledge (also called *Daawa*)

Taliban   Plural of *Taleb/Talib:* students

Tandoor   Clay oven

Tanqeed   Literary criticism

Tappa   Witty verse or proverb

Tariqa   Sufi way; order

Tarraka   Fried seasoning for daals (lentils), made of garlic, ginger, and butter

Tawwa   Hot plate

Tharra   Locally brewed alcohol

Tikka   Grilled meat pieces

Tonga   Horse-drawn buggie

Tumandar   Baloch head of tribal chieftains

Ulama Muslim religious scholars (pl. of *alim*)

Ummah Transnational Muslimhood

Urs Annual anniversary of a Sufi

Var Punjabi epic

Waaskat Waistcoat

Wadera Feudal landlord in Sindh

Waz Sunni sermon

Zakat Charity

Zarda Dessert of sweet yellow rice (with saffron)

Zenankhana Women's rooms

Zikr Recitation of Allah's (God's) names

Bibliography

REPORTS

Government of Pakistan. *Pakistan Year Book 1994–5*. Karachi: Finance Division, 1996.

Human Development Centre. *Human Development in South Asia 2002*. Islamabad: Human Development Centre/Oxford University Press, 2003.

———. *South Asia in 2001*. Islamabad: Human Development Centre/Oxford University Press, 2002.

Human Rights Commission of Pakistan. *State of Human Rights in 2004*. Lahore: Human Rights Commission of Pakistan, 2005.

Malik, Iftikhar H. *Pakistan at Fifty*. Brussels: European Institute of Asian Studies, 1997.

———. *Religious Minorities in Pakistan*. London: Minority Rights Group, 2002. http://www.minorityrights.org.

Runneymede Trust. *Islamophobia*. London: Runneymede Trust, 1997.

Transparency International. *Global Corruption Report 2004*. London: Pluto, 2004.

United Nations Development Program (UNDP). *Pakistan: National Development Report 2003: Poverty, Growth and Governance*. http://www.un.org.pk/nhdr.

BOOKS AND ARTICLES

Abbasi, M. Yusuf. *Pakistani Culture: A Profile*. Islamabad: National Institute for History and Culture, 1992.

Adamson, Hilary, and Isobel Shaw. *A Traveller's Guide to Pakistan*. Islamabad: Asian Studies Group, 1981.

Ahmad, Aftab. *Islamic Calligraphy*. Rawalpindi: Ahmad, 1984.

Ahmed, Ali, et al. *Angaray*. Lucknow: Sajjad Zaheer, 1932.

Ahmad, Aziz. *An Intellectual History of Islam in India.* Edinburgh: Edinburgh University Press, 1969.

———. *Studies in Islamic Culture in the Indian Environment.* Delhi: Oxford University Press, 1999.

Ahmed, Feroz. *Ethnicity and Politics in Pakistan.* Karachi: Oxford University Press, 1998.

Ahmed, Jalal Uddin, ed. *Zainul Abedin.* Karachi: Pakistan Publications, 2004.

Ahmed, Leila. *Women and Gender in Islam.* New Haven, CT: Yale University Press, 1992.

Ahmed, Q. *Pakistan Book of Cricket, 1991.* Karachi: Cricketpoint, 1992.

Ahsan, Aitzaz. *The Indus Saga and the Making of Pakistan.* Karachi: Oxford University Press, 1996.

Alam, Muzaffar. *The Crisis of Empire in Mughal North India: Awadh and the Punjab, 1707–48.* Delhi: Oxford University Press, 1986.

———. *The Languages of Political Islam in India, 1200–1800.* London: Hurst, 2004.

Ali, S. Amjad. "Forward Looking Art: Years before and after Independence." *Arts and the Islamic World,* 32 (1997): 33–45.

———. *Gulgee-Versatile Artist.* Islamabad: Amjad, 1984.

Ali, Salwat. "Mapping the Change." *Dawn,* 4 December 2004.

Allchin, Bridget, and Raymond Allchin. "Discovering and Preserving the Cultural Past." In *Old Roads, New Highways: Fifty Years of Pakistan,* ed. Victoria Schofield. Karachi: Oxford University Press, 1997.

———. *The Rise of Civilisation in India and Pakistan.* Cambridge: Cambridge University Press, 1982.

Allchin, F. R. *The Archaeology of Early Historic South Asia.* Cambridge: Cambridge University Press, 1995.

Amin, Mohamed. *Journey Through Pakistan.* London: Bodley Head, 1982.

Arberry, A. J. *Sufism: An Account of the Mystics of Islam.* London: Mandala, 1988.

Armstrong, Karen. *Islam: A Short History.* London: Phoenix, 2001.

———. *Muhammad: A Western Attempt to Understand Islam.* London: Gollancz, 1992.

Asad, Muhammad. *Islam at the Crossroads.* Gibraltar: Daral Andalus, 1982.

Askari, M. H. "Urdu Literature." In *Old Roads, New Highways,* ed. Victoria Schofield. Karachi: Oxford University Press, 1997.

Askari-Rizvi, Hasan. *The Military and Politics in Pakistan, 1947–1997.* Lahore: Sang-e-Meel, 2000.

Basham, A. L. *The Wonder That Was India: A Survey of the Culture of the Indian Subcontinent before the Coming of the Muslims.* New York: Sedgwick, 1954.

Bennet-Jones, Owen. *Pakistan: The Eye of Storm.* New Haven, CT: Yale University Press, 2003.

Bhalla, Alok, ed. *Stories about the Partition of India.* Delhi: Indus, 1994.

Bhutto, Benazir. *Daughter of the East.* London: Hamish Hamilton, 1988.

Butalia, Urvashi. *The Other State of Silence: Voices from the Partition of India.* London: Hurst, 2000.

Byron, Robert. *The Road to Oxiana.* London: Pimlico, 2004. Reprint.

Caroe, Olaf. *The Pathans: 550 BC-AD 1957.* London: Kegan Paul, 2000.

Chughtai, Arif Rahman, ed. *The Story-Teller: M.A. Rahman Chughtai.* Lahore: Chughtai Trust, 1997.

Cohen, Stephen P. *The Idea of Pakistan.* Washington, DC: Brookings Institution, 2004.

Cook, Michael. *The Koran: A Very Short Introduction.* Oxford: Oxford University Press, 2002.

Crile, George. *My Enemy's Enemy: The Story of the Largest Covert Operation in History. The Arming of the Mujahideen by the CIA.* London: Atlantic Books, 2003.

"Culture as Politics: An Interview with Seema Kermani." *The Times of India,* 10 December 2004.

Curran, Jim. *K2: Triumph and Tragedy.* London: Grafton, 1989.

Dalrymple, William. *City of Djinns: A Year in Delhi.* London: Penguin, 1998.

———. *White Mughals.* London: Flamingo, 2002.

Dani, A.H. *Chilas: The City of Nanga Parvat.* Islamabad: A.H. Dani, 1983.

———. *History of Northern Areas of Pakistan.* Islamabad: National Institute, 1989.

———. *The History of Taxila.* Tokyo and Paris: UNESCO, 1986.

———. *Human Records on the Karakoram Highway.* Islamabad: A.H. Dani, 1983.

Delancy, Richard. *Lonely Planet Hindi & Urdu Phrasebook.* London: Lonely Planet, 1998.

———. *Teach Yourself Beginner's Urdu Script.* London: Script Series, 2003.

Dickey, Christopher, and Carla Power. "Rocking the Casbah." *Newsweek,* 20 December 2004. http://www.msnbc.msn.com/id/6700425/site/newsweek/.

Durrani, Tehmina. *My Feudal Lord.* London: Corgi, 1995.

Edhi, Abdus Sattar. *An Autobiography,* narrated to Tehmina Durrani. Islamabad: National Bureau, 2000.

Farrukh, Nilofur. "Echoes of Socio-Political History." *Arts and the Islamic World,* 32 (1997): 59–61.

"Fifty Years-Fifty Questions." *Monthly Herald* (Karachi), January 1998.

Fisher, Michael H. *The First Indian Author in English: Dean Mahomed (1759–1851).* Delhi: Oxford University Press, 1996.

Francisco, Jason. "In the Heat of the Fratricide: The Literature of India's Partition Burning Freshly." *Annual of Urdu Studies,* 2 (1996).

Friskin, Sydney. *Going for Gold: Pakistan at Hockey.* Karachi: Oxford University Press, 1997.

Frith, David. *The Golden Age of Cricket, 1890–1914.* Guildford: Lutterworth, 1978.

Gascoine, Bamber. *The Great Moghuls.* London: Jonathan Cape, 1971.

Geertz, Clifford. *The Interpretation of Cultures: Selected Essays.* New York: Basic Books, 2000.

Gilmartin, David, and Bruce Lawrence, eds. *Beyond Turk and Hindu: Rethinking Religious Identities in Islamicate South Asia.* New Delhi: Research Press, 2002.

Guillame, Alfred. *Islam.* London: Penguin, 1990. Reprint.

Habib, Irfan. *The Agrarian System of Mughal India, 1556–1707.* New Delhi: Oxford University Press, 2000.

Habib, Miriam. *Painter-Teacher, Anna Molka.* Lahore: author, 1984.

Halliday, Tony. *Insight Guide: Pakistan.* London: Insight, 2000.

Hamdani, Agha Hussain. *Fatima Jinnah: Hayyat awr Kidmaat.* Islamabad: National Institute, 2003. Reissued.

Hamid, Mohsin. *Moth Smoke.* London: Granta, 2000.

Hasan, Khalid, trans. *Kingdom's End and Other Stories.* London: Verso, 1987.

Hasan, Khalid, ed. *Memories of Jinnah.* Karachi: Royal, 1990.

Hasan, Mushirul. *Legacy of a Divided Nation: India's Muslims Since Independence.* London: Hurst, 1997.

Hasan, Shaikh Khurshid. *Chaukhandi Tombs in Pakistan.* Karachi: Archaeology Department, 1996.

———. "Talpurs and their Tomb Architecture." *Daily Star,* 15 January 2000.

Hashmi, Salima. "The Visual Arts." In *Old Roads, New Highways,* ed. Victoria Schofield. Karachi: Oxford University Press, 1997.

Horrie, Chris, and Peter Chippendale. *What is Islam?* New York: Virgin, 1990.

Husain, Intizar. *Basti.* Lahore: Sang-e-Meel, 1983.

Husain, Irfan. *Pakistan.* London: Stacey, 1997.

Husain, S. A. *Muslim Cooking of Pakistan.* Littlehampton: Apex Books, 1983.

Hussain, Marjorie. "Pakistan's Art World Celebrated a Golden Jubilee." *Arts and the Islamic World,* 32 (1997): 62–63.

Hussein, Abdullah. *Udaas Naslain.* Lahore: Qausain, 1978.

Hyder, Quratulain. *Aag Ka Daryaa.* Lahore: Sang-e-Meel, 1994.

Ikram, S. M. *Modern Muslim India and the Birth of Pakistan.* Lahore: Research Society, 1995.

Ikramullah, Shaista S. *From Purdah to Parliament.* Karachi: Oxford University Press, 1998.

Iqbal, Muhammad. *Poems from Iqbal,* trans. Victor Kiernan. Karachi: Oxford University Press, 1999.

———. *The Reconstruction of Religious Thought in Islam.* Lahore: Ashraf, 1999. Reprint.

Jairazbhoy, R. A. *An Outline of Islamic Architecture.* Karachi: Oxford University Press, 2003.

Jalal, Ayesha. "The Convenience of Subservience: Women and the State of Pakistan." In *Women, Islam and the State,* ed. Deniz Kandiyoti. London: Zed Books, 1991.

———. *The Sole Spokesman: Jinnah, the Muslim League and the Demand for Pakistan.* Cambridge: Cambridge University Press, 1985.

———. *The State of Martial Rule in Pakistan: The Origins of Pakistan's Political Economy of Defence.* Cambridge: Cambridge University Press, 1990.

Jalbani, Abbas. "Breaking New Ground: Sindhi Books of 2004." *Dawn,* 6 February 2005.

James, C.L.R. *Beyond a Boundary.* London: Serpent's Tail, 2000. Reprint.

Jettmar, Karl. *Beyond the Gorges of the Indus: Archaeology before Excavation.* Karachi: Oxford University Press, 2001.

Jones, Owen B. *Pakistan: Eye of the Storm*. London/New Haven: Yale University Press, 2002.

Kardar, A. H. *Test Status on Trial*. Karachi: National Publications, 1955.

Kaul, Suvir, ed. *The Partitions of Memory: The Afterlife of the Division of India*. Delhi: Permanent Black, 2001.

Keay, John, *A History of India*. London: HarperCollins, 2000.

Keay, John. *When Men and Mountains Meet*. Karachi: Oxford University Press, 1993.

Kennedy, Charles H., ed. *Pakistan at the Millennium*. Karachi: Oxford University Press, 2003.

Kenoyer, Mark. *Ancient Cities of the Indus Valley Civilization*. Karachi: Oxford University Press, 1998.

Khan, Ahmad Nabi. *Islamic Architecture in South Asia: Pakistan, India, Bangladesh*. Karachi: Oxford University Press, 2003.

Khan, Imran. *All Round View*. London: Mandarin, 1988.

———. *Warrior Race: A Journey through the Tribal Land of Pathans*. London: Chatto and Windus, 1993.

Khan, Shahryar M. *The Begums of Bhopal: A Dynasty of Women Rulers in Raj India*. London: I. B. Tauris, 2000.

Khan, Yasmin Sabina. *Engineering Architecture: The Vision of Fazlur R. Khan*. New York: Norton, 2004.

Khuhro, Hamida. *The Making of Modern Sindh*. Karachi: Oxford University Press, 1999.

Kiernan, Victor. *Poems from Iqbal: Renderings in English Verse with Comparative Urdu Text*. Karachi: Oxford University Press, 1999. Reprint.

Kulke, Hermann, and Dietmar Rothermund. *A History of India*. New York: Routledge, 2004.

Lamb, Alastair. *Birth of a Tragedy: Kashmir 1947*. Hertingfordbury: Roxford, 1994.

———. *Kashmir: A Disputed Legacy, 1846–1990*. Hertingfordbury: Roxford, 1991.

Lamb, Christina. *Waiting for Allah: Pakistan's Struggle for Democracy*. London: Penguin, 1991.

Lambert-Hurley, Siobhan. "Contesting Seclusion: The Political Emergence of Muslim Women in Bhopal, 1901–1930." Ph.D. dissertation. University of London, 1998.

Lari, Yasmeen, and Z. Suhail. *The Jewel of Sindh: Samma Monuments on Makli Hills*. Karachi: Oxford University Press, 2002.

Lelyveld, David. *Aligarh's First Generation: Muslim Solidarity in British India*. Delhi: Oxford University Press, 1996. Reprint.

MacMahon, Robert J. *The Cold War on the Periphery: The United States, India and Pakistan*. New York: Columbia University Press, 1994.

Mahomet, Sake Dean. *The Travels of Dean Mahomet*. Berkeley: University of California Press, 1997. Reprint.

Majeed, Tehnyat. "1997 at the NCA." *Arts and the Islamic World* (50 Years of Art in Pakistan) 32 (1997): 97–101.

Malik, Iftikhar H. "The Afghan Conflict: Islam, the West and Identity Politics in South Asia." *Indo-British Review* 23, no. 2 (2002).

———. *Crescent between Cross and Star: Islam and the West after 9/11.* Karachi: Oxford University Press, 2006.

———. *Islam and Modernity: Muslims in Europe and the United States.* London: Pluto, 2004.

———. *Islam, Nationalism and the West: Issues of Identity in Pakistan.* Oxford: St. Antony's-Macmillan/Palgrave Series, 1999.

———. *Jihad, Hindutva and the Taliban: South Asia at a Crossroads.* Karachi: Oxford University Press, 2005.

———. "Pakistan in 2001: The Afghanistan Crisis and the Rediscovery of the Frontline State." *Asian Survey* 42, no.1 (2002).

———. *Pakistan: People and Places: Reflections on Living and Travelling.* Islamabad: Margalla Books, 1985.

———. *Religious Minorities in Pakistan.* London: Minority Rights Group, 2002.

———. *State and Civil Society in Pakistan: Politics of Authority, Ideology and Ethnicity.* Oxford: St. Antony's-Macmillan/Palgrave Series, 1997.

———. *U.S.-South Asia Relations, 1784–1940: A Historical Perspective.* Islamabad: Area Study Centre, 1988.

Malik, Rizwan, and Samina Awan. *Women Emancipation in South Asia: A Case Study of Fatima Jinnah.* Lahore: University of Punjab, 2003.

Mannheim, Ivan. *Pakistan Handbook.* Bath: Footprints, 1999.

Marshall, J. *The Buddhist Art of Gandhara.* Cambridge: Cambridge University Press, 1960.

Matheson, Sylvia. *The Tigers of Baluchistan.* Karachi: Oxford University Press, 1997.

Matinuddin, Kamal. *The Taliban Phenomenon.* Karachi: Oxford University Press, 1999.

Matthews, David, and Mohamed Kasim Dalvi. *Teach Yourself Urdu.* London: Hodder, 2003.

Mawdudi, Syed Abul Ala. *Purdah.* Lahore: Islamic Publications, 1972. Reissued.

McLuhan, Marshall. *Verbal-Voco-Visual Explorations.* New York: Something Else Press, 1967.

Meadows, Azra, and Peter Meadows. *The Indus River: Biodiversity, Resources, Humankind.* Karachi: Oxford University Press, 1999.

Memon, Muhammad Umar, ed. *The Colour of Nothingness: Modern Urdu Short Stories.* Karachi: Oxford University Press, 1998.

———. *An Epic Unwritten: The Penguin Book of Partition Stories.* Delhi: Penguin, 1998.

Menon, Ritu, and Kamla Bhasin. *Borders and Boundaries: Women in India's Partition.* New Delhi: Kali for Women, 1998.

Mernissi, Fatima. *Women and Islam: An Historical and Theological Inquiry,* trans. Mary Jo Lakeland. Oxford: Blackwell, 1992.

Metcalf, Barbara D. *Perfecting Women: Maulana Ashraf Ali Thanwi's Bihishti Zewar: A Partial Translation with Commentary.* Berkeley: University of California Press, 1990.

Miller, Charles. *Khyber*. London: Macmillan, 1977.

Moghal, Dominic, and Jennifer Jivan, eds. *Religious Minorities in Pakistan: Struggle for Identity*. Rawalpindi: Christian Study Centre, 1996.

Moorhouse, Geoffrey. *To the Frontier*. London: Hodder, 1984.

Moshaver, Ziba. *Nuclear Proliferation in the Indian Subcontinent*. London: Macmillan, 1991.

Mumtaz, Kamil Khan. *Modernity and Tradition: Contemporary Architecture in Pakistan*. Karachi: Oxford University Press, 1999.

———. "Reading Masjid Wazir Khan." In *Studies in Tradition*, 2, no. 2 (1993): 68–79.

Mumtaz, Khawar, and Farida Shaheed. *Women of Pakistan: Two Steps Forward. One Step Back?* London: Zed, 1987.

Murphy, Dervla. *Full Tilt*. London: Flamingo, 1965.

———. *Where the Indus is Young*. London: Century, 1977.

Murphy, Richard McGill. "Performing Partition in Lahore." In *The Partitions of Memory: The Afterlife of the Division of India*, ed. Suvir Kaul. Delhi: Permanent Black, 2001.

Naqvi, Akbar. *Image and Identity: Fifty Years of Painting and Sculpture in Pakistan*. Karachi: Oxford University Press, 1998.

Nasr, Seyyed Vali Reza. *Mawdudi and the Making of Islamic Revolution*. New York: Oxford University Press, 1996.

Newburg, Paula. *Judging the State: Courts and Constitutional Politics in Pakistan*. Cambridge: Cambridge University Press, 1995.

Nichols, Robert. *Settling the Frontier: Land, Law, and Society in the Peshawar Valley, 1500–1900*. Karachi: Oxford University Press, 2001.

Noman, Omar. *Pride and Passion: An Exhilarating Half Century of Cricket in Pakistan*. Karachi: Oxford University Press, 1999.

Noorani, Asif. "An Art Affair to Remember." *Star Weekend*, 4 December 2004.

Nye, Russel B. *The Unembarrassed Muse: The Popular Arts in America*. New York: Dial, 1970.

Palin, Michael. *Himalaya*. London: Weidenfeld, 2004.

Pandey, Gyanendra. *Remembering Partition: Nationalism and History in India*. Cambridge: Cambridge University Press, 2001.

Perkovich, George. *India's Nuclear Bomb: The Impact on Global Proliferation*. Delhi: Oxford University Press, 2003. Reprint.

Qureshi, Ishtiaq H. "Architecture." In *The Cultural Heritage of Pakistan*, ed. S. M. Ikram and Percival Spear. London: Oxford University Press, 1955.

———. *Ulema in Politics: A Study Relating to the Political Activities of the Ulema in the South Asian Subcontinent from 1556 to 1947*. Karachi: Maaref, 1972.

Rahman, Tariq. *Language, Education and Culture*. Karachi: Oxford University Press, 1999.

———. *Language and Politics in Pakistan*. Karachi: Oxford University Press, 1996.

Rammah, Safir. "A Dream Year: Punjabi Literature in 2004." *Dawn*, 30 January 2005.

Rashid, Ahmed. *Taliban: Islam, Oil and the New Great Game in Central Asia*. London: I. B. Tauris, 2000.

Richard, Yam. *Shi'ite Islam*, trans. Antonia Nevill. Oxford: Blackwell, 1995.

Robinson, Francis. *Separatism among Indian Muslims: The Politics of the United Provinces' Muslims*. Cambridge: Cambridge University Press, 1974. Reprinted in 1993.

Rodinson, Maxime. *Mohammed*. London: Penguin, 1979.

Rose, Leo E. and Richard Sisson. *War and Secession: Pakistan, India and the Creation of Bangladesh*. Berkeley: University of California Press, 1990.

Rutnagur, Dicky. *A History of Squash in Pakistan*. Karachi: Oxford University Press, 1997.

Safi, Omid, ed. *Progressive Muslims on Justice, Gender, and Pluralism*. Oxford: Oneworld, 2003.

Said, Edward. *Orientalism*. London: Penguin, 2003. Reprint.

Saiyid, Dushka H. *Muslim Women of the British Punjab: From Seclusion to Politics*. Basingstoke: Macmillan, 1998.

Schofield, Victoria. *Kashmir in the Crossfire*. London: I. B. Tauris, 1996.

Schofield, Victoria, ed. *Old Roads, New Highways*. Karachi: Oxford University Press, 1997.

Shahnawaz, Jahan Ara. *Father and Daughter: A Political Biography*. Karachi: Oxford University Press, 2002.

Shaikh, Farzana. *Community and Consensus in Islam: Muslim Representation in Colonial India, 1860–1947*. Cambridge: Cambridge University Press, 1989.

Shamsie, Muneeza, ed. *A Dragonfly in the Sun: An Anthology of Pakistani Writings in English*. Karachi: Oxford University Press, 1997.

———. *Leaving Home: A Collection of English Prose by Pakistani Writers*. Karachi: Oxford University Press, 2001.

———. "Rich Offerings—Pakistani English Literature, 2004." *Dawn*, 6 February 2005.

Shaw, Isobel. *Pakistan Handbook*. London: John Murray, 1998.

Siddiqui, Habib. "The Making of Manji: Her Master's Voice." http://world.media-monitors.net/content/view/full/12165/.

Siddiqui, Huma. *Jasmine in Her Hair*. Madison, WI: White Jasmine Press, 2003.

Singh, Sarina, et al. *Lonely Planet's Pakistan and the Karakoram Highway*. London: Lonely Planet, 2003.

Sirhandi, Marcella. *Contemporary Paintings in Pakistan*. Lahore: Ferozsons, 1992.

———. "Paintings in Pakistan: 1947–1997." *Arts and the Islamic World*, 32 (1997): 17–32.

Smith-Mackintosh, Tim, ed. *The Travels of Ibn Battutah*. London: Picador, 2003.

Sultan, Abida. *Memoirs of a Rebel Princess*. Karachi: Oxford University Press, 2004.

Tahir, Athar. *Lahore Colours*. Karachi: Oxford University Press, 1997.

———. *Punjab Portraits*. Lahore: Sang-e-Meel, 1992.

———. *Qadir Yar: A Critical Introduction*. Lahore: Adabi Board, 1988.

Taizi, Sher Zaman. "A Whiff of Fresh Air: Pushto Books in 2004." *Dawn*, 16 January 2005.

Talbot, Ian. *Freedom's Cry: The Popular Dimension in the Pakistan Movement and Partition Experience in North-West India.* Karachi: Oxford University Press, 1996.

———. *Pakistan: A Modern History.* London: Hurst, 1999.

Tenant, I. *Imran Khan.* London: Gollancz, 1995.

Thapar, Romila. *A History of India.* London: Penguin, 1979.

Titus, Paul, ed. *Marginality and Modernity: Ethnicity and Change in Post-colonial Balochistan.* Karachi: Oxford University Press, 1996.

Transparency International. *Global Corruption Report 2004.* London: Pluto, 2004.

Victoria and Albert Museum. *Colours of the Indus.* London: Victoria and Albert Museum, 2000.

Wheeler, R.E.M. *Five Thousand Years of Pakistan.* London: Royal India and Pakistan Society, 1950.

Winter, Dave. *Footprint Northern Pakistan.* London: Footprint, 2004.

———. *Footprint Pakistan Handbook.* London: Footprint, 1999.

———. *Zulfi Bhutto of Pakistan.* Karachi: Oxford University Press, 1993.

Wolpert, Stanley. *Jinnah of Pakistan.* Berkeley: University of California Press, 1984.

Woodward, Bob. *Bush at War.* New York: Simon and Schuster, 2002.

Yakas, Orestes. *Islamabad: The Birth of a Capital.* Karachi: Oxford University Press, 2001.

Yong, Lin, and Su Hua. *Pakistan.* Beijing: Pakistan Embassy, 1985.

Zaheer, Hasan. *The Separation of East Pakistan.* Karachi: Oxford University Press, 1994.

Zaidi, S. Akbar. *Issues in Pakistan's Economy.* Karachi: Oxford University Press, 1999.

Zaidi, S. Akbar, ed. *Regional Imbalances and the National Question in Pakistan.* Lahore: Vanguard, 1992.

Zajadacz-Hastenrath, Salome. *Chaukhandi Tombs: Funerary Art in Sindh and Baluchistan.* Karachi: Oxford University Press, 2003.

Zaman, Muhammad Qasim. *The Ulama in Contemporary Islam: Custodians of Change.* Karachi: Oxford University Press and Princeton University Press, 2004.

Ziring, Lawrence. *Pakistan: At the Crossroad of History.* Oxford: Oneworld, 2003.

WEB SITES

http://www.aiindex.mnet.fr
http://www.fashionpakistan.co.uk
http://www.hrw.org
http://www.jaring.my/just
http://www.sufiwisdom.org
http://www.un.org.pk.nhdr/.
http://www.urdupoint.com/cooking/Pakistan/
http:// www.visage.pk.com
http://www.zameeen.com

Index

About the Author

IFTIKHAR H. MALIK, a Fellow of the Royal Historical Society, is Professor of History at Bath Spa University, England, and is also associated with Wolfson College.